QUALITATIVE STUDIES IN PSYCHOLOGY

This series showcases the power and possibility of qualitative work in psychology. Books feature detailed and vivid accounts of qualitative psychology research using a variety of methods, including participant observation and fieldwork, discursive and textual analyses, and critical cultural history. They probe vital issues of theory, implementation, interpretation, representation, and ethics that qualitative workers confront. The series mission is to enlarge and refine the repertoire of qualitative approaches to psychology.

GENERAL EDITORS
Michelle Fine and Jeanne Marecek

Everyday Courage: The Lives and Stories of Urban Teenagers
Niobe Way

Negotiating Consent in Psychotherapy
Patrick O'Neill

Flirting with Danger: Young Women's Reflections on Sexuality and Domination
Lynn M. Phillips

Voted Out: The Psychological Consequences of Anti-Gay Politics
Glenda M. Russell

Inner-City Kids: Adolescents Confront Life and Violence in an Urban Community
Alice McIntyre

From Subjects to Subjectivities: A Handbook of Interpretive and Participatory Methods
Edited by Deborah L. Tolman and Mary Brydon-Miller

Growing Up Girl: Psychosocial Explorations of Gender and Class
Valerie Walkerdine, Helen Lucey, and June Melody

Voicing Chicana Feminisms: Young Women Speak Out on Sexuality and Identity
Aida Hurtado

Situating Sadness: Women and Depression in Social Context
Edited by Janet M. Stoppard and Linda M. McMullen

Living Outside Mental Illness: Qualitative Studies of Recovery in Schizophrenia
Larry Davidson

Autism and the Myth of the Person Alone
Douglas Biklen, with Sue Rubin, Tito Rajarshi Mukhopadhyay, Lucy Blackman, Larry Bissonnette, Alberto Frugone, Richard Attfield, and Jamie Burke

American Karma: Race, Culture, and Identity in the Indian Diaspora
Sunil Bhatia

Muslim American Youth: Understanding Hyphenated Identities through Multiple Methods
Selcuk R. Sirin and Michelle Fine

Pride in the Projects: Teens Building Identities in Urban Contexts
Nancy L. Deutsch

165101

PRIDE IN THE PROJECTS

Teens Building Identities in Urban Contexts

NANCY L. DEUTSCH

NEW YORK UNIVERSITY PRESS
New York and London

NEW YORK UNIVERSITY PRESS
New York and London
www.nyupress.org

Library of Congress Cataloging-in-Publication Data
Deutsch, Nancy L.
Pride in the projects : teens building identities in urban contexts /
Nancy L. Deutsch.
p.   cm. — (Qualitative studies in psychology)
Includes bibliographical references and index.
ISBN-13: 978-0-8147-1991-6 (cl : alk. paper)
ISBN-10: 0-8147-1991-0 (cl : alk. paper)
ISBN-13: 978-0-8147-1992-3 (pb : alk. paper)
ISBN-10: 0-8147-1992-9 (pb : alk. paper)
1. Identity (Psychology) in adolescence—United States—Case studies.
2. Urban youth—United States—Psychology—Case studies. 3. Youth
with social disabilities—United States—Psychology—Case studies.
4. Interpersonal relations—United States—Case studies. 5. After-school
programs—United States.   I. Title.
BF724.3.I3D48 2008
155.5'1825—dc22   2008004067

Contents

■   ■   ■   ■

Acknowledgments

This work is dedicated to my grandfather, Abraham William Deutsch. His enduring commitment to and valuing of education has filtered down through the generations to help make me who I am today.

Many talented scholars have been generous with their time and energy, yielding invaluable feedback throughout the process of researching and writing this book. Barton J. Hirsch has provided the intellectual support that has pushed my thinking and writing. My editors, Michelle Fine, Jeanne Marecek, and Jennifer Hammer, provided priceless advice in helping me develop the final product. Niobe Way and a number of anonymous reviewers offered critical insights that helped me develop my work. Brian Pusser went above and beyond the call of duty with an eye for fine details. Sara Rimm-Kaufman and the women of my junior faculty writing group at the University of Virginia lent me their minds and their hearts, pushing me intellectually while sustaining my soul. My thanks to Leslie Bloom, Marjorie Faulstich Orellana, Dan McAdams, Milbrey McLaughlin, Wendy Luttrell, Joe Allen, Gil Noam, and Ruthellen Josselson for their insightful comments along the way. I was financially supported during the course of this research by a variety of institutions, including Northwestern University, the Northwestern/University of Chicago Joint Center for Poverty Research, the Spencer Foundation, and the W. T. Grant Foundation. My thanks go to The W. T. Grant Foundation for linking me to a group of after-school scholars who are helping move the field forward.

The youth and staff at the East Side Boys and Girls Club deserve many thanks. The club and program directors have my unending appreciation for welcoming me and always asking how they could help. The youth opened themselves up to the inquiries of a stranger, and to them I am indebted.

There are numerous research assistants who have contributed to my work. Foremost among them are Leah Doane and Carrie Luo. The field-work of Terrenda White, Lauren Eslicker, Erin Higgins, and Susie Israel allowed me a deeper understanding of my research site.

I am grateful for the communities of which I have been a part at both Northwestern University and the University of Virginia. My colleagues over the years have pushed my thinking and provided circles of support.

And last but in no way least, I have been blessed with a large network of family and friends who have ceaselessly supported and influenced me. The creativity, scholarly questioning, and constant humor of the Deutsch and Lewis/Foley families inspire me and keep me on my toes. Thank you to my parents (all four of you) and Elizabeth and Jeff for believing in me. My many, many friends from across the country serve as a base for my work and my life. From childhood to college, Boston to Seattle, Chicago to Charlottesville, I trust that they know who they are, and that they know I love and appreciate them. I would not be who I am today, let alone where I am today, without my network of friends and family, who keep me sowing the creative, intellectual, and empathic seeds that allow me to thrive wherever I physically may be.

1

■　　■　　■　　■　　■　　■　　■　　■

"There Are Birds in the Projects"

The Ecology of Adolescent Development in Urban America

It is an early June evening in the Midwest, the kind of afternoon that suggests the end of school and the beginning of summer. The energy at the East Side Boys and Girls Club reflects this boundary land between structure and freedom, work and play. In the gym, the boys' softball team practices in preparation for the summer season. In the computer room, teenagers are working on final school reports and browsing the latest sneaker styles online. Scuffling feet and adolescent chatter fill the hallway as teens escape the heat emanating from the concrete expanse of the nearby public housing project. Inside the empty TV lounge, BJ and I sit, an African American teen and a White woman, shoulder to shoulder. Her 16-year-old body, athletic and strong, claims its space next to mine. Photographs are scattered across the table in front of us, the bright faces of BJ and her friends contrasting with the solemn tones of the buildings and landscapes of their urban neighborhood. One particular photo catches my eye. "What about this one?" I ask, pointing to a photo that shows nothing but sky and, in its center, a soaring bird (Figure 1-1). "Why did you take that one?" "Cause you wouldn't usually see, people think of the projects as

Fig. 1-1. BJ's Photo: The Bird in the Projects

bad," BJ says, looking me in the eye. "And that you wouldn't see birds or anything over here. So that's why I took that."

BJ's words strike me as both profound and obvious, hopeful and sad. In them I hear the echoes of media images of public housing projects like the one just outside the club's doors, of teens like BJ and her friends. But I also hear her resistance, her defiant response to those who would pigeonhole her and her home. And in the intersection of those two streams of consciousness, I glimpse her developing sense of identity, a self who exists within, but refuses to be defined by, her place in America's urban landscape.

BJ does not speak for all teens growing up in America's inner-city public housing. But she and her peers at the East Side Boys and Girls Club provide us a glimpse of how settings become sites for resistance and reconstruction, for recognition and relationships. Their narratives demonstrate the active, contextual, and relational nature of adolescent identity in today's complex world. Adolescents are in the process of exploring who they are, of envisioning and building a place for themselves in adult society. They are both individuating and socializing, separating and forming links. And they are doing so within multiple, overlapping social environments. American teens interact within and across an increasing number of contexts, from home to school to neighborhood to cyberspace. Yet too often our portraits of adolescence take on one of two extremes: erasure of the environment or dismissal of the teen's own agency. In our attempts to understand adolescence as a universal phenomenon we have overlooked the nuanced ways in which development is intimately tied to the inter-action of individual youth with particular people within specific social contexts.

Understanding the ways in which adolescents make meaning in and of their contexts, both local and societal, is key to understanding the process of adolescent development in 21st-century America. Only when equipped with such understanding can we support and promote positive develop-mental processes for all teens. And so it is with a desire to further such understanding that I offer up the stories of the East Side teens. Teens with whom I spent four years talking, playing, and learning. Teens who have much to say, and from whom we have lots to learn, about the process of development as they experience it within their mostly Black, economically poor, inner-city neighborhood.

My purpose in this book is twofold. First, and primarily, I seek to push forward developmental theory, specifically in the area of adolescent iden-tity development. I challenge researchers to reformulate our consideration of individuation as the primary goal of adolescence. In the split between psychological and sociological views of the self, the former of which fo-cuses on individual processes, the latter on structural constraints, the mid-dle ground of interpersonal connections often gets lost in the shuffle. Yet we all develop our individual sense of self within the contexts of our rela-tions and interactions with other people. Whereas relational development is now seen as important for studies of girls and women, we have been less attentive to relational development among males.[1] I focus on the ways in which all of our identities, female and male, are negotiated and con-structed within and through interpersonal relationships in local contexts.

Traditional psychological studies of identity focus on differences in out-comes by race and gender alone while social class, until recently, was virtu-ally ignored as a category of influence. I expand the consideration of rela-tional development to include the negotiation of social categories, such as gender, race, and social class. The experiences of youth living at the inter-section of multiple marginalized social categories are a growing presence in the research literature. But laboratory studies, which have served as the basis for much psychological research into identity, use primarily college students as their subjects, thereby excluding non-college-bound populations. Furthermore, lab-based methods strip psychological processes from their real-world contexts. Development and context are not isolated. They are interactive. And to better understand and address the issues facing diverse teens, we must understand the contexts—physical, social, and psychological—in which they are developing and the relationships formed in those contexts, through and within which their identities are negotiated.

Second, I seek to inform youth practice and policy, particularly in the realm of after-school programs. Foregrounding context and relationships as key influences on the process of development naturally leads to the opportunity to apply this knowledge to settings that serve youth. In recent years there has been increasing attention paid to the role of such programs, often fueled by public concerns for community safety and policy initiatives such as California Proposition 49, which provided earmarked funds for after-school programming statewide. Research on out-of-school time programs for youth have primarily focused on them as settings for improving academic achievement or reducing specific behaviors that put youth at risk (e.g., drug use, sex, gang activity). Yet for youth in such programs, these settings serve as broad developmental spaces and contexts for building self and identity.

On the theoretical side, adolescent identity has been studied in the context of peer groups, families, and schools. Yet after-school contexts, too, serve as sites for the construction of self and, as such, have the potential to serve as spaces that support positive youth development in a more holistic manner than much research would suggest. Examining how youth negotiate and build identities in after-school contexts, settings in which they voluntarily choose to participate, can help researchers understand how youth use their social contexts and relationships in their construction of self and, thereby, how these and other settings can best support youth development. Without a better understanding of *whether* and *how* after-school programs function in youths' development, we will not maximize the potential of these settings to best serve youth.

I spent four years at the East Side Boys and Girls Club learning about the lives of the club's members and staff.[2] The adolescents' stories and experiences are the guiding voices of my work. In thinking about these youths' lives, I weave together the interactive influences of local contexts and larger society. I work from Uri Bronfenbrenner's ecological systems model of development, conceptualizing the various levels of a youth's environment as a dynamic, interconnected system of relationships.[3] In this model, individuals are involved in experiences and activities within their immediate surroundings, their microsystems. These relationships are bidirectional; youth both influence the microsystem and are influenced by it. These microsystems also interact with each other. Parents visit the school or help with homework. A Boys and Girls Club staff member calls a member's teacher or parent. These connections between settings become their own developmental contexts, mesosystems. Beyond this lies the exosystem, settings in which the youth is not directly involved but which have their own influence on the youth's development, such as a parent's workplace. The final, overarching system is the macrosystem, the laws, customs, resources, and values of the culture in which the other systems are nested.

I locate my fieldwork in the microsystem, the activities and interactions in a youth's immediate environment. Yet I keep an eye firmly trained on the outer circles of youths' lives, considering the ways in which social norms and categories filter down into individual identity construction. I build from the groundwork laid by the authors in Lois Weis and Michelle Fine's volume on local contexts as construction sites for youth identities.[4] I focus on an after-school program as such a site and examine how this micro context serves as a setting in which youth negotiate, through their activities and relationships within the Boys and Girls Club, macro social structures and the processes of self-construction. In doing so, I link theory and practice. I explore theoretically how identity development is influenced by multiple levels of ecology. I then look to the ways in which local environments and relationships can help youth negotiate the larger social world. Throughout, I consider the developmental stage of adolescents, who are on the doorstep of adulthood, attempting to balance childhood with their emerging sense of themselves in the grown-up world.

Adolescents' Developmental Needs

The adolescent's physical presence embodies the social meanings we give to this age. Capriciously changing clothes, hairstyles, and body piercings; increasing height, budding breasts, and sprouting hair; fluctuating voices, and abundant energy taken over by sleeping binges: the adolescent is in flux. Her body and mind are changing, as is her place in the social world.

She is growing into who she will become as an adult. And yet she is also holding onto her past, taking with her the experiences and ideas that have made her who she is today. And she is doing all this quickly. After infancy, adolescence is the period of greatest and most rapid developmental change.[5] The outcomes of these processes form the foundations of adulthood.

Since midcentury, western psychologists have identified identity integration as the primary developmental task of adolescence.[6] Increased cognitive abilities and expanded social worlds allow for both a more abstract construction of self and the consideration of a greater number of social roles and relationships. The expansion of social roles sets the stage for the consideration of possible selves (things we may be in the future), as well as the acknowledgment and integration of multiple selves (the different faces we display across different contexts). The process of self-reflection and identity integration begins early in adolescence, as youth notice contradictions between the self-attributes they display across various social roles. Teens may realize that they are outgoing, funny, and talkative with friends but are more reserved, responsible, and argumentative with family. During early adolescence they first identify these contradictions and consider them in relation to their overall sense of self.

During middle-to-late adolescence, youth consolidate these discrepancies through the process of identity integration, developing a stable self-concept that allows for different personality displays in different contexts but maintains an inner, core self. According to stage theorists, these contradictions can be disturbing and harmful if not resolved, as the identity that results from integrating one's different identifications serves as a basis for future development and as the connection between childhood and adult roles. The danger of not resolving the "crisis" of identity integration, as it is termed by Erik Erikson, the influential psychoanalyst and identity theorist, is identity diffusion (or confusion), which prevents one from moving forward into future stages of development.[7] Yet the existence and consideration of possible selves can also be a positive motivating factor. Some have suggested that a balance of positive and negative possible selves, which youth strive to achieve and avoid, is optimal.[8] Wanting to be a good student, therefore, is not enough. We must be able to imagine who we will be if we do not achieve that goal. The image of the school dropout motivates us to work hard to become a good student. Thus, youth integrate their identities toward images of possible future selves, both positive and negative. These images are based on their view of themselves in relation to the larger social world, as well as their daily experiences and local environments.

This linear and stable portrait of identity development has been challenged over time. Psychologists and sociologists have struggled with questions about the nature of self and the processes by which we construct identities. Stemming from William James, George Herbert Mead, and Charles H. Cooley, and moving on to Erik Erikson's stages of identity development and James Marcia's identity statuses, psychologists have framed identity development as an intrapsychic activity that takes place in a sociocultural framework.[9] Sociologists have urged us to examine identity in terms of the meanings that individuals construct through human interactions and the structural and relational constraints placed on identity.[10] Social psychologists have studied how group identity influences behavior, particularly through the lens of social identity theory, a model of group affiliation developed primarily through laboratory research.[11] In recent years, postmodernists have pushed us to consider identity as shifting and contextual, suggesting that there is no such entity as the stable identity posited by traditional theories.[12]

In addition to the split between those who consider identity fluid and decentralized and those who consider it unitary, the disciplinary juncture in identity studies has led to differing foci of research, with psychologists situating identity in the individual and sociologists locating identity in social interactions and societal structures.[13] I emphasize the ways in which these three influences intertwine within our local contexts, negotiated within and through our relationships with other people. Thus, I fall somewhere in between traditional and postmodern theories of identity, attempting to balance individual agency with social constraints. I find postmodern notions to have a kernel of truth to them. Yet I believe we strive, nonetheless, for a coherent sense of self, which serves as a uniting thread across contexts. We may shift aspects of our presentation of self, but we retain an internal and coherent sense of identity. I view our relationships and interpersonal interactions as the essential contexts within which we negotiate and balance these self-presentations and internal identities.

Researchers examining racial and ethnic identity have largely worked from an Eriksonian notion of identity stability, focusing on universal, progressive stages that result in defined identity statuses (i.e., you have "achieved" ethnic identity or you have not).[14] Although Erikson considered sociohistorical context in his writings on identity across the lifespan, he has been interpreted as privileging identity stability and stages. Researchers of racial and ethnic identity have followed suit, primarily focusing on identity statuses and assuming that, once achieved, racial or ethnic identity will persist across contexts. In line with traditional developmental research, studies have focused on the influence of ethnic and racial identity on outcomes such as psychological adjustment and academic achievement. More recently, researchers exploring the influence of race and gender on youth outcomes have begun to consider the intersection of personal experiences, perceptions, and racial/ethnic identity development, particularly with regard to discrimination and social barriers.[15] Some have specifically examined how racial and ethnic identities are negotiated within local cultural practices and social interactions.[16]

In addition, researchers are taking a closer look at the intersectionality of social categories. Scholars using such a frame examine how social constraints operate differently depending on the confluence of social categories, considering, for example, the joint influence of race and class on access to and experiences of education.[17] Others have pushed us to consider identity development through the lens of intersectionality. These researchers consider how the interlocking of gender, race, and class shapes the "Others" against which we define our selves and the stereotypes to which we respond, thereby affecting our own identities.[18] Despite this increased focus on intersectionality, a recent editorial in the *Journal of Adolescent Research* still highlighted the need for more work with non-White populations, poor adolescents, and middle and high-school-aged youth. Such research, it was noted, is needed to help us move beyond the focus on identity statuses to "a more multidimensional model of identity that integrates personal and social aspects of self" and that would be more useful in the applied arena.[19] I attempt to answer that call.

I work from the growing body of literature that explores the lived experiences of youth growing up at the intersection of marginalized social categories. The intertwined influences of gender, race, and social class that come together in the cultural image of the "urban teen" are becoming the focus of research by many in psychology, sociology, education, and a variety of interdisciplinary fields.[20] For those interested in adolescence and identity, the role of these social categories in shaping both experience and sense of self must be a topic of exploration. In the late 1990s, Michelle Fine and Lois Weis suggested that three material bases shape our sense of self and Other: the body, the economy/economic opportunities, and the state/social policies.[21] I locate the processes by which these bases influence our identities in our local contexts, occurring within and through our relationships with other humans. In doing so, I retain the Eriksonian idea of an integrated identity as the healthy endpoint of adolescence. I acknowledge that we strive to reconcile and consolidate identities displayed across relationships and contexts into a stable self-concept. Yet I also refute the primacy of individuation, emphasizing how deeply relational the process of identity construction is for all people. Our relationships are the sites in which we negotiate not only our individuated sense of self, as both autonomous and connected to others, but also our identities in relation to macro social categories such as gender, race, and class.

The Context of Development

Context has been called an "essential feature of self."[22] Our identities are both sent out to the world and reflected back to us. They are profoundly social and contextual, and so is the process of their construction. We rely on both our own view of ourselves and our understandings of how others recognize us. The sense of stability and continuity posited by the Eriksonian model of identity assumes that, for most people, a coherent self exists across contexts. Yet we all occupy multiple social categories at once. I am a woman, a daughter, a researcher, an artist, a White, half-Jewish, American. None of these categories alone captures my experiences of the world. Recent theories have pointed out that women and many ethnic minorities have more fluid senses of self than initial identity theories suggest. This is because, historically, we have been required to move between contexts that expect different self-attributes of us.[23]

Furthermore, as W. E. B. Dubois indicated at the turn of the 20th century, a double consciousness exists for minorities in the United States, who must make sense not only of their own self-image but also of the possibly divergent image that others have of them.[24] In the postmodern world, this may apply to men as well. The complexity of modern life, including the multiplicity of roles we take on, the number of people with whom we interact, and the large variety of situations in which we find our-selves, forces us to continually reformulate ourselves for each emerging situation and context.[25] Although the "looking glass self" may still exist, the number of looking glasses has been exponentially increased, resulting in an infinite number of identities and evaluations from which to choose and to which to conform.[26]

Over the past 30 years, theorists and researchers have been increas-ingly focused on the contextual and interactive nature of all human de-velopment. The relationship between humans and our environments is bidirectional and multilayered; we develop through our participation in communities and cultures.[27] Humans have a uniquely long developmental trajectory and are more dependent on learning, a social activity, than are many other species.[28] Increasingly, therefore, theories of human develop-ment are highlighting the relationship between the human and her con-text as the pivotal force in development.[29] For those of us concerned with adolescent development, the contextual nature of identity development, in particular, is key.

For too many youth today, the developmental context is one of oppres-sion. Overall, 15.3% of American teens live in families whose incomes fall below the official poverty line. This number is vastly increased for Black adolescents, 24.7% of whom live in poverty.[30] Even more teens live in neighborhoods characterized by high rates of poverty; 29.4% of youth under age 18 live in census tracks with poverty rates of 40% or more, with a greater percentage of racial and ethnic minority youth living in such neighborhoods.[31] In addition, high-stakes testing; school segrega-tion (both interschool and intraschool, via tracking); large, disorganized, and underresourced schools; and the mass incarceration of young, Black, males—all these contribute to creating climates in which the number of developmental stressors is great.[32] For racial and ethnic minority youth and young people living in poverty, it is not simply the categories of race or social class that influence their development but the everyday, personal experiences of discrimination that accompany these categories.[33] These experiences shape how youth see themselves within society. They send a message that some identities, such as that of a college student, for exam-ple, are not open to these youth.[34] And these experiences are determined not only by the relationships between people but also the relationships between people and social structures.[35]

For example, new work by Anne Galletta and William Cross complicates the famous oppositional identity theory of John Ogbu, which placed the onus of the Black-White achievement gap on the development of an oppositional culture by Black youth. According to Ogbu, Black youth develop identities that actively reject traditional schooling as part of White culture. Galletta and Cross, who examined the same school district where Ogbu did his seminal work, emphasize educational policies and practices as instrumental in shaping the educational attitudes of African Americans. Rather than considering youth culture as the seed of the achievement gap, they highlight how Black families' history of interactions with the school district, both administrators and policies, shape their expectations of the educational system. Thus, school policies become instrumental in creating the context for the achievement gap.[36]

My own work, which emphasizes macro social structures as they interact with and influence local activity and identity construction, builds on this frame. The intersection of categories within which we live determines others' reactions to us, our relationship to power structures, and our images of our self. It is thus at the crux of our interactions with other people, relations with social structures, and group-identity alignments (both chosen and assigned) that our identities are constructed. Because our positions and relationships may change across contexts, our identities, and the meaning we give to particular identity categories, may also shift. This complicates what has traditionally been considered "normative" developmental processes.

Such issues began to come to light in the 1990s, as researchers pushed us to consider the dynamic and contextual nature of identity processes as they unfold within local settings and ecological systems. A number of volumes of work brought the unique developmental features and needs of minority and economically disadvantaged youth to our attention. Work by Margaret Beale Spencer and her colleagues, Shirley Brice Heath and Milbrey McLaughlin, Michelle Fine and Louis Weis, and Bonnie Leadbeater and Niobe Way, among others, took on race, ethnicity, gender, and social class as contexts for development. These researchers considered the experiences of youth from racial and ethnic minority backgrounds growing up in low-income urban neighborhoods, schools, and youth organizations.[37] They pointed to the need for more in-depth research on developmental processes in context and a linking of theory with practice to help improve

youth. I search for the meaning of actions rather than their causal explanation. Although some criticize interpretive frameworks as trying to increase communication without examining where and when communication is possible,[45] I believe my approach to adolescent identity helps us better understand youths' daily experiences and thereby better address their needs. This approach focuses on how youth who are often marginalized in local schools and larger society use an after-school program, and the relationships within it, to negotiate their place in the world. In doing so, these teens construct/resist/reconstruct their identities and the boundaries that both unite and define them.[46]

The Self and Identity

I am not interested in identity as a static construct. Nor am I interested in selfhood as a primarily internal concept. I work from and beyond the symbolic interactionist tradition by examining the dynamic relationship between the social world and the activity of selfhood. I insert George Herbert Mead's "Generalized Other" into Uri Bronfenbrenner's ecological model of human development.[47] I explore the process through which adolescents come to understand and create their selves in the world. I start from the premise that reality is socially constructed and that everyday activity is an entry point into understanding the larger social world and its relations of power. Social constructionists reject the idea of a single, empirically true reality. Rather, we all actively construct our worlds. These personal meanings are not developed in isolation but in concert with our culture and with other people's perceptions.[48] Self-making depends on the shared ideologies of one's society.[49] The categories that we use to communicate reflect the shared meanings of our culture.[50] Gender, as the most common of categories, reflects our assumptions of a binary sex/gender system, with particular meanings ascribed to each gender.

I combine the perspective of those who view gender as an activity, something we "do," and thereby create, in our everyday actions, with those who view gender as structural, a category that has been constructed through institutions and policies.[51] I expand this examination of the creation and re-creation of gender to other domains of identity, especially race and class.

Although I acknowledge the relevance of newer theories of identities, such as those that reframe the discourse around subjectivities that shift across settings, I maintain allegiance to the Eriksonian idea of an integrated identity. I steer away from traditional ideas of stages and statuses but lean toward narrative and symbolic interactionist theories of identity, which still emphasize internal coherence over contextual decentering. In 1968, Erikson wrote that "psychosocial identity is necessary as the anchoring of man's transient existence in the here and now."[52] Nearly four decades later, in a review of the field of identity studies, James Côté invokes Erikson's ideas in challenging the shift away from a stable, integrated identity. Côté suggests that by rejecting the notion of a "stable psychological base," postmodernists remove the possibility of individual agency in identity construction; people, therefore, are at the mercy of social forces, leading to context-defined subjectivities that have no stable unity across time and place.[53] This approach does not align with my own beliefs in the power of self-definition or with my experiences with adolescents. The teens with whom I have worked recognize the contextual nature of subjectivity but also strive to integrate the various subjectivities that they enact in different settings or that are thrust on them by different people.

Work taking a listening-centered approach to adolescent development supports this assertion. A number of researchers have found that adolescent boys experience tensions between their public and private identities, facing pressure to present a certain type of masculine identity that does not always correspond to their own internal sense of self.[54] Thus, the intersection of individual lives and social structures may require some shifting of identity presentation, but it does so within constraints and does not do away with an internal need for coherence between our internal and external selves. In *The Unknown City*, a study of working-class young adults, Fine and Weis struggle with the tension between essentialist and social constructionist approaches to identity with regard to social categories such as race and gender. Despite their desire to position race and gender as social constructions, they continually confront the material realities of these categories in their participants' narratives. This problematizes their aspirations, as researchers and theorists, to "play with" and deconstruct these categories.[55]

Similarly, despite radical critiques of identity and postmodern desires to destabilize and fragment the self, I come up against narratives that lead me back to a more durable and traditional sense of self. This durability does not make irrelevant the contextual nature of our identities. Rather, it argues for the integration of these subjectivities as an underlying task of adolescence. The meaning of my own "Jewishness," for example, is different in the urban northeast than it is in the rural south. Those meanings influence how I both view and present myself as a Jewish woman. But such a stance of shifting meaning does not deny that I seek some stability across those contexts. Our subjectivities are not so postmodern that multiple contexts release us from our embodied self and sense of internal identity. Thus, I cannot do away with the idea that we seek a stable sense of identity across time and contexts, even if we shift aspects of our identities (or subjectivities) across settings and relationships.

After-School Programs as Sites of Development

From this nested set of contexts, relationships, and individuals, we come to the crux of my question. How are youth within a particular after-school program interacting with the environment and the people within it in the process of their own self-construction? And how do these local contexts and relationships interact with and mediate larger social structures? If adolescents are having their developmental needs met and cultivating a sense of self within such sites, then these environments should be helping youth to integrate multiple roles, providing a sense of both individual validation and belonging, and granting a balance of autonomy and adult support.

Settings lacking in such supportive processes can give way to negative outcomes. When local contexts do not provide opportunities that fit adolescents' developmental needs, harmful psychological changes can occur. Indeed, youth may be attracted to gangs because they meet needs, such as a sense of belonging, safety, and self-worth, not met by the larger environment.[56] Research on urban after-school programs suggests that supportive adults and settings that help minority youth think critically about society may support positive group and individual self-worth as a form of resistance. This can help adolescents mediate between macro social structures and personal experiences and identities.[57] It is my contention that using a developmental lens to consider after-school programs as a setting for adolescents will enhance their potential. Increasingly, after-school program researchers are emphasizing the importance of promoting positive development in addition to problem prevention and intervention.[58] Because identity is a key task of adolescence, considering youth organizations as settings for self-construction may augment these settings' functioning, better enabling them to support specific and necessary developmental processes.

The positive youth development (PYD) movement serves as a foundation for this type of setting-based, developmental research. Researchers working from a PYD frame take an asset-based approach to youth. We assume that all youth have inherent competencies, which are fostered through contexts aligned with their assets. Supportive contexts provide positive adult-youth relationships, skill-building experiences, and opportunities for community involvement. Whereas the concept of resilience has been traditionally located within the individual, PYD suggests that environments and youth interact to promote or impede the development of positive cognitive, affective, and behavioral characteristics. These characteristics have been identified and defined as the "5 C's" of PYD: competence, confidence, character, connection, and caring. Although development is a process, the 5 C's describe the goals of positive youth development and assume that a proper balance of these characteristics is a desired outcome of adolescent development.[59] As fields, psychology and sociology have not drawn on PYD, which often takes an applied approach. This is a shortcoming of the literature. By returning to the roots of identity theory and examining how youth construct identities within contemporary settings, we bring together the strengths of theory, basic research, and applied developmental research to better understand the process of identity construction as it occurs for adolescents in today's complex world.

I assume that the actuality of adolescents' lives and daily activities are key to understanding both their localized sense of self and their views of where they will fit into society in the future. I assume that to understand the world we must understand the meanings people give to actions and how these meanings are created through our interactions with others.[60] Whereas the bulk of literature on youth growing up at the intersection of marginalized social categories points to the importance of interpersonal relationships to their identities and overall development, researchers have continued to focus on the negative aspects of relationships or on the lack of positive relationships in these youths' lives. But I believe BJ when she says there are birds in the projects. Understanding the influence of gender, race, and class on young lives and identities requires examining how these categories are enacted within local contexts and relationships. Such a frame, molded of interpretivist and interactionist perspectives, works from detailed personal narratives of lived experiences.[61] These ideas, concepts, and theories sensitize my investigation and help to frame my book's main themes.

The Journey through East Side

Throughout this book I consider both abstract theory and local environmental factors, foregrounding the ecological contexts in which identities are developed. I uncover unexpected and important information about the process of self-construction for adolescents living at the intersection of multiple social categories, teens who are often marginalized by mainstream society. I explicate how they engage in the space of an after-school program, using their relationships and activities in the club to negotiate the construction of their identities within the social world, both local and macro. I have organized the book around three main themes of self-construction: (1) interpersonal self, (2) self in relation to society and Others, and (3) the influence and construction of gender and its intersectionality with race and class. And in each of these themes, youths' relationships with other people play a key role.

The results of this research are presented in seven chapters. In chapters 2, 4, and 6 I focus on the three main themes. Each chapter is followed by a case study of an individual youth (chapters 3, 5, and 7). The case studies provide in-depth portraits of how these themes are enacted in the lives of individual teens and expand on the theoretical developments in the preceding chapter. In the final chapter, chapter 8, I consider the findings in relation to the needs of after-school programs and practitioners concerned with creating positive developmental spaces for teens. Therein I link the process of self-construction with the potential of after-school programs, yielding practical implications rooted in adolescents' developmental needs.

The Interpersonal Self

In chapter 2, I examine the construction of self in relation to interpersonal others. From talk shows to pop psychology to sitcoms, American culture seems obsessed with perceived differences in the relational styles of men and women and the importance of interpersonal relationships to each gender. In the spring of 2004, *Newsweek* magazine got into the act, asking why women are "the more social sex."[62] The article focused on evolutionary and biological evidence for the importance of female friendships to human survival, leaving readers with the impression that women have a naturally stronger impetus for forming and maintaining bonds through prosocial behavior. Yet nowhere does the article consider the role of socialization in the development of gender differences. Neither does it ponder the changes in the human social world since prehistoric times which have altered the skills necessary for survival for both men and women. This focus on dichotomy without serious consideration of context, cause, change, or overlap is typical for mainstream considerations of human development. The insistence on looking at gender differences in social relations as a Venus versus Mars issue ignores the fact that we all grow up in relation to others and that human connection is important to all of us and to the continuation of civil society.

In chapter 2, I listen to youths' self-descriptions for indicators of how they see themselves, both as individuals and in connection to others. My findings do not mirror much of the past work on relational identity. Yet they support the assertions of researchers such as Niobe Way, who have argued that boys are as relational as girls, if only we would listen to their stories with a more attuned ear.[63] Both boys and girls at East Side depict themselves in rich relations with others. The teens describe themselves using a balance of individuated and connected words, demonstrating an ability to see themselves in relation to, but not subsumed by, their interpersonal relationships. Four youth (two boys and two girls) use only connected words in their self-descriptions. The narratives of the East Side teens challenge our assumptions about the greater importance of relationships for girls over boys.

Two words emerge repeatedly in the voices of the teens: respect and responsibility. Youth talk about these as key characteristics that are important to their overall sense of self. Many report that these qualities are encouraged and developed at the Boys and Girls Club. Respect is a term that can be used in myriad ways, especially by teens as opposed to adults. I use the term in a "ground-up" fashion, listening to the various meanings it has to youth in different contexts and exploring its meanings within and upon their interpersonal relationships. A majority of the youth say that they would not be the same person they are today without the club. Many indicate that these prosocial characteristics would be different without the support of the club and its staff. The importance of respect and responsibility as qualities that are emphasized by interactions within the club is supported by data from field notes. These characteristics are encouraged and expected as well as modeled. This is a key finding for youth programmers and policy makers to consider as we think about how to promote prosocial traits in youth.

Self and Society

In chapter 4, I discuss the construction of self in relation to society, particularly social categories such as race and class. In addition to developing our identities in relation to those with whom we have personal contact, we are also aware of our positions in the larger world. And those positions influence our relationships with other people. We construct our sense of self in part based on knowledge about and reaction to how we are seen by others. Historically, research in this area has focused on the development of specific ethnic and racial identities.[64] Yet the intersection of race and class in America has made problematic an approach to identity which attempts to isolate the influence of each category. We are all some combination of categories that together influence our social positioning and sense of self. As a result, researchers are increasingly tackling the complex knot woven by the intersection of social categories. Much of this work has been conducted in the context of schools and classrooms.[65] Whereas education is an important venue to explore, understanding how adolescents negotiate social categories and construct self and Other in sites in which they voluntarily participate is also imperative. In this exploration, we learn more about how to shape settings in ways that align with youths' developmental needs and innate competencies.

The East Side teens have a strong sense of themselves as constructed as Other by society. They refer to experiences of being treated as "project kids," stereotyped because of where they live. The boys in particular describe differential treatment by authority figures based on the confluence of their race and neighborhood. When talking about experiences of discrimination, the teens shift between attributing prejudice alternately to race, neighborhood, and gender. Their narratives demonstrate the importance of looking at the interactive process of social categories in self-construction. The boys' narratives highlight the ways in which the bodies of minority males are read by society. This complicates our thinking on the influence of gender on identity, a topic that is the subject of the next section.

Within this chapter, I also explore the ways in which East Side serves as a site of both resistance to and reconstruction of stereotypes with which the youth are in dialogue. Like other aspects of ourselves, race and class identities are negotiated within our relationships and interactions with others.[66] All but one of the youth feel respected at East Side. Many contrast this to their experiences outside of the club, where they feel that people judge them based on external characteristics. Yet they are prone to using similar images to differentiate themselves from other kids in their neighborhood. An after-school program can serve as a site in which youth grapple with social boundaries and hierarchies, using the site and people in it to help define self and Other.[67] Club members tend to fall back on stereotypes of urban teens as images against which they construct their own identities.

This section demonstrates the active engagement of East Side youth in the complex, cultural discourse of race and class. Despite assertions that race "doesn't matter," a phrase the teens sometimes used in response to my questions about the role or importance of race in their lives, the East Side teens describe experiences of both race and class discrimination. These are often melded together into singular experiences. Their awareness of other people's perceptions of them influences the ways in which they socially identify. Most important, their words demonstrate the fallacy of examining self-construction through the lens of one variable. They also illustrate the importance of having a local setting, such as an after-school program, within which the whole teen is seen and respected and in which social stereotypes can be laid down and resisted.

The Gendered Self

In chapter 6, I consider gender as an influencing social category and explore its construction within these teens' lives and activities, as well as its intersectionality with race and class. Gender has been deemed an essential feature of the self. As an organizing social category, perhaps none can match its power. Our brains quickly recognize and process the gender of those with whom we interact.[68] From birth, when a clothed baby is itself androgynous, many parents seem committed to ensuring that the "proper" gender of their child is recognized, swathing their newborns in layers of pink or blue. A trip to a children's clothing store will affirm how important society considers this gendered marking.

Likewise, research has prioritized the study of gender difference, seldom looking at within-group differences or between-group similarities. A growing body of work points us to the overlapping influences of gender with other social categories. Boys' constructions of masculinity and girls' constructions of femininity are responses to their raced and classed positions within the gender structure.[69] Research in this domain typically focuses on boys *or* girls, examining the construction of gender within single-gender groups. Yet masculinity and femininity rely on each other; boys and girls both participate in the construction of each. Considering only girls' constructions of femininity and boys' constructions of masculinity gives us only half the picture.

The youth at East Side demonstrate knowledge of traditional gender norms and use such stereotypes in their abstract discussions of gender. Yet when describing real people and goals, they make no such attributions of gendered traits. Teens appear to differentiate between what they recognize as gendered expectations and gender as a lived experience. The citing of traits of independence and responsibility for both women and men may be linked to the sociohistorical context of African American culture, particularly for minority youth growing up in an urban neighborhood with high rates of poverty. Yet there are two areas in which gender norms appear to be strictly enforced: sexuality and physical appearance.

When discussing gender in the abstract, East Side youth talk about femininity and masculinity as acting. Girls describe femininity as something that is put on and taken off in different contexts, often related to clothing and makeup. Femininity, as a personality characteristic, tends to be deemed negative, associated with qualities such as talking too much and being "fussy." For both boys and girls at East Side, definitions of the masculine and feminine rely heavily on personified images of the Other. They sometimes evoke a gay man to define the word feminine or a woman not wearing makeup to describe masculine. Other times, particularly in the realm of sexuality, the Other is used to define the boundary of appropriate norms through demonstration of inappropriate gender behavior. East Side itself serves as a site in which norms are resisted (through participation in cross-gender activities) and reconstructed (through peer-group interactions).

The East Side youths' constructions of gender demonstrate the ways in which discourses of social class and race intersect with gender and influence our relationships to the gender structure. Youths' narratives also reveal the differential salience of gender in various areas of their lives. Thus, they urge us to consider gender as an entity whose meaning is fluid and constructed in our local contexts and through our relationships with others.

Case Studies

The three case study chapters, 3, 5, and 7, present the stories of Lorenzo, Nicole, and John. Each youth provides an in-depth look at themes explored in the chapters preceding them, explicating how these issues are played out in individual lives. Yet each adolescent's narrative also expands on the topics covered in the prior chapter(s) and foreshadows issues yet to come. The case studies serve not only to illustrate matters considered previously but also to move the thesis forward, providing new information and patterns, ideas and themes not uncovered in the more general discussions.

In chapter 3, we meet Lorenzo, a 17-year-old African American male, who has spent much of his young life caretaking for younger siblings, leading to a feeling that he missed out on being a kid. At the Boys and Girls Club, Lorenzo develops a close relationship with Charles, the physical education director, who becomes a father figure to him. At the same time, Lorenzo begins to see himself as a role model for younger club members, using his interpersonal and caretaking skills to develop leadership abilities as a coach for the younger kids' sports teams. Lorenzo helps us see how interpersonal relationships can provide a supportive base from which to develop a prosocial identity that meets developmental needs, leads to greater social integration, and changes one's self-perceptions.

In chapter 5, I present the story of Nicole, a 15-year-old African American female, who is a good student and active club member. She has been involved in club programs since she was little. In recent years she has taken

on how those programs should be run. Youth who participate in such programs often get the opportunity to travel to conferences to meet club members from around the country. Yet, on the other hand, national and regional rules are sometimes at odds with what individual clubs consider the best practice for their own neighborhoods.

The tension between levels of governance was apparent at all the clubs I visited. East Side is no exception. Staff complain of required paperwork that takes them away from activities with youth. Directors wrestle with how to follow national rules while still meeting their local community's needs. One way in which I see East Side as unique is in the creative and determined ways in which Rick and Sean work with staff to serve the youth of the community. They do so even though it sometimes requires bending official rules. Rick and Sean both believe that their primary purpose is to serve the youth of the neighborhood and, in line with the organization's mission statement, to serve those kids who need them the most. Their attitudes are reflected in their actions. Whereas most clubs only allow teenagers into the building after 6:00 in the evening, East Side changed its policy to make sure that the teens have somewhere to go in the immediate after-school hours. Staff meetings include discussion of kids both inside and outside of the club. Rick makes an effort to employ community members, giving him eyes and ears in the neighborhood and a way to find out what is going on with the kids after club hours. When problems are noted, Rick and Sean work with staff to address the issue. This includes reaching out to parents who are having trouble and trying to bring in youth from the neighborhood whose family situations are difficult. Club staff wrestle, at times, with ethical dilemmas stemming from their commitment to do the best they can for the youth while balancing individual child and group needs and complying with the organization's overarching policies. But this commitment translates to an active and caring environment in which youth get support for their developing selves.

This does not mean that the club always runs smoothly or that there are never tensions between administrators, staff, kids, and families. Rick himself refers to East Side as having its "ebbs and flows," yet his ability to acknowledge the ebbs and remain optimistic about returning to a flow is unique. At times, he would look at me and say, "You know, Nancy, last year we were in a down slump. But now, we're getting back on track." Such slumps often seemed to stem from issues with staffing. Staff members and administrators left, and Rick struggled to fill empty slots with capable, competent, and personable replacements. But kids' attachment to individual staff members sometimes thwarted such efforts. When Charles and Cheryl left, many of the older teens, who had close ties to them, stopped coming to the club. Although some of the male teens stuck around to play ball, Charles's absence was palpable, and even those remaining boys did not take easily to his replacement. When Charles returned to East Side a few months later, the older boys reappeared.

Cheryl's case was more complicated. She had started a number of popular girls' programs and had a celebrity-like following among the preteen and adolescent girls. Cheryl was initially well liked and given wide berth by club administrators, likely due to her ability to get innovative girls' programs up and going. So her exodus came as a bit of a surprise. The full story behind her leaving never emerged, but it was apparently not a voluntary resignation. The club members were not given any warning of her departure, although Cheryl spoke individually to a few girls to whom she was particularly close. This lack of any official recognition made it all the more difficult for the girls to adjust to Cheryl's absence. The rumor was that a group of parents had begun to object to Cheryl's girls' discussion groups, feeling that the groups had devolved into discussions of sex. The girls, for their part, felt that these discussions actually helped keep them from engaging in sexual activity too early. The club director, possibly under pressure from the parents, decided that Cheryl had begun to cross the line between staff and peer and that, despite her impressive record of service, she could no longer work at East Side.

The period after Cheryl's leaving was one of the "ebbs" in East Side's tides. The timing overlapped with Charles's departure, leaving a hole in the teens' adult support networks at East Side. The situation with Cheryl may have had less drastic impact if it had been handled differently by the club's leadership. In particular, communicating more with the youth may have helped salve the wound. Yet I believe it was actually Rick's desire to carefully place the club at the center of its local community that led to the tension around this particular issue. The adults clearly perceived the teens' needs differently than did the youth themselves. Cheryl seemed to be aligned with the teens' view of their needs, putting her at odds with club directors and some parents. Rick's need to balance these two competing groups of stakeholders led him to make decisions that, in the short term at least, were not productive to youths' attachment to East Side. In the long run, most of the members returned to East Side, even those girls who were closest to Cheryl. Rick was able to hire new staff and retain the club's positive reputation among parents in the community.

For youth who come from homes without a lot of positive adult support, East Side helps them negotiate the tasks of growing up. I saw East Side staff arrange for youth to get glasses, have clean and seasonally appropriate clothes, and obtain work permits when their parents did not or were not able to do so. For those youth who did have family support, East Side provided an additional buttress on which they could lean when needed. This does not mean that East Side is without its flaws. As you will see throughout the book, there are issues of youth-on-youth harassment. Staff are not always as proactive as they could be in addressing issues, particularly regarding gender. Opportunities for more critical engagement with social issues are sometimes missed. As with any organization, there is room for growth and the potential for more proactive and transformative activity is often overlooked amid the daily demands of keeping the club functioning with limited funding and staff.

East Side's Neighborhood

The majority of club members live in the nearby public housing project. The neighborhood has been in a state of uncertainty in recent years as residents wait to hear whether their units will be torn down. Like other inner-city housing projects, both a high level of gang violence and a sense of supportive community characterize the neighborhood. Evidence of the latter was witnessed at a meeting when the housing authority announced that the project would be renovated but not torn down. Residents erupted into a loud cheer. For the most part, it seems that residents, although desiring improvements in their living conditions, do not want to be separated from the community. The apartment buildings are in better condition than much public housing, but it is still not very safe at night. Nearby are railroad yards and single-family houses. The surrounding neighborhood has experienced extensive gentrification. In fact, police crime statistics and census income data appear to be highly confounded by the middle-class to upper-class housing that has gone up in nearby blocks in recent years.

Fig. 1-2. Bob's Photo: "It's Just My Home"

The space around the club is not immune to the violence in the projects. Three local gangs operate in the area. There have been shootings outside of the club, and many youth have experienced the deaths of relatives, friends, and fellow club members. Kids as young as five know the local gangs' colors. On my first day at the club, I was informed by a small boy that if I had parked my car outside the club, "there'll be bullet holes in it!" The club director was quick to assure me that this had only happened to him once in his many years in the neighborhood. In fact, I never experienced any property damage or personal safety issues in my four years there.

The lives of the youth outside of the club, however, are marked by violence. Some youth talk about strategies they use for staying safe, such as taking alternate routes home. Bob, a 14-year-old male, articulates the conflicted feelings that many youth have about their neighborhood and the challenges it presents to them psychologically and physically. When describing a photograph of his building in the housing project (Figure 1-2), he says:

> I feel comfortable there cause I've lived there all my life. It's just my home.
> It's real convenient, two bus stops, pay phone if I need it, store across the
> street, restaurant. Girl was stabbed to death by the woman who lived beneath me . . . someone got shot on this side. Nicole's brother was shot

across the street here, by [Deuces]. I almost got shot. They were shooting at me. Antonio and I were playing baseball, and there were some Hispanic guys walking by us, and these Black guys started shooting at the Hispanic guys, [Kings], near us . . . I'm gonna have problems when I grow up.[74]

This is the neighborhood in which the vast majority of youth from the study live. It is typical of the experiences of many of them outside the club walls.

The difference between youth who live in the projects and those who don't is a continual issue at the club. These divisions are recognized by staff and youth alike. Virtually all the club members live in the projects. Some who don't have difficult relationships with other youth.[75] These types of splits are even more apparent when the club takes kids on trips outside of the neighborhood. Charles, the physical education director, notes that participants in a sports program at a nearby park see the club youth as "scavengers" because they are from the projects. He sees this attitude displayed whenever the club team plays against the local park team. The teens are well aware of these stereotypes. The fact that virtually no youth from outside the projects attend the club, despite the fact that it is equally accessible to youth from other parts of the community, is striking and demonstrates the deep social class divisions in the area.

The East Side Youth Who Participated

The larger ethnographic sample comprises all the youth and staff who were present at East Side during four years of fieldwork by myself and five other research assistants. The specific study sample consists of seventeen youth ages 12–18, nine females and eight males. Seven of the youth were between the ages of 12 and 14, and ten of the youth were 15 or older at the beginning of the interview portion of the study. Ten of the youth describe their race or ethnicity as Black or African American, two as African American and Hispanic, two as African American plus two additional ethnicities, and one each as Hispanic, White, and Other.[76] Fourteen youth live in the housing project near the club. The remaining three have close ties to the neighborhood. Only one lives with both her parents. Eleven live with their mother and a number of siblings. Two live with only their mother, and three live with either another relative or other nonfamilial adults. All participants are active club members, who had been coming to the club for a number of years and/or came to the club on a regular basis during the study years (for details on sampling, see appendix A).

Methodology

My goal as I began the study was to explore the underlying and often invisible societal influences on youths' identity development. I wanted to examine how youth make meaning of, resist, and re-create social categories and relationships within their local settings and daily activities as they construct their sense of self. I was interested, too, in understanding the role of interpersonal relationships to boys and girls, to hearing how youths' connections with other people inform their own identities. I further wanted to examine how knowledge about these processes could be applied to create more supportive environments for teens.

My methodological approach stems from feminist and social constructionist bodies of research that privilege subjective knowledge and emphasize social positioning. I take an interpretive, rather than an explanatory, approach, using qualitative methods to examine individual experience, which I then relate to broader themes in identity development. Qualitative data provide the opportunity to identify mechanisms and process, showing the connections between individual stories and larger variables.[77]

Because of my interest in the role of local environments in self-construction, it was important for me to draw on methodology that links situated contexts with larger social relations. Theories that consider local activity as a key to understanding both society and personal identity were, therefore, influential to my project.[78] To study the self without examining its activity is to miss the actual site and process of self-construction. Furthermore, the self is constructed in relation to both local interpersonal relationships and macro social structures. The intersection of identity and feminist frameworks provides a lens through which to see how social forces (stereotypes, expectations, roles) come together with individual self-construction in the process of identity development in daily life.

My research process was one of both seeking and discovery. I knew I was interested in the role of Others in youths' self-concepts. I thus formulated questions to get at this issue. I was also concerned with the influence of interpersonal and group relationships on self-construction and gender, race, and class as social categories. During the process of analysis, however, I discovered themes, such as respect and responsibility, that I had not previously considered.

One of the beauties of qualitative research is the live nature of the process. Data collection and analysis are interactive. This allows the researcher to discover threads of meaning that may be missed if theorizing and analyzing took place in separate spheres. Through this process I uncovered themes that may have remained hidden if I had relied only on a "wish list" of research questions. This is not to minimize my physical or intellectual presence within this project. What I recorded was filtered through my eyes and ears. The analysis was worked through in my brain. The data, therefore, was never truly free of me (for details on the methodology and methods used in data collection and analysis, see appendix A).

My Place in This Project

Research is bidirectional. As a researcher, I am both subject and object. My participants are subjects, objects, and actors. The idea of an unattached, unbiased observer is not only unattainable but also a false idol. It is in the relationships between researchers and participants that knowledge is co-constructed.[79]

This was never more apparent to me than during my time "in the field." Over four years I spent anywhere from one to four days a week at the club. From coaching volleyball to judging a baby contest to attending a funeral, my activities diverged greatly from traditional, empirical research. Anyone who has worked with adolescents knows that it is impossible not to be affected by their energy, their intensity, their unique combination of cruelty and charm. And anyone who has spent any length of time within a community knows that it is impossible not to feel emotionally connected to those within that circle. To deny such influences would be to deny the humanity of both researcher and participant. Through examining the humanity of both, we learn more about our topic and ourselves, we bring richness and honesty to our research. Such self-reflexivity is part and parcel of feminist methodology.

This self-reflexivity requires acknowledging the multiple positions that we occupy in relation to our participants, as well as in the world as a whole.[80] My own social positions and values influenced the choices I made and the methods I used in this project. They also affected what I was willing and able to see.[81]

I have written elsewhere about my subjectivity and relationship to the East Side community and this research.[82] My own position as a White, female, adult, academic immersed in an after-school program with mostly low-income, Black, teenagers influenced what appeared salient to me, as well as how I interpreted what I saw. In addition, the power relations that are constituted from a blend of gender, race, class, age, and my position as a researcher, influenced my interactions with youth.[83] Throughout my time in the field, as well as during the entire process of analysis and writing, I attempted to keep these power dynamics present in my mind.[84] At various points in this book I highlight my own position and the context of youths' self-construction in relation to me, as the researcher. This is dealt with in-depth in chapter 7, where the story of John emphasizes this self-reflexive work.

Methods

I used four methods as entry points into the adolescents' experiences of self: focus groups, interviews, photography projects, and ethnographic observations. In addition to carrying out four years of participant-observation at East Side, I conducted two focus groups and two sets of semi-structured interviews with seventeen selected youth. The interviews included discussion of photographs that the teens took with disposable cameras I provided as part of this research. I also conducted formal and informal interviews and group discussions with East Side staff, administrators, and parents over the course of the four years (for details, see appendixes A–D). The ongoing nature of analysis, however, helped to reduce data overload at the completion of data collection. Throughout the years I reread and reflected on field notes and analyzed data from pilot interviews and focus groups to help guide my future data collection. As I conducted the final sets of interviews with youth, I searched the transcripts for emerging themes so I could follow up with youth and staff before leaving the field and focus future observations. I also began to reread field notes from over the years to get a sense of how themes emerging from interviews may be observed in youths' interactions over time. Once I had left the field, I read through the entire data corpus making notes on themes and categories of interest. I then compiled and analyzed the data in multiple forms, within and across participants and sources. I coded data based on both my beginning theoretical frames, rooted in identity theory, and on emergent themes, such as respect. Examining themes through in-dividual youth narratives as well as across the corpus of data deepened my analysis (for details of analysis, see appendix A).

Seeing the Birds

The foundation of this work is my focus on the contextual and rela-tional nature of identity construction. A common theme is the necessity to move beyond considerations of dichotomous differences. I aim for a process-based approach to identity that considers the confluence of social categories and positions in our lives and the role of local environments and relationships in helping us negotiate and balance these positions in our own identities. Youths' narratives support this and demonstrate the complicated nature of contemporary adolescent life.

In the pages that follow I set forth an exploration of the process of identity development in context and in relation, to others and Others, to individuals and society. I seek to provide insight into how individual and social identities are formed in and through our relationships. It is the in-teractive effects of social categories, through social positioning and seg-regation, that lead to different contexts of development for minority and low-income youth.[85] To understand processes of development, we have to examine the role of social structure in creating the contexts in which development takes place. We must then consider how youth engage with and in these contexts, and their multiple activities and relationships, as spaces for self-construction. I highlight how youth at East Side construct connected, often prosocial, selves. But, just like adults, teens are not al-ways nice to each other. The process of self-construction, while exciting, can be messy and hard to watch. No setting can ensure that all interactions within it are positive. It is the responsibility of adults to create settings that help youth positively direct their creative, self-constructive energies. Do-ing so requires a better understanding of the developmental opportuni-ties provided by settings for teens and the ways in which they can support youth in reaching their potential.

2

■　■　■　■　■　■　■　■　■

"I Give People a Lot of Respect"

The Self in Interpersonal Relationships

> Respect is not something one can imitate, but something one must embody . . . "Respect" as an integral aspect of life, both personal and social, is maintained by the respectful acts of individuals.
>
> —Sarah Lawrence-Lightfoot (2000), p. 57

If I asked you for the first five words that come to your mind when I say "teenager," the chances are that "respectful" and "responsible" would not be among them. Adolescence in America has been characterized, at least since the turn of the 20th century, as a time of turmoil, of crossing the stormy seas from childhood to adulthood.[1] As a society, we have constructed an image of adolescents that inspires a vague sense of both awe and fear. When my brother and I were teens, my mother got used to receiving nods of sympathy when she told people that she had two adolescents at home. Yet she remained perplexed by peoples' reactions. To her, my brother and I proved energetic and exciting, challenging, perhaps, but never boring.

This view of adolescence as a time of inspiring growth that can be rewarding and invigorating, as well as challenging and frustrating, is not the mainstream one. Nor is it typically considered for its potential to positively shape adolescent development. We seldom recognize that our stereotypes of adolescents construct the images youth have as models for their emerging identities.[2] Although the role of adult expectations in academic achievement has been documented, we have not extended this to the broader sense of self. And when we consider the role of other people in identity construction, we often turn to discussions of girls versus boys, relational selves versus individuated selves. The East Side teens' stories of self-construction help explicate the role of such interpersonal processes and make clear the importance of personal relationships and characteristics such as respect and responsibility to both male and female teens.

Identity Development in Adolescence

One of the key tasks of adolescence is the formation of an integrated identity.[3] During adolescence, the age-old question "who am I" emerges and quickly becomes a vital concern. When we think of adolescents, and especially their subcultures and peer groups, we often picture the ways in which they mark themselves physically. Clothes, hairstyles, and accessories serve as a billboard to the world: "this is who I am." Or at least, this is who I am today. During adolescence, such physical markings can be tried on and discarded, as teens experiment with different identities.

But identity is more than who one is as a unique individual. Identity also entails figuring out where one fits into the world at large. Thus, identity is an intrapsychic activity that takes place within sociocultural context. This is facilitated by changes both in the individual adolescent and in the adolescent's social worlds.[4] During adolescence, increased cognitive abilities make it possible for youth to consider themselves abstractly; metacognition permits identity to become a pressing issue. Social worlds also expand, as youth have increased contact with people outside their families. These changes bring about recognition of both possible selves (things we may be in the future) and multiple selves (different identities that we may display in different contexts). While possible selves can motivate us, multiple selves, if not integrated and resolved, can result in role conflicts, whereby different aspects of the self seem to contradict, rather than complement, each other.[5]

Part of the task of adolescence, therefore, is to integrate and resolve the myriad selves we experience in different contexts. This may be a particular challenge for minority youth, who often experience more role conflicts at earlier ages than their majority peers. This can stem from social stereotypes, which lead some adults, such as potential employers and teachers, to characterize adolescents in ways contradictory to their own self-perceptions. For youth growing up in poverty, role conflict can also result from the stress of economic hardship, which may require adolescents to take on adult roles, such as financial provider or caretaker.[6]

As part of identity construction and integration, adolescents individuate from their families of origin and stake out an autonomous sense of self.[7] Yet this separation, as it is often characterized, is not a severing of ties. Adolescents need relationships with supportive adults. In some cultures, in fact, separation is not given the precedence it is in the United States.[8] Autonomy can, and should, exist within a community of support. Supportive adults and environments can help adolescents bridge the conflicting roles and contexts that must be integrated during identity formation. They provide a balance of autonomy and support, allowing adolescents to experience both individual validation and a sense of belonging.[9]

Some scholars have argued that society's power structure and socialization processes, on both macro and micro levels, have specific impacts on individual identity development that differ based on an individual's position within the social structure.[10] Such a stance leads to the consideration of identity beyond the level of individual characteristics and demographics, grounding identities in our sociopolitical system. This also points to factors beyond gender that influence self-concept. The social positioning of East Side youth around axes of race and class is a central factor in their lives. These positionings influence self-concept in ways that confound what we traditionally think of as gender difference, pointing out the role of perceived social power in self-development.

"I Don't Disrespect Anybody": The Connected Self

American rock anthems may valorize man as a rock or an island, but John Donne was closer to the truth when he wrote:

> As therefore the bell that rings to a sermon, calls not upon the preacher only, but upon the congregation to come: so this bell calls us all. . . . No

man is an island, entire of itself . . . any man's death diminishes me, because I am involved in mankind; and therefore never send to know for whom the bell tolls; it tolls for thee.[11]

Humans are interdependent. The human baby requires nine months of gestation and years of close protection, care, and supervision. And this is only the beginning. We exist within webs of relationships that support us throughout our lives. Group identity may be a more basic, evolutionary need than individual identity; our survival as a species required interdependence.[12] Yet, as Donne was penning his verse, across the sea the Puritans were founding the first settlements that would spawn the American ethos of individual success through hard work and independence. This saga of American character has informed the ways in which researchers have positioned identity as a developmental task.

Early psychological theories posited that the self was created in dialogue with the social world. These theories emphasized the ways in which people are worked into our self-concepts through our "looking glass self" and the "generalized other."[13] Although self is a distinctive notion from identity, the two are linked. Erik Erikson, who developed the influential stages of identity development in the mid-20th century, clearly drew on these theories in creating a portrait of the struggle of the individual to find a place for herself in society.[14] Theorists of the self focused on internal constructions and systems such as self-esteem and self-concept. Identity theorists pushed the self into the public world; they explored how the intrapsychic self-concept is expressed in individual behavior and presentation of self, encompassing but not limited to the various self-systems.[15] Whereas the self is influenced by the social world but exists solely within individual consciousness, identity exists within both the world and the individual psyche.

Recently, the concept of a unitary and stable identity has come into question. Postmodernists suggest that identity is better thought of as subjectivities, emphasizing the multiple and contextual nature of identities in a postmodern world. Kenneth Gergen, for example, has provided the idea of a "saturated self," the contemporary individual who is bombarded with numerous contexts and interactions within any single day.[16] These frameworks are necessary but not sufficient. They leave identity as a floating entity with no stable link to the individual self. It is important to acknowledge the power of context in shaping identities. But it is essential to also consider the individual at the center as an active agent bringing cohesion to her experiences in the world through the process of identity-making. In such a view, the process of coalescing context and self is key and transpires within the local settings of our lives.

Ever since Erikson, developmentalists have viewed adolescence as the period of life when issues of identity construction come to the fore. The focus of adolescent development has been on separation, on the ways in which adolescents become their own people, individuating from their families, exploring possible future roles, and developing integrated identities that serve as a foundation for understanding themselves and their place in the world. This focus on separation may be an artifact of the Western emphasis on individual independence. Cross-cultural research reveals differences in the process of separation. Adolescents in some eastern cultures report strong interdependence and greater happiness with their families.[17] Although researchers recognize that identity is developed within social relationships, relationships have tended to serve primarily as a backdrop to the process of separation in developmental theory.[18] My work suggests that relationships need to be moved to the fore of identity studies. The East Side teens describe themselves as embedded in rich relationships with others; many of their narratives involve the club as a site for the nurturance and enactment of their relational identities.

"I Am . . .": Youths' Self-Descriptions

At the beginning of the first interview, I asked youth for the five words that best describe them. I coded these self-descriptors into two categories: connected and individual (see appendix E for coding criteria).[19] Connected words refer to youths' relationships with others. Individual words describe a trait that is an individual characteristic, independent of connections with other people.[20] All but one youth used at least one connected word among their five self-descriptors. Four (two males and two females) used only connected words. The majority used an almost equal split of connected and individual words. Some of their answers are below.

> Lover, respectful, fun, happy, smart. Happy and smart are the most important. Lover means fun to be around, caring. Respectful means honest,

trustworthy. They mean a lot [to me]. —Dynasty, 15-year-old African American female

Intelligent, relaxed, clever, responsible, mature. Responsible [is the] most important. I think I'm intelligent because I can hold my own wherever I'm at . . . If I work hard I can accomplish anything. It's like I'm relaxed cause I ain't really the type that gonna be all out in the open and wild and crazy. It takes people a while when they first meet me to figure me out. . . . Responsible because I take on everything and I complete the tasks I need to to get where I need to be. —Kelly, 16-year-old African American male

Kindness, truthfulness, helpfulness, attitudes. Kindness is most important. I help out with the club when they need help. I tell the truth no matter what. . . . I help my momma around the house and stuff. When people tell me something I know is not true I get mad . . . [at the club] I be kind to kids and stuff. Whatever [club staff] ask I tell them the truth. I help out with Sean and stuff. —Moonie, 12-year-old Hispanic female

[I'm] nice, at points respectful, outgoing, funny, a good person. They . . . mean I'm an okay guy. . . . I'm not perfect. I'm not bad either. Most important are respectful and a good person. —Antonio, 14-year-old Black male

As these quotes demonstrate, most youth combine connected and individualistic words in their self-descriptions. They are able to balance relational qualities with individual talents to create holistic identities that exist in relationship to, but are not subsumed by, others.

Moonie's reference to the club as a site for this relatedness is not unique; many of her peers also emphasize the role of the club as a location for such connected selves. Although contrary to our stereotypes of American teens, these youths' voices underscore the importance of human connection to other people. Particularly notable is the lack of gender difference in youths' self-descriptions. Contrary to what prior theories of development might suggest, girls do not use connected words in their self-descriptions more frequently than boys. The words retain some stereotypically gendered traits. The girls are "caring" and "kind" as opposed to the boys' less feminized choices of "responsible" and "a good person." Yet beneath the surface of those words, both boys and girls are talking about their relationships with other people.

Scholarship on women's psychological development is the one arena in which the role of interpersonal relationships in identity has been emphasized. Researchers who have explored the experiences of girls and women propose that for many girls identity development is more relational than the process which Erikson described. Supporting this hypothesis, gender differences in morality, sense of self, and independent versus interdependent self-concepts have been found.[21] Gilligan's work on girls' moral development, in particular, has influenced the field to consider how individuals balance abstract developmental tasks with on-the-ground personal relationships.[22] In her seminal work *In a Different Voice* she pointed out that girls are often more concerned with maintaining personal relationships than with upholding abstract notions of morality or law. This, she points out, does not make females less developed morally but, rather, concerned with the more personal dimensions of human relationships.

The East Side youth do not reflect this gendered dichotomy of relational development. Boys and girls both blend characteristics such as intelligence and humor with respectfulness and kindness. Furthermore, no qualitative differences in the types of individual or connected words are apparent. Kind, respectful, responsible, fun, funny, and smart are common words for all the East Side participants. The one exception is that whereas two boys describe themselves as athletic, the only girl to refer to athleticism in her self-description uses the word "good-sportsmanship" rather than the more individualistic "athletic." These voices support an emerging body of newer work that considers relational development as integral. These theories consider interpersonal processes as essential to self-concept. But the self is still not a passive recipient of the social world; the self is active in its construction.[23] There is evidence from experimental work in social psychology that both independent and interdependent self-construals coexist as distinct dimensions within individuals rather than as wholly different constructions of self.[24] Although gender differences may exist in individuated and interdependent self-concepts, human psyches are designed for connections with others.[25] Although cultural discourse tends to link images of community and family-tied selves to women and ethnic populations, these images have historically been an important facet of American identity, despite an emphasis on individuality.[26] This is reflected in the identity narratives of the East Side teens.

East Side teens' racial and social class positioning may influence the role of relationships in their identity construction. This is supported by earlier research at Boys and Girls Clubs that found no gender differences in the importance to youth of relationships with adult staff. Ties to adults may be important in helping youth integrate into the adult world, especially for youth in economically or socially marginalized groups.[27] The relational climate of schools has been suggested to be particularly important for African American males. Researchers examining African American males' school experiences have found that teacher-student relationships characterized by distrust, disrespect, and stereotyping are associated with students' acting out and disciplinary conflicts.[28] Some studies found that Black males have more intimate friendships than do white males. Although some have found that African American peer ties are complicated by concerns of trust and betrayal, strong ties and the desire for intimate friendships have been reported.[29] Cross-cultural research indicates that in some societies interdependence is fostered among all adolescents.[30] Thus, the theorized gender differences in the importance of interpersonal relationships to development may be an artifact of research samples. White, American males may be not the "norm" but the exception to the relational rule.[31]

A study of Israeli youth found that adolescents' relational experiences and identity construction were linked. Sharing of experiences and trust were major themes in teens' narratives about their relationships. It appeared that adolescents' relationships with others provided them with a safe base from which they could explore how others see them without threat to their own self-concept.[32] Similarly, a Dutch study suggested that young adults receive a sense of fulfillment from their interpersonal relationships that is critical to psychological health.[33] Research with urban populations in the United States indicates the importance of adolescents developing relational skills and of having a network of relationships on which to rely for social capital, as well as the importance of interpersonal relationships to the development of morality.[34] Opportunities for bonding with peers and adults, building supportive relationships, and practicing prosocial norms have all been highlighted as important features of positive developmental settings for youth.[35]

As the East Side youths' narratives indicate, close personal relationships both influence the self and provide a powerful context for shaping identity. They are often incorporated into our self-concepts.[36] Relatedness has even been named as one of three basic human needs, along with competence and autonomy; relationships and autonomy are not mutually exclusive.[37] Both men and women develop in the context of relational demands. Emerging work on boys challenges our notions of the role that relationships play in boys' identity development. Relational approaches to studying boys' lives and friendships, with both middle-class White and urban, racial-minority teens, demonstrates the important role of friendships and other interpersonal relationships in their lives.[38] Over the past decade, Niobe Way's work has consistently shown that the urban, racial minority boys with whom she works strongly desire close relationships.[39] More broadly, Ruthellen Josselson's work has demonstrated how part of all individual development is the integration of relational contexts and the cultivation of multifaceted forms of relatedness. Adolescent identity achievement, therefore, becomes a matter of balancing individuation and relatedness, not eschewing one for the other.[40]

Group social ties are also important. Being a part of a group may be critical to adolescent development, in that it gives the individual a mirror in which to see herself reflected and provides a sense of being part of a culture with positive traditions and opportunities. Feeling connected to a group may also protect self-esteem.[41] Some have suggested that the true conflict of adolescence is connection versus disconnection, indicating that individual identity development cannot be separated from relational concerns.[42]

Adolescents' feelings of connection to others and their resulting constructions of self will affect society's structure in the future. In fact, adolescents' perceived connections to others have been linked to a sense of purpose and morality. Studies of moral exemplars and youth activists in adulthood have demonstrated the overwhelming importance of a sense of linkage to others and collective responsibility as precipitants to both moral and civic action and identity. These studies have also led to the realization that such action stems from the construction of an identity that is in relationship with others, linked by a common humanity.[43] Developmental psychologist William Damon contends that "the genesis of [a person's ability to act as a civil member of community] can be traced back through the person's entire history of interpersonal relationships."[44] Thus, the importance of a relational sense of self goes far beyond addressing the typical talk show debates over whether men and women are doomed to stare at each other across an abyss of misunderstanding resulting from entirely different self-concepts. The importance of social contexts and relationships is linked to the continued development of a prosocial, civil society.

The East Side teens' self-descriptions suggest that many of them are developing identities strongly linked to other people. The words they choose highlight their connections to others. Two words in particular are remarkable for the sheer volume with which they appear in youths' self-descriptions. "Respect" and "responsibility" emerge consistently in the narratives of East Side members. Not only do they use these words to describe themselves, but also their stories of self-construction often revolve around these themes. Narratives of respect and responsibility frequently involve the club as a setting in which these traits are developed and nurtured.

I opened the first interview with the directive "tell me about yourself. Describe yourself to me." Four of the seventeen participants (24%) included the word "respectful" in their response. Three (23%) used the word "responsible." Seven (41%) used words such as "caring," "nice," "kind," or "loving." In their five-word self-descriptors, six youth (35%) included "respectful" and ten (59%) gave some version of words such as "nice," "helpful," "caring," "kind," or "responsible." Four (24%) said "respectful" was their most important quality and three (23%) listed "kindness" or "responsible" as most important.

That is not to suggest that youth portray themselves as 24-hour-a-day stand-up citizens. Many acknowledge contradictions in their self-descriptions. "I'm nice to get along with . . . I'm mean sometimes." "I'm caring. I can be mean sometimes." "I'm nice, respectful, but I have a bad attitude." One 12-year-old girl notes that she is "kind to people who are kind to me." These selves are contextual, and self traits are subject to shift depending on the situation. Yet what these statements also reveal is that the self is not shifting in relation only to activity or role but in relation to other people.

The youth at East Side suggest that they developed their relational selves, or at least important prosocial qualities, at the club. Eleven of the youth feel they would not be who they are today without East Side's influence. Many of the boys, in particular, couch this development in the language of a "redemption" story. They describe growing into responsible and respectful teens from the "little terrors" of their youth. According to many of their stories, these changes occurred within the walls of East Side, in part through the relationships they developed there. Adult staff helped the youth learn to be respectful, offering respect to them in return. As they grew older, teens began to see themselves as being responsible for role modeling positive behavior and identities to the younger members. Thus, their individual identities began to be tied to their relationships with others. As part of the East Side community, they were respected as individual contributors to it. In turn, they had a responsibility toward the club and the people in it, as well as toward themselves.

The fact that more boys than girls discuss East Side as a site of "redemption" for a prosocial self, suggests a difference in the ways in which boys and girls are socialized into and experience the world. Boys have fewer opportunities for developing their relational selves in their everyday environments. This has consequences. Prior work indicates that pressures associated with socialization into masculinity put boys at risk for disconnection from other people, making the development of personal relationships more challenging for young males.[45] East Side, however, successfully makes connections with urban, minority males—youth who have been traditionally difficult for program and policy makers to reach. In the coming sections, I examine the meaning of respect and responsibility and then explore how these traits in particular, and the connected self more generally, emerge through teens' words and actions at East Side.

Respect and Responsibility: The Meaning of the Words

Respect

Academia and the American media have largely built their images of adolescence around the notion of "storm and stress," emphasizing the emotional upheaval of the teen years. Although contrary to this mythology of adolescence, the image of a respectful and responsible teen is one that sustains traits which have been traditionally valued in African American culture and community. Sarah Lawrence-Lightfoot, in her exploration of respect, notes that respect is part of the legacy of slavery for African Americans, who traditionally had to find "codes of behavior" that showed deference to Whites while maintaining their own dignity.[46] Respect has been noted to be more valued than being liked by African American women. This is in contrast to images of White femininity in which being liked is prized.[47] Some in the African American community have noted that being respectful can save your life. Respect has been linked to traditional African codes of honor and community, especially in the African American religious community, where there has been a call to reconnect with the "covenant of respect."[48] African American teens have been noted to demand personal respect, which may be associated with a strong sense of right and wrong that permeates notions of self, friendship, and community. Respect is tied to authority; adolescents are aware that power and respect are connected and that to lose one is to lose the other.[49]

Respect is also shaped by economic and social structures. As minority and working-class men have faced displacement from the labor market, traditional masculine routes to respect have been removed for them. The decline of the manufacturing sector, the movement of jobs from inner cities to the suburbs, and the increase in service jobs have left many men without the means to achieve respect through the labor market. Fathers and sons may even find themselves competing for the same jobs. In such circumstances, respect may be sought through alternative modes. Hypermasculinities, participation in the underground economy of drugs and violence, and consumerism as a display of status have all been noted as means of seeking respect for individuals dislocated from more traditional pathways.[50] Thus, the youths' discourses of respect point to the world beyond the borders of their bodies and psyches, demanding that we address the individual need for respect from a more structural level.

Returning to the interpersonal, respect, as it is constructed by both Lawrence-Lightfoot and the East Side youth, is not a one-way street. Respect, rather, is bidirectional, requiring mutuality for its honest enactment. To both demonstrate and earn respect, you must be willing to appreciate and listen to those with whom you are interacting. Respect can be a mutual trait that reflects values of community orientation.[51] Youths' descriptions of respect illustrate this.

> I talk more like I'm older but I don't disrespect anybody. Unless they disrespect me. I tell people when I first meet them, just treat me nice, that's all I ask. —Dynasty, 15-year-old African American female

Respectful [is my most important trait]. I like to treat others as others will treat me. —Lorenzo, 17-year-old African American male

I respect staff and so they respect me. —Alyiah, 15-year-old African American female

The staff echo this theme of reciprocal respect.

Pausing a moment, Charles [the physical education director] added, "at first these girls would be gettin' pregnant and stuff. . . . When we have dances or sleep-overs they be trying to sneak over together or what not. . . . But they know not to try anything, because they know what me and Cheryl [another staff] expect of them and they respect us just like we respect them. But these guys were bad when I first came . . ." [*As Charles was talking, teen boys were filtering into the room, getting ready for a group meeting. As one boy came into the room talking loudly and trying to get Charles's attention, another boy said, "Be quiet, he talking, man!"*][52]

The quotes and observations above demonstrate the importance of symmetry in respectful interaction. Both the youth and staff recognize that giving respect is required to receive it. Charles's acknowledgment (that the boys "were bad" when he was first getting to know them but that they now understand and live up to his expectations) illustrates his understanding of the time and energy it takes to earn respect. Charles recognizes the teens' requirement that adults treat them as the adults themselves expect to be treated. The boy shushing his peer shows that respect in action: Charles respects the boys so they will demand respect for him.

Angela, the mother of John, a 17-year-old Black male, reinforces this idea when she shares her thoughts on the mutual nature of respect.

You know, John, if you respect him he'll respect you but if not, he'll be honest about what he thinks. But like all kids, if you respect them they respect you. With teens you gotta respect them if you want them to respect you. I tell kids, you know, treat me the way you want to be treated. If you treat me like shit I'll treat you like shit. But if you give me respect I'll do the same for you.

John is the one boy who does not express a close attachment to the club. He feels disrespected by most of the staff. A few hours after I had this conversation with Angela, I observed John standing in the entranceway of the club. He bumped into an adult African American woman and immediately turned around and said "excuse me" before continuing his conversation with other teens. John's tendency toward respectful interaction, even if he disrespects those from whom he does not feel that he receives respect, illustrates Angela's words.

Some youth acknowledge that there are situations in which respect is required regardless of whether it is returned, especially with adults. This type of respect mimics the outward behaviors without the inner affect of respect. This is reflected in youths' statements that they may act in a certain way around adults but would not respect people who did not respect them.

> I'm around my teacher or somebody, my auntie or somebody, I'm not really bad. Or if I'm around an adult. But when I'm hanging out with my friends I may curse or say mean things, be bad. . . . I have respect for the adults and I don't want to get in trouble if I say something I have no business saying. So I just hold my peace until I'm away from them. But if they don't give me respect then I don't respect them. That's just how I am. If they cuss at me I'll cuss at them. —Carla, 14-year-old African American female

This kind of respect is notably different from mutual respect. Carla says she does not want "to get in trouble" and hence curbs her behavior. She does so not out of reciprocal respect but out of fear of consequences. Respect for authority is an important type of respect, and the ability to understand and respect legitimate authority is an important part of citizenship.[53] This process is enhanced, however, if youth also feel respected by the individuals in authority.

The significance of bidirectional respect to the East Side teens has important consequences for how we think about settings for youth. Many adults proceed with the notion that teenagers should respect them simply because they are adults. They don't feel the need to earn respect, believing that their age and status should confer respect on them. Rick, the director of the East Side club, noted that this was one of the biggest misjudgments made by new staff: "It takes a long while for teens, alums, preteens, to give anyone respect. . . . Just myself and Charles get a lot of respect 100% of the time." But Rick went on to note that both he and Charles had to earn that respect over many years of work at East Side. He says that if you get frustrated and yell at kids, you only fuel their anger and disrespect. Rick tries to remind staff of this.

His own path to respect involved demonstrating not only that he had respect for the kids but also that he held them all in the same regard. One night, an alumni of the club, a large 20-year-old man nicknamed Mad Dog, walked into the gym with a friend cursing up a storm. Rick was sitting on the bleachers and called out to Mad Dog to quit that kind of talk in the club. Mad Dog immediately came over, apologized, and shook Rick's hand. A younger teen boy who was sitting behind Rick reacted with shock. "Man! You get respect from everyone!" the boy said, shaking his head in amazement. The boy was impressed both that Rick had called Mad Dog on his behavior and that Mad Dog had reacted in such a respectful manner. Rick sees this type of consistent respectful behavior from the staff as key to helping youth develop a sense of respect.

It is clear from youths' statements and from Rick's discussions of the process of earning respect at the club that assumptions of automatically conferred respect often backfire. Without bidirectional respect, adults are seen as being disrespectful and thus not deserving of respect. If adults view youth as deficient, youth are also unlikely to respect them. Furthermore, respect accorded out of fear of retribution is seen by some as the "worst type" of respect.[54] Resistance to such one-sided respect must be understood within the cultural-historical framework of African Americans and other minority groups in the United States. In light of the legacy of slavery and the continued plight of racism, the requirement of unidirectional respect can be seen as in direct opposition to the need for self-dignity. Because respect is often accorded to us by default, White middle-class and upper-class individuals, especially men, may be unable to understand resistance to demands for respect.

Due to structural positioning, race and class privilege in the United States confers individual respect automatically on certain individuals. If part of adolescence for all of us is validating a sense of individual self-respect, for some that battle is already half won. For other adolescents it is a constant fight against stereotypes and historically rooted discourses of race and class. Research conducted with early adolescent males who were identified as at risk for gang involvement suggested that they had to fight for a sense of dignity and respect. Supportive relationships helped them counter the pressures they faced in their local environments, providing respect through those human connections.[55] Thus, respect is intimately tied to both the construction of a positive identity and the role of relationships in forming that identity.

Is it any wonder that teens will disengage from classrooms or institutions in which they do not feel respected? Is it surprising that youth may be resistant to work environments in which they feel demeaned by supervisors? I see in East Side youths' narratives not an opposition to authority, as disrespect is sometimes assumed to be, but a desire for individual respect as human beings and the willingness to return such respect when it is given. This theme has particular relevance in thinking about school experiences, which many youth contrasted negatively to their experiences in the club. Early research on African American school success suggested that teacher respect for students may be an integral part of creating a classroom environment conducive to learning.[56] Contemporary work also points to the importance of trust, which is linked to respectful interaction, as a key component of successful schools, especially for African American males.[57] In a recent study of the experiences of Latino students, participants talked about being disrespected by some teachers. These students used a "community living room" space within their school to resist that disrespect and to co-construct positive ethnic identities.[58]

The willingness to display respect in response to receiving it is evident in youths' actions in response to East Side's rules. There are codes of behavior and dress that are enforced in the club. These include prohibitions on cursing and wearing hats. At times, club members admonish each other for breaking these rules. The statement "we're in the club, man" often punctuates such reprimands, indicating that a respect for the rules is an important part of respecting the club as a whole. As Charles notes, the youth feel respected in the club and therefore are willing to respect the club in return. Such consistent expectations and promotion of positive behavioral norms is a common characteristic of successful youth programs.[59]

Rick also feels that the models of respect that youth see in the club help them develop prosocial behaviors: "They get respect in so many ways. [They see it demonstrated] staff to staff, staff to parent, staff don't yell at kids. We say please, we say thank you." Rick sees this rub off on kids in their behavior toward the club. He acknowledges that kids will police themselves when it comes to club rules and points to the lack of damage to club property as demonstrating the respect that the youth have for the club.

> I don't see any real damaged equipment. There's no graffiti, writing on the walls. But that makes a good point. Back in the day you would go to other clubs and you'd see broken pool sticks [and other damaged equipment]. [The fact that that doesn't happen at East Side] shows that kids respect the club and treat it as their own.

When Sean, the assistant director, first began working at the club, he did not feel that the club members were respectful toward each other or staff. He saw this rooted in a lack of self-respect, further underscoring the multilayered nature of respect.

> "There's no respect here," Sean said. I asked him what he meant, and he said the kids don't respect anyone. "Not staff, not each other. How you gonna respect someone when you don't even respect yourself? That's where it starts, with self-respect."

Two years later, asked whether East Side helps youth develop respect, Sean reiterates the linkage between respect for oneself and respect for others: "I radiate, and basically with no excuse expect, first and foremost respect for yourself. Don't be looking, acting, talking like an idiot and in return I will give you the respect you deserve." Sean is in good company. Writers in the African American community have called for greater self-respect as being the foundation of "intraracial atonement" and the passing on of respect to the younger generation.[60]

During my time at the club I noticed that staff infused respect into their interactions with youth. This came in the form of gentle reminders about behavior, as well as through staff's own modes of interactions. Often, while I was talking with staff, club members walked up and interrupted.

Each time this occurred, the staff member would look at the youth, acknowledge his or her presence, and say something to the effect of "you can see that I'm talking with this person. It is disrespectful to interrupt. If you need to speak to me now you have to say excuse me." Every time the youth would nod, apologize, and say excuse me. The staff would nod, say "excuse me" to me, and turn to the child. "Okay, now tell me what's up." In doing so, staff members respected youths' needs but also insisted on giving respect in order to receive it. Attention, particularly in the form of appreciation and validation of others, has been described as a key aspect of respectful interaction. In interaction with youth, this can come in the form of validating youths' voices, ideas, and needs.[61] Respect for the individual youth is one of the traits of the club that makes it a safe and supportive environment for members.

Responsibility

The bidirectional nature of respect is one of the characteristics that separates it from responsibility, according to youths' uses of the terms and the ways in which these modes of behavior are played out in the club. Responsibility, in contrast to respect, is something that an individual takes on and "handles." Although it expresses a sense of self in connection to others, as one demonstrates responsibility toward or to another person, it does not require mutuality. Whereas respect exists in symmetry, responsibility may be one-sided.[62] Youth talk about the importance of "taking care of your business" and living up to your responsibilities. This is linked to gaining the trust of adults and proving themselves to others. Thus, responsibility can be an individually based characteristic. But it exists in relation to others. Kelly, a 16-year-old African American male, indicates this when describing why being responsible is important to him.

> Responsible is [my] most important [trait] 'cause I feel people can trust me and they know if they need something from me if there's any way in my power I can do it I will do it. . . . Being . . . responsible is appreciated at the Boys and Girls Club cause [the staff] know if one of their bosses from downtown come I gonna come and ask the questions that need to be answered. I ain't gonna act the fool in front of them. [The staff] know I know there's a time to be serious.

For Kelly, being responsible is a personal trait that demonstrates to other people his positive character. This is enacted and supported within East Side. Similarly, Daniel, a 16-year-old Hispanic and African American male, describes himself as a "responsible young adult." He defines successful adults as those who "can handle whatever responsibilities come their way." Daniel says that his responsibility is encouraged at the club because "I have an image. Everyone expects me to be up, want to do stuff and I know everybody likes that about me here. I'm always willing to help. Like if they're short staff or something. I'm always up and rolling."

Prior studies have found a heightened sense of responsibility among non-White adolescents that is associated with strong attachments to family and community.[63] Some African American religious leaders have called for adult Blacks to take personal responsibility for teaching young Blacks the traditional African values of respect and community, thus fusing personal responsibility with one's ties to the group.[64] Whereas responsibility may indicate self-reliance, it can be learned within a community. Social support is viewed by some as the basis for independence and accountability. Others have found that teenage autonomy actually benefits from connections and a sense of belonging.[65] Cross-cultural work has demonstrated that adolescents in collectivist societies are sometimes given familial responsibilities that are distinct from independence.[66] In the United States, research on after-school programs has highlighted the need for youth to have opportunities for both individual recognition and social bonding, demonstrating the need for a balance of autonomy and group belonging.[67]

Responsibility, on both personal and group levels, is encouraged at East Side by individual staff, as well as by the overall environment. Cheryl, a female staff member at the club, emphasizes both respect and responsibility with the girls on her cheerleading team.

> [During a cheerleading squad meeting] Cheryl begins to ask the girls what happened on Saturday. Apparently, they were supposed to perform and only a few of them showed up. Cheryl talks firmly to them, saying, "just because I am not there doesn't mean you can just not show up. You treat them just like you'd treat me. That hurt me and embarrassed me that you didn't come. Someday you have to commit to something." She talks about responsibility and how you can't just be a member of the squad

when it is fun. "You can't just show up for sleepovers and not when it's hard work. Because I know who was here Saturday and if you think you didn't come Saturday but you're coming to the sleepover you're wrong. Because I'll be standing out there with a clipboard and you won't come in." Cheryl explains that once they are in high school they would get kicked off the squad for not showing up for practice or a performance. "This isn't for me, you know. I've got mine, you've got to get yours. . . . I know that I'm being hard on you and you may not come back because you'll be mad at me, but I want you to be responsible." Cheryl will occasionally stop and look at someone: "Are you okay?" she'll ask, with concern in her voice.

Cheryl balances her lecture on responsibility with a clear respect for the girls as people. While they have a responsibility to the group and to Cheryl, each girl is also responsible for her own future. It is the combination of these responsibilities that Cheryl emphasizes.

Cheryl is not the only staff member who sees it as her job to infuse a sense of personal responsibility in club members. One evening I observed a conversation between staff members, instigated by the club's report card party that day.

In the computer room Steve [the computer instructor] was sweeping up while Sheila [another staff member] was standing talking to him. "I just don't think that if you say [the pizza party] is for bringing in your report card that you should go ahead and give the pizza to everyone. It defeats the purpose," Sheila said. "We're tryin' to teach the kids some responsibility. That is part of our job," Steve said. They continued to talk about what that meant and how much you should bend rules or change requirements for kids. . . . "I mean, I am taking the kids [on a field trip]. And there are kids who are always up in here disrespecting me and not listening when I tell them to stop jumping on the furniture and whatever and they're not gonna go. And now they all want to go; well, too bad . . . my decision is that if you have been disrespectful to me this whole time then I am not going to take you on the trip. . . . I'm taking those who have earned it by participating in here in the right way." Sheila nodded. . . . Steve noted that he, [another staff member], and Sheila taught kids to be responsible by not letting them do whatever they wanted and by setting rules and boundaries with them. . . . . "Because part of what we're here for should be to teach them to be responsible," Steve said.

The staff encourage responsibility and respect through special rewards, such as pizza parties and field trips, as well as the designation of responsibility. They often give members tasks that require youth to be responsible, such as fundraising for a group trip, planning a club-wide event, or helping watch younger members. After turning 16, teens can also work at the club for pay. Youth who work at East Side have assigned hours and tasks and must treat the job just as they would any other employment, although the club is fairly flexible in dealing with scheduling conflicts. Club staff also monitor the grades of some club members and stress the importance of being responsible about schoolwork. In another interaction between Cheryl and the cheerleaders, Cheryl says that she makes exceptions in the team's requirements for older members who are in high school and have jobs because she understands that they have other responsibilities. This includes respect for competing youth programs. Some of the older teens at the club also attend a youth group at a local church. East Side helps arrange for members to be able to attend programming in both places without conflict. Thus, at its best, East Side serves as a bridge between the various spaces of youths' lives and provides an additional source of support that is rooted in their community. Staff help youth juggle multiple, even conflicting, responsibilities.

This concern with balancing responsibility to others with responsibility to one's self was demonstrated in a particularly poignant manner by Diane, East Side's former program director. Diane had a close relationship with Te Te, a 15-year-old multiethnic girl. During my third year at the club, Te Te was going through a difficult time. She was struggling with self-esteem issues and family difficulties. Te Te made extra money by babysitting a neighbor's child. She was supposed to meet the boy at his school, but he was rarely there when she went to get him. This was a source of stress for Te Te. When it became clear that Te Te was having difficulty handling all the stressors in her life, Diane sat down and had a long talk with her. In addition to other issues, Diane addressed the fact that Te Te had to stop babysitting. She told a researcher, "[Te Te's] just a child. She's tryin' so hard to do good . . . it's too much. She's got her own activities." Diane even spoke with Te Te's mother about it. Diane recognized Te Te for demonstrating positive responsibility. But she also pointed out where this became problematic and emphasized the need to protect Te Te's own self-interests. This links Te Te's self-esteem issues to her overall sense of self-respect. Part of respecting ourselves is recognizing our boundaries and limits. If you want respect from others, you must take responsibility for treating yourself with respect and demanding respect from others.[68]

The teens acknowledge East Side's role in nurturing respect and responsibility in them. Many youth refer to themselves as having gained prosocial characteristics in their years at East Side and talk about how participation in the club has changed them.[69] Eleven of the seventeen youth interviewed feel that they would not be who they are today without the Boys and Girls Club. Sometimes teens talk about activities that they would not have had access to without the club. Others mention academic support. But many youth talk specifically about the people at the club and how staff have influenced them. This ranges from Bob, who says that "different traits of the children and staff members rubbed off on me," to Alyiah, who believes that the help she got from staff she "probably wouldn't have gotten from no one else." Seven youth say that East Side helped them change their attitudes or develop self-characteristics such as maturity and respect. Kelly, a 16-year-old male, says that if he had not come to East Side, "I think I'd be, the person that people don't wanna see me as, the one who comes around and people say 'oh no not him!' . . . If I never came here I'd probably still be childish, goofy, running around, nothing to do, irresponsible, like a little kid, not taking responsibility for what I do." Like Kelly, many youth see themselves as having developed prosocial traits at the club. In some of these narratives, East Side becomes a setting for self-transformation. This use of the club as a site of "redemption," a place wherein one grows from an unruly kid to a mature teen, was not uncommon. A number of youth describe a process of self-development within the club. Many youth have literally grown up at East Side, having attended since they were quite young. Through their interactions with adult staff and kids at East Side and participation in activities over the years, they have developed a sense of themselves as more connected and prosocial than when they entered.

It is important to note that East Side does not view itself as a "redeemer" of youth. Nor do any of the staff (or I) consider the population that East Side serves as in need of redemption. Rather, the youth themselves describe East Side as a site of self-change. This may be in part linked to the natural maturation that occurs from childhood to adolescence. Yet the specific narrative of respect and responsibility appears to be unique, not previously captured by theories of adolescent development. It is a narrative distinctly linked to youths' participation in East Side; they were given respect by adults and expected to return that respect and act responsibly toward both the staff and club members. The use of the club as a site for the construction of a redemption story is reminiscent of the life stories of highly generative adults, some of whose desires to contribute to future generations are rooted in life stories revolving around themes of redemption. It also calls up narratives of empowering communities, a concept from community psychology which considers how communities serve as sites for the construction of group-based narratives that empower their members. These ideas have been previously examined primarily in adults.[70] The appearance of this type of narrative among the East Side teens suggests that this setting holds promise as a model for creating positive developmental environments for adolescents, as well.

Conclusion

The role of relationships in both boys and girls' self-constructions has theoretical and practical implications. On a theoretical level, researchers are too quick to look to gender as an explanatory variable for individual differences. Chalking relational differences up to gender does not challenge society to ask the important questions about structural factors that may lead to the emergence of differences along gender lines. We must explore similarities and differences within and across gender, as well as other social categories. Only by doing so will we begin to explain differences in self-concept. On a practical level, relationships and our sense of connection to others have an effect on the well-being of society. If we want to support adolescents in becoming productive and positive citizens of the world, then we need to know the processes by which teens develop identities that are congruent with prosocial community values.[71]

What comes through from the East Side teens' narratives of respect and responsibility is a sense of the person in relation, individual youth embedded in webs of social relations that inform their identities. This vision—of adolescent identity developing in relation to interpersonal and group relationships—moves beyond the stereotypical view of the adolescent self.

While much is made of the negative role of peers in adolescence, the focus of such work is rarely on the positive ties that bind youth to others. Yet the youth at East Side describe themselves as rooted in rich relational milieus that provide a context for their developing identities and allow them to define themselves positively in relation to others. The themes of respect and responsibility are important parts of the youths' self-descriptions. East Side serves as a site for the development of respect and responsibility through a combination of giving, expecting, and role modeling these traits. Our country is on the verge of a crisis of care, a crisis rooted in our failure to tend to the ties that bind us.[72] The East Side teens are telling us that they are capable of developing into adults who value their connections with others. They need settings that will foster such identities, where they are appreciated for who they are and what they bring to the community.

3

■ ■ ■ ■ ■ ■ ■ ■ ■

"I Never Thought Kids Would Look Up to Someone Like Me"

Lorenzo's Story

Volunteering with the kids [at the club influenced what I want to be in the future]. To reach out to people and see different prospects of how people see life. Charles [the club's physical education director] . . . has been like a father to me. He talks to me. He cheers me up. At the same time we have fun. He taught me everything I know about basketball . . . the club teaches me. I know kids look up to me, and I like to set a positive vibe for them. . . . [If I hadn't come to the club] I feel I wouldn't be open. People wouldn't understand how I feel.

—Lorenzo

Lorenzo is a 17-year-old African American male who has been coming to East Side for four years. He is dark-skinned, broad, and tall with cornrowed hair that hangs down to the bottom of his neck. Usually clad in t-shirts and loose pants or athletic clothes, Lorenzo tends to don a serious facial expression. A small tattoo peeks out from the blue sweatband that is a consistent presence on his right wrist.

Lorenzo is in 12th grade. He currently resides with his aunt and her children in the housing project near the club, having moved in with them a few years before at his mother's request. Lorenzo says that he would have preferred to stay with his mother and younger brothers and sisters but chose to move in with his aunt because his mother didn't want him. Despite wanting to stay with his mother, or perhaps as a result of not being able to, Lorenzo names his aunt and cousins as the people to whom he is the closest. At age 14 he took care of his younger siblings for a few months while his mother was away. Lorenzo describes himself as "misused," as if his childhood "was took from [him]" by "having to play the parent role at a young age."

Lorenzo appears somewhat aloof to outsiders yet clearly enjoys playing the clown to younger club members. When he speaks in interviews and focus groups he is serious and seems to give his honest thoughts. His facial expression tends toward indifference, but he breaks into a smile when something strikes him as funny. Despite his somewhat tough demeanor, in his interviews he was quite open with me. Lorenzo is articulate and thoughtful and speaks often of responsibility and respect. In both the focus group and his one-on-one interviews he discusses being a role model for younger kids at the club.

Lorenzo's story expands on themes of the connected self. At East Side he develops relationships that influence his sense of self. These relationships stand in contrast to those with adults from his school as well as, to a lesser extent, his family. Thus, East Side provides needed supports to Lorenzo and, in his words, has helped him become the responsible and respectful young man he is today. His story demonstrates how a youth organization can serve as a site for self-transformation.

Lorenzo's Role at East Side

Lorenzo constructs himself as someone who has connections to other people. He prides himself on being respectful and responsible. At the same time, he is proud of his individual talents. This is evident in his participation at East Side. He is a star player on the teens' basketball team. Lorenzo has aspirations of playing basketball professionally, although he balances this with an interest in majoring in computers in school. His basketball skills are important to him, and he spends a good deal of time at the club on the court. He says that playing basketball at the club has shown him that he is talented and "has what it takes to succeed." The most common place to find Lorenzo is in East Side's gym. But in addition to playing ball at night with his peers, Lorenzo spends most afternoons there, helping Charles coach the younger kids. Thus, the combination of his love of basketball and his close relationship with Charles leads to his having a distinct place in East Side's gym.

Lorenzo credits the staff at East Side for encouraging him and telling him that "whatever I feel I'm very talented and to stick with it. Not to accept anything but success." Because of the club Lorenzo says that he can "set goals and strive to reach them." Over his time at East Side Lorenzo feels that he has become more active, concerned, and open minded. He now tries to participate more at the club and to "give everything a fair chance." Lorenzo thinks that the club is an important place because it is an alternative to the streets. Beyond being a safe haven, we will see that East Side also provides specific supports for Lorenzo's developmental needs.

Lorenzo's Sense of Self

At the start of the interview, Lorenzo describes himself as nice, caring, respectful, honest, and "very talented." When asked later for the five words that best describe him, Lorenzo provides four connected words: honest, respectful, dependable, and responsible. His fifth word is athletic. His talents, especially in the area of sports, are important to him because they are his "whole life" and represent what he wants to do when he grows up. He likes to write songs and rap in addition to playing ball. Yet at the same time he feels that his most important quality is being respectful because he likes "to treat others as others will treat me." He also likes people to be able to trust him and that people can "rely on me to get the job done." Seeing other kids happy and everyone at peace makes Lorenzo feel good, while seeing innocent people die and "poor kids suffer" makes him feel bad. In describing himself this way he reinforces the theme of personal responsibility within a community of mutual respect.

Lorenzo's definitions of successful adults reflect the importance of respect and responsibility to him. He describes a successful man as one who is "smart, intelligent, responsible, works, takes care of responsibility." A successful woman, according to Lorenzo, is an "independent woman who can also take care of herself, raise a family on her own." Notably, independence is prized as an important female trait. This is not surprising, since Lorenzo's father left his family and Lorenzo was raised by his mother and his aunt. But independence, in Lorenzo's description, includes taking care of others. Thus, it is an independence that exists within a network of relationships.

Although intelligence is part of being a successful man, being smart, in Lorenzo's view, is not enough. One also has to live up to his responsibilities—presumably responsibilities to other people. This is an important fact when considering Lorenzo's life. Lorenzo does not live with either of his parents and has not for some years. He openly states that he does not want to be like his father, who "don't take care of his responsibilities." At East Side, Lorenzo developed a relationship with Charles, whom he describes as being like both a big brother and a father to him. In addition, the club director demonstrates to Lorenzo that there is always "someone out there to give you a helping hand." Thus, at the club, Lorenzo learns what it means to be part of a community of support. In contrast to his home life, where he was thrust into an adult role at an early age, at the club Lorenzo receives needed assistance. He learns that he can accept help in addition to taking care of others. Through these relationships and interactions he begins to see himself as a responsible member of that community. He also begins to contribute to it in his own right, by serving as a role model to younger club members.

In line with this connected sense of self, Lorenzo reports having close relationships with his aunt and cousins, as well as his best friend. He credits his aunt with having been there for him when he needed her and having taken care of him for "my whole life. She is my mother and my aunt." Lorenzo is a popular boy at the club and in the neighborhood. His best friend is male, and they share an interest in basketball. Lorenzo says that they come from similar backgrounds and "both have a rough life. Rough childhood." According to Lorenzo, the two boys "have faith in each other" and each knows the other can do anything to which he sets his mind. Lorenzo tries "to stay positive and do whatever it takes to keep our friendship good." Thus, despite his difficult family ties, Lorenzo is able to build close connections to other people, both peers and adults. These relationships are important to him and to his sense of self.

Lorenzo does not think that he would be the same person he is today without the club. Without East Side Lorenzo says that he would not "be open. People wouldn't understand how I feel." He believes that his responsibility, respectfulness, and honesty are encouraged and appreciated at the club. The prevalence of his position as a role model to younger club members in his self-descriptions and overall narrative also indicate the important role of the club in his life. Given the significance he places on his relationships with others, the club serves as a key site in helping Lorenzo develop and maintain his positive self-concept.

"Getting Back to Yourself": East Side as a Developmental Context

Lorenzo feels he can learn more at the club than at school but "be free" while doing so. In part this is because he better understands what is expected of him at the club. In the focus group Lorenzo also mentioned this issue: "It's like at school you're always trying to adjust but here it's like you know what's it like. When you get here it's like a relief. You get to go back to your regular [self] . . ."

Although this statement makes no reference to race, it is notable that the only incident of racism that Lorenzo reports experiencing took place at school, when a substitute teacher used a racial slur against him. Given the research on African American males' school achievement and the stereotypes that they face in academic environments, the club may be particularly supportive for boys like Lorenzo, who do not feel comfortable in school.[1] A significant number of studies document that African American students, males in particular, have more difficulty developing positive and supportive relationships with teachers.[2] Some suggest that after-school programs may meet the developmental needs of Black males better than schools.[3] In fact, many participants, both boys and girls, contrast the club and school environments, saying that they feel more like themselves at the club.

> I feel more free at the club. . . . The staff and I've been around here so long. I'm used to how everything goes, being around everybody. . . . I feel comfortable at school too, but I don't feel as comfortable around teachers cause . . . at school you have to . . . like adjust . . . be more of a good student. —Daniel, 16-year-old African American–Hispanic male

When I'm at the club I can do a lot more than what I can do at school. At school I have to rush . . . at the club I can take my time. . . . At school I be bunched up. —Dynasty, 15-year-old African American female

Like if I'm at school I don't really be how I am. I change to be better, to make them say, "Oh he's a good kid, he don't get in trouble." At the club I just be myself. . . . At the club I know what I can say and what I can't say . . . I can just be myself. There's more freedom. —Kelly, 16-year-old African American male

I got some type of disguise for each class [at school]. I'm different. . . . When I come to the club it all come together. —Peaches, 16-year-old African American female

These quotes are typical of youths' descriptions of the differences in their school and East Side experiences. At the club, youth can express their "authentic," whole selves. Although this is partially due to greater freedom in terms of autonomy in movement and activity choice, it is also due to youths' perceptions of more consistent behavioral expectations at the club and the fact that the people at the club know them. Recent work examining the organizational climate of schools has pointed to the importance of trust and respect for creating and sustaining successful schools. In part, relational trust between individuals within the organization is key, including clearly understood and consistently enacted expectations.[4]

Work with African American boys in schools echoes this, underscoring the important role of interpersonal trust and respect to students' behavior in classrooms. Such work highlights the fact that interactions occur between two people and involve each person both reading and responding to the behavior of the other. When teachers and youth perceive each other as untrustworthy and disrespectful, interactions can spiral downward to confrontations that jeopardize students' school success.[5] High levels of trust of and support from individual teachers appear to help Black male students negotiate academics more successfully, countering some of the negative processes common in their school environments.[6] The racial and cultural divide between many African American males and their teachers makes these relational issues especially salient in today's schools.

East Side youths' descriptions of the club environment echo some of the tenets of relational trust and respect. Although youth may adjust their presentation of self or behaviors for different teachers, they feel generally accepted at face value by club staff and peers. The term "code-switching" has been coined to describe this idea of going back and forth between behavioral expectations and modes of speech and interaction in different contexts.[7] The distinction that youth make between club and school experiences is important. Whereas "appropriate" code-switching is often viewed as a necessary skill for ethnic and racial minority youth, when expectations conflict with perceptions of the self or are seen as necessary to manage stigma, the process can cause stress or conflict. Thus, the club allows adolescents to "live and be with each other" without the pressure or concerns of code-switching.[8]

Becoming a Team Player

Part of Lorenzo's comfort at East Side stems from knowing that he is accepted there. He feels that his responsibility, respectfulness, and honesty —traits that he considers important to his sense of self—are encouraged and appreciated at the club. This is not just rhetoric. Conversations with staff and observations of Lorenzo support his view of East Side as a place where these qualities are nurtured. Sean initially thought that he could not trust Lorenzo but was proven wrong. He eventually got Lorenzo into a leadership role: "You know, he used to be the one who wanted to make all the moves and be the star of the game. But in a leadership role he's still getting attention and it's positive." Thus, the club helped Lorenzo to balance his need for validation as a talented individual with his need for group affiliation. He has found a valued role within the social environment of the club.

Providing youth with a sense of identity and purpose is a common trait of successful youth organizations. In addition, East Side helps Lorenzo develop an identity that has traits valued in the adult social world. East Side is a place where he can validate an identity and accrue social capital in a way he is not able to in school.[9] Lorenzo is given opportunities to demonstrate prosocial behavior and is positively recognized by staff for doing so. These factors have been identified as important aspects of positive youth development programs.[10] The teaching of social and emotional skills and ethical values through direct interaction and respectful, supportive relationships has also been pointed to as a key characteristic of effective prevention programming.[11] Thus, Lorenzo's activities at East Side are linked to specific, positive developmental tasks.

The balancing of individual validation and relational respect is particularly evident in Lorenzo's sports and coaching activities. Lorenzo is able to go back and forth between playing serious basketball with his peers to respecting the space that the younger members need to develop their skills. Some of his ability to walk this line may come from his close relationship with Charles, who also balances his "hard" and "soft" sides in his relationships with the kids.[12] In his daily activities at the club Lorenzo demonstrates his skills in shifting his level of play depending on the situation. The field notes below are from one evening when Lorenzo was playing basketball with the older teen boys and two adults, including Charles.

> As the game went on, Lorenzo ran hard up and down the court. . . . Lorenzo guarded Charles a lot during the game, trying to block his shots and getting up into his face. At one point they sort of collided and each had an arm around the other's shoulders, patting each other's shoulders in a bit of an embrace as they straightened back up and walked over to get the ball from where it had gone out of bounds. All the guys played hard, running [up and down] the court quickly and making a lot of long passes [leading to] inside shots. Lorenzo ran around the court a lot, often maneuvering his way under the basket to be free from the crowd and open for a shot. He missed three shots in a row at one point and the male [coach] yelled to him to get with it. Lorenzo made the next shot he went for, an inside shot after a pass with someone on him. He smiled and made a quick, sharp, downward motion with his fist. Throughout the game Lorenzo would clap his hands as his team made a shot or smile and clap if they got the ball on a turnover. . . . For most of the game the score hovered around a 1 point difference, with each team being up at various points. Then, with about 3 minutes left, Lorenzo's team got up by 10 and remained there, winning the game.

In the above instance, Lorenzo demonstrates his basketball skills and love of the game. Yet even amid the competition, his close and comfortable relationship with Charles comes through. In the excerpt below we can see how Lorenzo adjusts his effort level and competitive nature to respect the playing of younger kids.

> Lorenzo was playing basketball with a bunch of much younger boys and one teen girl. . . . Lorenzo was about twice the height of the rest of the boys. Lorenzo only shot the ball twice himself. Every other time he rebounded the ball and then either threw it in a long pass down the court to the girl or to one of the small boys or he brought it down the court quickly himself and then passed it to the girl or one of the boys. The one time he [himself took a] shot was on a fastbreak when he ran down and [dunked the ball]. The other time was when he had passed it to the girl and she missed the shot and then passed it to him. Often when he ran down the court with the ball he ran in a straight-legged run, moving the top half of his body from side to side and making googly eyes and grinning, making the boys laugh. He would always pass it to a small boy or the girl and once, when one boy missed his shot, Lorenzo rebounded the ball and threw it back to him. "Try again," he said. The boy tried the shot again. Even in passing the ball Lorenzo would goof around and have fun, tossing it against the wall to make it go behind him or sometimes rolling the ball down the court. Only once or twice, when there was little time left in the game or when someone stole the ball did Lorenzo guard any of the shorter boys. Generally he just stood aside and waited for them to shoot and then rebounded. The only time I saw him guard was not near the basket but after they had rebounded or stole the ball and were trying to take it up the court and pass it. Lorenzo stood in front of the boy with the ball and waved his hands and made a face and funny noises and then put his arms down and let the boy go on his way. He would sometimes play sort of hard, but also kept it mostly in a joking way and even if he ran the ball hard down the court himself he would pass quickly to a younger boy or the girl. Sometimes he would fake a pass or fake shooting, but he always ended up passing it to a younger boy or the girl to shoot.

Lorenzo tailors his playing to the situation. His involvement with the younger boys is not because he can't hold his own with his same-age peers. On the contrary, Lorenzo is an active member of the older boys' basketball team and plays with them every night. He is also a popular guy in general, throwing parties for his friends and socializing with the

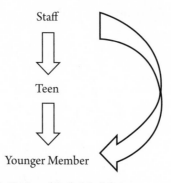

Fig. 3-1. Tri-Level Role Modeling

neighborhood teens both inside and outside the club. Thus, his relationship with the younger kids does not stem from social necessity. Rather, it is an important part of Lorenzo's identity and gives him a valuable place in the club.

Tri-Level Role Modeling

One of the ways in which East Side allows youth to develop new roles for themselves in the club as they grow older is by providing them with opportunities for what I have termed tri-level role modeling (Figure 3-1).

Through this process teenagers simultaneously receive needed support from adults while also serving as role models to younger club members. As we have begun to see with Lorenzo, these relationships not only help solidify a place for him at East Side but also influence his overall sense of self. Lorenzo's recognition of himself as a role model is a repeated theme during his interviews and interactions at the club. A number of other youth also note that seeing themselves as responsible for modeling positive behavior to younger kids influences their own behaviors and leads to changes in the way they see themselves.

Alexis, a 15-year-old African American girl, says that "the young kids, you better teach them things, teach them right from wrong." Daniel and one of his friends say that they influence each other. Nearly all the youth in the focus groups talk about how the staff trust the teens, talking to them in a peer-like way. Yet they all agree that the staff still demand, and receive, respect as adults. Scott, a 16-year-old male, says that the staff help the youth to "see ourselves in the future." Thus, the interaction of having adult role models and feeling responsible for modeling positive behavior to younger members influences the teens' sense of themselves and also gives them a role in the club that develops along with their changing needs.

Kelly, a 16-year-old male, points out that the club is a place to be both young and mature. This is tied to the issue of being a role model.

> At the Boys & Girls Club it's the place I can go back and be a kid again. It's the place where you don't gotta carry all that. But sometimes it's the opposite cause you gotta take on more. 'Cause it's like, people expect more of you sometimes. It's like "Why you doin' that? Why you actin' immature like a little kid?" Like people expect you to be more, set an example for the younger kids.

Thus, East Side gives youth adult support in dealing with stressors in their lives. The club is a place where they can forget about their troubles and experience the freedom and frivolity of childhood.[13] Yet staff expect older teens to be role models for the younger kids. In doing so, the club recognizes the dual nature of adolescence: children becoming adults and needing aspects of both worlds to support their development.

Lorenzo in particular appears to benefit from this tri-level relationship, using both his relationship with Charles and his relationships with younger club members as supports for his developing self. During the focus group Lorenzo says: "I just learned, it just got brought to my attention that some things you do you have to watch out for your actions. I never thought that actually little kids would look up to someone like [me]." He continues on to say:

> I feel that, when I'm here I got to like, act like a role model cause I know like the staff they like probably expect more of me cause I been here so long and they work with me for long so I just try to, ya know what I'm saying. Be a good example for the little kids and all that.

By the time of his interviews, a year after the focus groups, Lorenzo has incorporated this aspect of the club into his identity at East Side. In addition to serving as a role model for younger members, something which

Lorenzo sees as important to his own sense of self, he also prizes his relationship with Charles. Lorenzo receives important support from Charles and also appears to replicate positive aspects of his relationship with Charles in his interactions with the younger East Side kids. Nearly every day I was at the club Lorenzo was there. In the afternoons he was almost always in the gym with Charles and the younger boys, either playing ball or coaching.

Lorenzo's relationship with Charles is a nice example of the tri-level role modeling that is possible at the clubs. "[Charles] has been like a father to me. He talks to me, he cheers me up." Lorenzo refers to Charles in the two interviews as both the "big brother I never had" and a father. "When I was down he always wanted to know why I was down. He always influenced me to want to do new stuff, to never give up." Lorenzo says that helping Charles with the kids has made him think about what he wants to do in the future. It allowed Lorenzo "to reach out to people." Lorenzo and Charles have fun together, but Lorenzo also credits Charles for teaching him all he knows about basketball. He says that Charles has influenced him, teaching him that life is worth living.

In the focus group Lorenzo talks about how Charles gave him more motivation to focus on school.

> First like, I go to school just to play just to go and play sports but [Charles] told me I had to be more serious than just sports cause there's no guarantee that I'm going to make it or whatever, but, actually to put sports behind education, behind. Education first, and stuff like that. And so he helped me a lot decide what I want to do when I get older. . . . I still want to go to the NBA but . . . to do like graphic design or something.

Lorenzo does struggle with school. He has a spotty attendance record and dropped out more than once. Charles worked to get him back into school when he dropped out and continually tries to convince him to stay in school. While appreciating Lorenzo's participation in the club and his talents with the kids, Charles also wishes that Lorenzo would put the same energy he puts into the club into school.

> We got him back in school one time but he quit again. If he put the energy he put to coming here to play basketball he'd do great. And he was

great with helping me coach kids. If we could get him here as staff with me he'd be great . . . the kids respect him. Sometimes he'll just take charge and he's respected a lot.

Charles recognizes his own limits as a mentor to Lorenzo. He worked to get him back into school but eventually stopped talking to him about getting a job. He feels that Lorenzo wants to "do good" but that he doesn't have the drive he needs to succeed. This disjuncture between expressed desires, future plans, and action is not uncommon among adolescents from low-income communities. Youth recognize the chasm between what education promises to American citizens and what they see in their own communities. The intersection of race, social class, and gender presents challenges to traditional models of returns to schooling. Youth recognize the lack of high-paying jobs in their communities, persistent income disparities between educated working-class and upper-class men, and the continued presence of racism.[14] Furthermore, high rates of incarceration among young Black males in some urban neighborhoods make it all the more difficult to envision an identity that includes a high school or college degree.[15]

Lorenzo's split between what he says and what he does when it comes to school may be tied up with the search for an identity that both reflects the perceived societal importance of academic aspirations and meets his needs for feelings of competence.[16] Yet Lorenzo does feel supported by Charles. And Charles continues to work with him, providing needed encouragement even in the face of his frustration over Lorenzo's school habits. Furthermore, Charles recognizes Lorenzo's potential to be a "great" staff person. He is able to balance his disappointment in Lorenzo's academic record with appreciation of his talents as a youth leader.

While Charles is serving as a role model for Lorenzo, Lorenzo sees that he can also be a role model for younger kids. An example of the tri-level role modeling between Charles, Lorenzo, and younger members is a softball game in which both Charles and Lorenzo were playing with the kids. The interactions between Charles and Lorenzo, as well as Charles and the younger players, and subsequent interactions between Lorenzo and the kids demonstrate the ways in which these relationships reflect each other.

Lorenzo hit a home run and kissed his two fingers, touched his chest with them, and then pointed up to the basketball basket. He looked at Charles and grinned. Charles laughed. . . . Lorenzo stood at the sidelines now and then, shuffling his feet back and forth, doing a little dance, and grinning at the boy who was running the scoreboard. He clapped a lot when his team made a good play and also teased [a young girl]. [The girl] smiled at him and ran to hit him with the bat when he teased her. Lorenzo grinned and hid behind a large mat that was propped up against the wall. They went back and forth like this for a while, with him teasing her while she was up to bat and her running after him threatening to hit him with the bat. Charles joked around with the players and smiled when people made good plays. He made faces when he was up to bat. There was a lot of laughter and good humor overall in the game, and they decided to play a second game when they finished the first one.

During this game Lorenzo has the opportunity to interact with Charles as a mentee, showing off a bit when he makes a good play and receiving validation from Charles. Yet he is also able to act as a mentor, mimicking Charles's style of friendly and fun interaction with the younger kids, both encouraging them and making them laugh. At other times, Lorenzo acts as the actual coach for the younger boys' teams, giving them advice on playing skills, calling players in and out of the game. The younger kids benefit from both these relationships, as well as from their own direct interaction with Charles. While they have Charles as an adult model of who they may be down the road, they also have Lorenzo as a model of who they may be in a couple of years. Furthermore, Lorenzo provides a model of self that includes individual traits and achievements, as well as a position within the community. Youth observe Lorenzo's relationship with Charles and the role he himself plays within the club. Thus, younger members can see a possible future role for themselves in the club.

The process of tri-level role modeling grants youth respect as contributing members of the community, as individuals with an important role within the group. Yet in order to achieve that status, youth must first demonstrate both respect toward club staff and members and a level of personal responsibility. It is clear from Lorenzo's description of his relationship with Charles that he respects him. Furthermore, his interactions with the younger kids demonstrate both respect and responsibility. He acts as coach, encouraging and training them, but he also uses respectful modes of interaction to communicate and interact with them.

Being able to model oneself on an adult, both as an individual achiever and as an example to others, is a unique aspect of the clubs. There are few settings in adolescents' lives, outside of families, in which they come into simultaneous contact with adults and children. In fact, our social settings are becoming increasingly age-segregated. With this segregation come fewer opportunities for cross-age interaction and modeling and, therefore, fewer opportunities for youth to learn important social skills, including caretaking.[17] Yet such cross-age contact allows adolescents a special developmental opportunity: to meet their own needs for support from an adult while also demonstrating their independence and value as responsible people in their own right. It provides a balance of assistance and autonomy.

Sean, the assistant director, notes that it took time for Lorenzo to come into this role. At first Lorenzo acted as a "star." Over time, Lorenzo was able to demonstrate that he is capable of more prosocial values and modes of interaction. Sean responded to this, helping move Lorenzo into the leadership role that Lorenzo eventually took on with Charles in the gym. Lorenzo recognizes this. He took a photograph of Sean and some younger boys as a group of people who are important to him. In describing why they are important to him, Lorenzo says that the little boys look up to him and that Sean gave him chances when no one else did. As noted earlier, he says that his realization that kids looked up to him led him to change his behavior. Thus, Lorenzo recognizes both his responsibility as a role model and the respect that was given to him by club staff, allowing him to move beyond first impressions to prove himself.

Lorenzo's responsibility and skills in working with the younger children is widely recognized at the club. Carlos, an East Side staff member, recommended that Lorenzo look for a summer job at East Side or another club specifically because of his skill in working with youth. Charles, too, notes that Lorenzo is good with the kids and has the potential to be a good staff member. In fact, Lorenzo was given a job at East Side for the summer. Thus, he learned that he could transform his talents and abilities into productive job skills. This emphasizes not only his ties to other individuals but also a possible location in larger society. The value of this type of experience cannot be overemphasized. As noted, Lorenzo is not a successful academic student. Having an alternative identity that is prized allows Lorenzo to achieve validation in another area that has links to real-world job possibilities.

East Side as a Site of Self-Transformation

In addition to what Lorenzo says about East Side's role in his life, the way in which he constructs his story is also of interest. His narrative follows the structure of what has been called a "redemption story." In such tales, the protagonist, through lessons learned, experiences a self change, turning off of a negative path onto a positive one. These redemptive narratives are common among highly generative adults, those who give back to future generations through volunteering and/or work such as teaching or mentoring.[18] Lorenzo's self-construction involves not only the development of prosocial traits but also the overcoming of past adversity to become a responsible and respectful adolescent. This transformation of self occurred at least in part through his relationships at East Side, in which Lorenzo feels that he developed the qualities that he prizes in himself today.

Lorenzo mentions numerous times, and in myriad ways, that he did not have a childhood, that he had to "grow up fast." Lorenzo describes himself as having been angry, misused, unloved, and worthless as a child. He lived a "rough" childhood, one in which he "never had a bond with [his] mother or father." When he was younger, Lorenzo says, he didn't see a reason for living. Yet he transforms this early adversity into a positive growing experience. By the time of the study, Lorenzo was one of the most active and involved teen members at East Side.

An example of his redemption narrative is the event that Lorenzo cites as the most significant in his life. When Lorenzo was 14, his mother went away for two months. He took care of his brothers and sisters. Lorenzo describes this event as showing his courage and demonstrating how his life was taken from him because he had to "play the parent role at a young age." Lorenzo's choice of this event as a significant one is in line with his own view of himself as having had a more difficult childhood than other youth. It is revealing that Lorenzo chooses an event that highlights the difficulty of his childhood and early entrance into adulthood. It is also noteworthy that he constructs the story in such a way as to show its silver lining—the strength and responsibility that he demonstrated and which he considers to be important parts of his present self. Thus, he links his past and present selves through this incident and paints a picture of progression of his self from unloved child to responsible teen.[19] Lorenzo is happier now. He has a good relationship with his parents. Although he does not live with either of them, Lorenzo says, "I get and give love to both my parents. I love my life."

Lorenzo says that these changes in him came about from "saying what I feel and never letting anyone put me down." He feels he developed these qualities at East Side. He ascribes the changes in him since childhood as partially due to the Boys and Girls club because he has been able to open up to people and "receive opinions and help, ask people for help. I can rely on people." Rick, the club director, "showed me that there's always someone out there who can help you, give you a helping hand." He feels that the club is the group that has had the most influence on him, making him "more active, more concerned, more open minded."

Lorenzo appears to have learned a sense of interdependence at the club. In addition to serving as a role model, he has learned to ask for help. He appreciates that he can "tell one of the staff a problem and they can help you with it . . . they can influence me." This ability to ask for help should not be underestimated for its importance to positive youth development. Adolescents must learn to balance both their desires for independence and their needs for adult support.[20] Psychologists such as Ruthellen Josselson have emphasized how important mutually caring relationships are to human development. Learning to care for others while also allowing others to care for you is an important part of self-development.[21] Lorenzo's narrative demonstrates the importance of these ideas to adolescent boys, for whom relatedness is often not viewed as a primary concern. His story supports findings by other researchers who work with urban boys, especially Niobe Way, who have been urging us to hear the desire for close relationships embedded in boys' narratives.[22] Given Lorenzo's family history and his adult role in the family, it seems that it was particularly important for him to find a space in which he felt he could ask for and receive help from adults.

Lorenzo takes a picture of the mother of a club member, who also works at the club, as an adult that he is close to because she cares about how he feels and "I'm comfortable around her. I can tell her anything." Lorenzo says that she is like a mother to him because he doesn't live with his mother. He says that they share the same character, in that she is very respectful, and he can come to her if he is down or needs something. The relationships that Lorenzo forms at the club are something that he talks about during the focus group, as well.

4

■　■　■　■　■　■　■　■　■

"I Can't Act Ghetto in the Ghetto No More"

Self, Society, and Social Categories

> The great social collectivities which used to stabilize our identities—
> the great stable collectivities of class, race, gender, and nation—have
> been, in our times, deeply undermined by social and political devel-
> opments.   —Stuart Hall (1989), p. 12

When I answer the question "who am I," I am in part providing
a definition of myself as an individual, a unique psychological entity. Yet I
am also describing where I exist in relation to others and within society.
Knowing how I am perceived by others influences my own sense of self.[1]
It is not only others' perceptions that influence our sense of self; it is also
whom we see as our own Other. We define ourselves in part by who we
are not.[2]

Race has historically been a powerful axis around which Othering has
revolved. Ideologies of race developed in the late 17th century as a means
to stratify the social system. The process of Othering helped to consolidate
race and class norms during colonial expansion and in nationalist movements. Knowledge of the Other simultaneously created both the native

or racial Other and the colonizing self.[3] This process of self-definition through the body of others occurs not only via macro level narratives and images; these constructions occur within and through our daily interactions and interpersonal relationships.

Today, the inner city serves as a site for the construction of an Other that blends race and class. Media and cultural images provide us with the often unconscious tools we use to produce the raced (and, I argue, classed) Other.[4] These productions structure our local interactions, but they are also re-created within them. The adolescents at East Side understand the ways in which they are constructed as Others by society and how this influences their daily lives and relations with other people. Their own self-constructions are in dialogue with these images. East Side serves as a site in which they negotiate social stereotypes, forming a safe space within which youth can resist dominant discourses and see themselves as subjects rather than objects.[5]

These youth articulate a need for a new model of identity development that goes beyond singular categorizations of gender, race, and social class. They voice with great prowess the ways in which society constructs them as Others and that this construction rests on more than race or class alone. The portrayal of "poor Black inner-city teens" affects not only how these teens are viewed by others and how they see themselves but also their opportunities for social advancement. East Side members actively engage with the dominant discourses of race and class, even as they downplay the importance of these categories in their own self-definitions. They also demonstrate that in the process of their own self-construction their activity, interactions, and relationships both resist and reconstruct societal images of urban youth.

The Multiply Othered Self

Traditional ways of defining self and Other do not adequately capture the identity-building process of youth who are Othered on multiple axes of power.[6] Psychological theories of group identity rest on the assumption that discrimination between "me" and "not-me" is the most basic conceptual level on which humans operate. They start from the premise that we seek to identify categories on which we can both separate ourselves from and link ourselves to others.[7] Assumptions of universal group identities identification with the racial/ethnic group? Class and race both influence the lives of minority youth in poverty-stricken neighborhoods. Recent research on the relationship between racial identity and academic achievement found that, in contrast to the "acting White" theory, which suggested that African American youth reject academics as not compatible with a Black identity,[22] positive identification with one's minority racial group decreases the effect of discrimination on academic self-concept and achievement. The authors suggest that this variation from prior studies may be due to the socioeconomic makeup of the sample, which included greater economic diversity than prior studies, indicating the interactive nature of race and social class.[23] Likewise, research on racial identification of multiracial adolescents has demonstrated that racial identity changes over time and may be influenced by socioeconomic status.[24]

But despite a call for more ecological models of development that examine the interactive systems of racism, classism, and sexism,[25] there is still a dearth of empirical work that studies how these overlapping -ism's actually play out in local contexts. The voices of the East Side teens help us understand the interactive nature of race and class in the process of self-construction and the importance of after-school settings as spaces for engagement with these social categories. The youth simultaneously resist and reconstruct the image of the Other, often using the club as a site of subjective agency. Their relationships with other people in this site provide important contexts for these negotiations. Yet the club does not always live up to its potential for critical engagement with these issues. Discourses of race and class are sometimes reinforced rather than challenged. Whereas staff at times broach issues of racism and classism or point out when youth are being hypocritical, there is no overarching sense of collective action around these issues. Youth are not always challenged to engage critically with these structures in ways that could lead to social action. Despite this, their narratives demonstrate a profound recognition of social categories and their role in shaping the teens' lives. The club is used as a staging ground for negotiation of these identities.

"Project Kids"

One of the dominant ways in which East Side youth describe how society sees them is as kids from the projects. BJ, a 16-year-old African American female whose words opened this book, demonstrates that she and her peers are in dialogue with this construction of themselves. You may recall that one of the photos BJ took was of a bird flying in the sky (see Figure 1-1). When I asked her why she took this photograph, she said: "I just, cause you wouldn't usually see, people think of the projects as bad and that you wouldn't see any birds or anything over here so that's why I took that." BJ expresses a keen awareness of the image that society holds of housing projects. She exerts her own agency in engaging with that dialogue to disprove the stereotype and demonstrate her own personal experience of self in the projects, which includes things of beauty. In taking this photograph, BJ is attempting to "break the gaze" of others. She is creating a counter-narrative of growing up in the projects that directly resists dominant social discourses.[26]

Many youth mirror this awareness of people's images of their neighborhood. Bob, the only White boy in the study, says that although he has never been treated differently because of the neighborhood he lives in, he believes this is only because people don't know where he lives: "But I think if they did know where I lived they'd have a different opinion at first of me. . . . Because a lot of people tend to, even though they may not say so, make judgments based on appearance or background." Bob is both pointing out that youth expect people to perceive them based on where they live and highlighting the conflation of race and class in the United States. Bob is White, and not automatically recognized by others as being from the projects. This allows him to escape that social identity in a way that his Black peers cannot.[27]

African American boys from East Side are especially aware of being identified outside of the neighborhood as kids "from the ghetto."

It'll be like, me and a few of my friends we'll go outside the neighborhood to get away and relax and people be like lookin' at us and say they from the ghetto, think we've got no manners. Some people think all the people from here don't know how to act. —Kelly, 16-year-old male

Like I can go to a classy place and I don't know if it's racist or where we come from and, not to be racist, but a little Caucasian kid will ask his mom why is this person from the projects up there with change. Like people from the projects never got change in their pockets. [*How often does this happen?*] Every . . . it depends on places I go. If I go to classy place it will happen. —Antonio, 14-year-old male

East Side boys are aware of being treated like "project kids" based in part on their place of residence but also on their race. They recognize their bodies as socially marked and are unable to escape this recognition of themselves by certain segments of society.[28] These boys have developed an understanding of the intersubjectivities of their identities.[29] They recognize that their identities sometimes have little to do with their own sense of self. Rather, these identities are often shaped by the ways in which others recognize them. Our identities are circumscribed by social relations, the conditions of which we do not control.[30] For boys at East Side, their neighborhood carries with it a relationship to larger society that they must learn to negotiate in their interactions with the world.

It is not only the boys, however, who experience being characterized as "from the projects." Nicole, a 15-year-old Black girl, says that her cousins, who are "totally preppy cause they live in the suburbs," sometimes make comments to her about where she lives. They will say things like "you don't have parties out and you don't like, there don't be kids runnin' around with no parents. Little mean stuff." She says that she does not get treated differently very often. She attributes this to the fact that she does not go many places outside her neighborhood.

Similarly, Kay, a 16-year-old Black female, says that "people used to think I was ignorant cause I grew up over here." When I ask her how that makes her feel, she replies, "I don't care. I'm used to it." Being thought of as ignorant has become typical for Kay. Her experience demonstrates the way in which stereotypes filter down from what Uri Bronfenbrenner calls the macrosystem into the micro levels of our environments.[31] These macro level stereotypes play out in our local interactions and experiences, eventually infiltrating individual level consciousness. Whether or not youth accept these representations of themselves, they are part of their subconscious images of themselves in the world. As such, they are images that youth must choose to resist or accommodate. This choice, resistance or accommodation, dramatically changes the ecological contexts of their development.[32] Within the club, youth can resist these images through a combination of language and activity. Their relationships with other teens and adults who share their social positioning allow for this activity.

Language and Discursive Resistance

Because we exist within a system of language that gives words historical and social meaning, our discourse of identity is partially bound by that language.[33] The language of self-definition is learned through interaction with culture and others. Teens at East Side exert their own agency in reconstructing the image of the "project kid" through using the dominant discourse as a form of joking. By acknowledging and using cultural images in their own activity, East Side youth claim the power of self-definition and use language to respond to others' misrepresentations of them.[34] In the interaction below, taken from my field notes, youth make explicit their own awareness of outsiders' construction of their identities. They use their long-standing relationships with each other to play with that construction and test my position as an outsider.

"Hey, hey, you know Shelby [a young female staff member from the neighborhood] runs with a King," Sammy said looking at me and making the finger sign of the Latin Kings. "I don't believe that," I said. Sammy looked surprised. "You know what a King is?" he asked me. "Why do you think that I wouldn't?" I responded. "Really? You know the Kings? . . . Oh, oh you must be a queen. Were you a queen? You run with them?" he asked me . . . Sammy repeated that Shelby's man is a King. BJ was laughing and saying "Yeah, yeah, he's right!" . . . And Eric was nodding his head and laughing as well. "Will you all cut it out? You giving me a bad name," Shelby said. "It's true it's true! Her man's . . . a King," Sammy said making the hand gesture for the Kings. "I mean, he's Black, but he's a King. I'm a King," he said. I rolled my eyes at him. "I don't believe you." "Nah, he's true, ——'s a King. He's in lockdown. He's Shelby's man. She used to run with him," BJ said. "Yeah, yeah, she's gangbanging." Shelby opened her mouth and eyes wide and shook her head, letting out her breath as she did. "Would you all cut it? You giving me a bad name here. Come on," Shelby said.

For the next half hour Sammy asked every kid who came into the room who and "what" was Shelby's man. Each kid named him and said he was a King. Many kids made the Kings' hand gesture as they answered. I eventually told Shelby I thought she was losing ground.

[Shelby] shrugged and smiled. "I mean, he's a friend of mine, yeah. But I don't gangbang. That's not me." Sammy shook his head. . . . "They run drugs and you did too. You smoke," Sammy said, grinning. Shelby shook her head. "You know I don't do that. I'm always in here telling you all not to do drugs. Don't get involved with all that. You know that I'm always telling you to stay away from that," Shelby said shaking her head. . . . "Yeah, you know, she's from the projects so you know she's gotta gang bang and do drugs, right?" Sammy said to me. . . . Shelby stood up and said, in an overly serious tone, "I am not from the projects," then she started laughing.

During the course of this interaction, the image of the "project kid" is constructed and reconstructed a number of times. Sammy, Eric, and BJ use stereotypes of teens from the projects to tease and test each other and me. It is psychologically safe for them to do so; I am the only person in the room *not* from the projects and am clearly in the cultural minority within this local context. Social distancing from group identities that carry negative stereotypes has been found to serve as self-protection in both lab-based and naturalistic research with teens.[35] Yet here the youth are not distancing themselves from their neighborhood. Even Shelby's final defense, "I am not from the projects," is followed by her laughter. Rather, the teens are using their relationships with each other and Shelby, formed within the club, to create a shared identity based on their insider status, an identity that excludes me, the racial and class Other.

The discourse of "ghetto" is used frequently as a negative descriptive by the East Side teens. One afternoon Kelly, a 16-year-old Black male, walks into the computer room and starts talking about his high school science fair. He laughs and shakes his head, complaining about the quality of the fair. "We had a ghetto fair in school today. It was so projectish." The computer instructor asks him what he means. "Man, it was a science fair but it was such a ghetto fair, so projectish," Kelly replies, shaking his head. Although he himself lives in "the projects" Kelly uses the words "projectish" and "ghetto" as good-natured insults. In doing so, he reclaims the word but also reinforces the meaning, maintaining its negative connotation. In another interaction, Moonie expresses a need to change her "ghetto" behavior when she learns the purpose of one of the research assistants.

"What do you do?" [Moonie] asked. "Research," I said. "On us?" she asked. "Yeah, the kids, the staff, the club—what makes it good, bad, or better . . . that kind of stuff," I said. "No you don't!" she said. I nodded. "Ooh, and I been acting so ghetto around you!" she said. "I got to change my behavior. I can't act ghetto in the ghetto no more," she said.

Moonie expresses a concern about how her behavior will be written up by the researcher. Her anxiety over her "ghetto" behavior supports a stereotypical use of the word, constructing an Other juxtaposed to her self. But it also demonstrates an attempt to resist the construction of "project kids" by others; she does not want to portray stereotypical behavior to the researcher, who she suspects will portray her as a "ghetto kid" to outsiders. Her relationship with this researcher and the interactions between them are suddenly brought to Moonie's attention as spaces for the reification of stereotyped identities.

Moonie's use of the term "ghetto" is further complicated by her apparent comfort with "ghetto behavior" as long as it is not shown to outsiders. Nicole, a 15-year-old Black girl, demonstrates a similar comfort with the word "ghetto." At the same time, she distances herself from it. Nicole says that at home she acts, "I don't want to say ghetto but, you know, relaxed." "Ghetto" appears to be synonymous with "relaxed" in her sentence, yet she backs away from its use. Perhaps this is because of her recognition of what the word has come to mean, particularly to White people.

One afternoon a couple of young teens demonstrate that constructions of the Other are also used as a form of teasing. Te Te (a 14-year-old female of mixed ethnicity), Eric, and a few others, are talking with one of the research assistants. Te Te asks Eric if he has change for a ten and, when he gives it to her, she says he got his money from selling drugs. Eric tells her not to say things like that. Te Te laughs and says that Eric is a gangbanger.[36] Eric again tells her to be quiet. The conversation turns more serious when Eric asks the research assistant if she has ever been shot at and adds that he has "plenty of times." Te Te manages to lighten the mood by returning to the theme of Eric as a gangbanger, eventually making Eric laugh. The seriousness of gang violence in their neighborhood, and the construction of urban youth as gangbangers, is used by Te Te as a humorous device. In doing so she relies on the fact that Eric is *not* actually in a gang. Their shared identity as club members exists in relation to the Other urban teen, the gangbanger. This shared space gives Te Te the freedom to play with stereotyped social identities.

Eric was also present when Sammy was teasing Shelby. As an adolescent male growing up in a housing project with a large gang presence, Eric is at a time in his life when he has to make decisions about how to negotiate his safety. The question of whether or not to join a gang is quite salient for boys in violent neighborhoods. Some researchers have noted that an environment such as a youth organization can serve as a "holding ground," allowing teens to delay the decision by associating themselves with the club.[37] In this way, the club serves as a site of identity moratorium, a period when teens can consider their options. By engaging in talk about gangs, especially in teasing and joking, youth can explore the issue safely, without making a commitment to any particular identity.

Discourse is one means of resistance. Actively attempting to escape the social context is another. Many of the youth say that moving out of the neighborhood is one of their goals. John, Antonio, Kelly, and BJ all name "getting out of the projects" as a goal or as part of their definition of success. BJ is the only girl to explicitly list escaping from the projects as a sign of success. Seven additional youth name owning a house as a goal or something they consider part of being successful. Only two of those seven are girls. Although most of those youth do not explicitly name getting out of the projects as a goal, it can be assumed that is part of their plan. Those who live in the projects do not own their own homes.

Boys talk more frequently than girls about getting out of the projects. More boys than girls also report being treated differently because of their neighborhood (five versus two). The boys' experiences of being recognized as "project kids," and their transference of these experiences into goals, indicate the ways in which youth negotiate the social implications of their physical presence. Social scientists often talk of girls' bodies as having social meanings. The East Side youths' discussion of being recognized as "project kids" highlights that minority boys' bodies are also inscribed with social meaning. Being Black and male has a particular meaning in America which may at times lead to gender being a more salient social category than race.[38]

The social reading of minority teens' bodies can lead to both aspirations to escape and anxiety at the prospect of leaving the projects. Antonio's and Kelly's comments suggest that, based on past experiences, they expect to be treated outside of their neighborhood as if they do not belong. The suburbs, city parks outside the bounds of the projects, the library, and even school are places in which these teens experience being recognized, and treated by other people, as "project kids." East Side, for most youth, serves as a space to escape these anxieties. Yet, as we will see later, race and class divisions are at times brought inside the club, making it a site of at once resistance to and reconstruction of racial and class identities.

The desire to escape their neighborhood influences youths' daily activities. Some teens say they prefer to spend time with friends from school who will explore other parts of the city. A number say that club kids don't leave the neighborhood; some express a desire to leave the neighborhood more often than they do. One of the photographs taken by Rashad, a 13-year-old Black male, is of a sporting event that he attended on an East Side field trip. He says that this event is important to him because it got him "out of the projects." Being able to leave the projects is generally desired. But youth are also cognizant of the way in which they are stereotyped outside the neighborhood. Leaving the projects requires negotiations of others', both Blacks and Whites, representations of them.

The Breakdown of Black Power

The separation of "project kids" from the larger racial group creates an experience of prejudice that resists group identification. Blacks and African Americans are groups with which the teens identify themselves, but the boundaries of their neighborhood influence their experiences. Their geographic location within the projects complicates their identification with other Blacks. America's socioeconomic structures divide people by both class and race, destabilizing social categories that used to mark group identities.[39] The Black Power movement of the 1960s and 1970s saw the inner city as a powerful site for resistance and solidification of Black identity; the socioeconomic situation in the inner city today has removed such unity. Middle-class Blacks and Whites have left these neighborhoods. The image of urban housing projects as sites inscribed with racial meaning and negativity pervades cultural discourse.[40]

In the 1980s and 1990s, "urban" became a signifier for racial or ethnic minority, poverty, teen parenthood, and gangbanging.[41] The inner city itself was racialized and became a metaphor for lax moral values.[42] In the past few years, urban has taken on a new, hip connotation. "Urban chic" is all the rage. There is an influx of young professionals into cities. Yet when paired with "teen" or "youth," urban still conjures up an image of poverty. Today, a distinct separation exists between the "urban" of gentrification and the "urban" of public housing. The neighborhood in which East Side sits is indicative of this. The blocks just outside the projects are being quickly populated with new condominiums and refurbished row houses. The teens at East Side, on the other hand, are living in "the inner city," "the projects." This geographic space has a culturally inscribed meaning, leaving youth open to discrimination from both Blacks and Whites who do not live within its borders.

The splitting of social identities by geography (and thereby class) is obvious in interactions with youth and parents who do not live in the projects. One evening during a girls' volleyball game, Jade's mother, who is White, struck up a conversation with me.

> I told her that I practiced volleyball with Jade. . . . [Jade's mother] nodded "Yeah, she loves volleyball, all night she hits the ball against the wall. We don't live in the projects. We live down by . . ." She also told me that the girls go to [a local] magnet school. I said that I thought the Club was a great place and that it was nice the kids had somewhere to come where they could play volleyball and other games. . . . At one point while the game was still going on [Jade's mother] tapped me on the shoulder and said, "You know, the one thing I don't like about them coming here, the influence of the other kids. I mean, they're half Black, but they're not being raised like that. You know, with the slang and all, and it's rubbing off on her," she said pointing to [her younger daughter]. [The younger daughter] looked up and said something that I couldn't quite hear. "See?" [Jade's mother] said, shaking her head.

Jade's mother clearly and purposefully separates herself and her daughters from the majority of East Side's population on the basis of both race and class. My own identity as a White woman likely made Jade's mother comfortable expressing these thoughts to me.

Jade's mother relies on a shared cultural understanding that "projects" equals "Black" and differentiates herself in part on race. But a similar attitude is reflected by African Americans in the youths' lives. Some teens talk about both Black and White teachers at school who judge them on the basis of where the teens live. Others mention suburban relatives who say "mean" things about the projects. I occasionally heard kids at other local clubs express negative opinions about certain clubs, including East Side, whose members are seen as "project kids." The geographic space that East Side members inhabit affects their ability to form collective identities with others who may share similar experiences of prejudice. Because of the cultural saturation of the image of the inner-city projects, some teens may even seek to identify with the dominant Other, separating themselves from the stigma associated with the dual categories of Black and poor.[43]

"We All Grew Up Here": East Side as a Shared Space

We can return to Jade to see how such "ghettoizing" of East Side youth affects their interpersonal relationships at the club. Two years after the incident described above, Cheryl is attempting to socialize Jade into the girls' peer group at the club. She tells me that she is having difficulties because of Jade's "better-than-thou" attitude.

> I have tried and tried with that girl, but forget it. I am done. She just walks around here thinking that she is better than everyone else. She has that stuck-up expression on her face. . . . She won't talk to the other girls on the volleyball team. . . . I mean, she thinks that she is so much better than anyone here. . . . Her conflict with the girls on the team is that she is stuck up and thinks she is better than them. . . . And I would meet with the girls and talk to them about Jade before practices because they just couldn't deal with her. And I tried to tell them that they had to just understand how she is. And I've tried to talk to her about how she acts, but she doesn't want to hear it from anyone. I feel badly for her because . . . she will never be able to get anywhere if she acts like this with people all the time. . . . Yeah, they don't live in the projects, big deal, they live across the street. And so what if they go to the [magnet] school. What's so big there if you're getting Fs? 'Cause I've seen Jade's report card, I know her grades. And she gets Fs. So what if it's an F at the [magnet] school? And please, her mother is an addict. I mean she's getting better and don't get me wrong it's great that she's getting her life back on track, but she was a junkie. So don't be thinking you're all above everyone else.

The social distinctions that most youth locate outside the club are here brought inside by the internalized attitudes of a member. Cheryl does not hesitate to point out the hypocrisy of using a neighborhood boundary to divide self and Other. In general, East Side members use the club as a place to assert their own positive identities against outside constructions of them. Jade's attempt to carry these images into the club is met by resistance from her peers. Inside the club, youth have the power to draw their own social boundaries and exclude those who define them as negative Others. Their shared social positioning allows the teens to band together to form a group identity within East Side. This identity provides a shared relational space in which to safely challenge dominant discourse.

Daniel, a 16-year-old biracial boy who used to live in the projects, illustrates this use of the club as a safe space to avoid negative Othering. He thinks that outside the club, people, including teachers, make assumptions about the kids who live in the projects. He talks explicitly about how people characterize youth who live in inner-city, low-income housing. He says that "people judge you because of the neighborhood you live in," that he gets treated differently all the time, and that "it's just a stereotype." Daniel articulates an awareness of how other people sometimes view him because of where he grew up. He also confronts that stereotype through his own actions. He attempts to "prove 'em wrong" by succeeding where some expect him to fail. But Daniel says that he does not feel stereotyped at East Side. He attributes this to the common background of his fellow members and staff: " 'Cause everybody's the same. Everybody grew up in the same community so you can't really stereotype anyone like that."

East Side offers a safe space in which Daniel and other youth can enact their own notions of race and class. In focus groups, many youth echoed Daniel, noting that people at the club are "like them." Michelle Fine and colleagues have coined the term "homesteading" for the use of a shared space to construct positive identities that resist public representations. "Homesteading" was prevalent at the Boys and Girls Clubs.[44] This phenomenon has also been discussed by bell hooks and William Cross in terms of spaces in which Blacks can come together and be "themselves" beyond the reach of public representations of Blacks. For minority adolescents, associating with teens who share similar social positioning can provide support and understanding for their experiences.[45] Youth organizations have been found to serve as settings for the crystallization of shared racial meanings among White working class youth. They also serve as sites where minority teens and youth from low-income backgrounds can subvert social hierarchies and construct a sense of self-efficacy outside of the rubrics of race and class.[46] Community psychologists have looked at this phenomenon in terms of shared stories, whereby communities adapt dominant cultural discourse to their local situation, creating narratives that express their experiences through a sense of positive, shared identity.[47] East Side gives youth two levels of narrative: a shared culture of the club as a local context and a common discourse by which to construct their own identities while negotiating dominant discourse.

Part of what makes East Side such a safe place is the staff. Staff respect youths' rights to construct themselves as individuals outside of rubrics of race and class while still acknowledging the importance of recognizing the race/class system and helping youth negotiate it. Staff members are aware that youth do not always have the power of self-definition. They sometimes try to help youth understand how others see the youths' neighborhood and the ways in which the youths' self-presentations shape that image. Sean told me that he did "experiments" when he took taxis to and from the club. "I'll ask the taxi driver what does he think when I give him the address. They usually say they think they're going to get robbed." Some drivers refuse to drive to the projects, and some won't come to the club. Sean takes this information back to the kids at East Side. He does this in part to make the youth aware of the images that they present. He reminds them that certain clothing styles signify particular meanings to adults, especially those not from the projects. In doing so, he points to the way in which identity is located at the intersection of the individual and society, making the individual presentation of self socially relevant as it feeds back into cultural and political images of youth.[48] Because social identities rest not only on one's own self-definition but also on the recognition of that identity by others, it is necessary to understand your own relationship to the social world.[49]

Relationships with supportive adults may be particularly important for youth who are negatively stereotyped by society. These adolescents' self-perceived locations in the social world may be problematized by the knowledge that the "generalized other's" view of them does not correspond with their subjective experience of self. The East Side teens' demonstrate this in their narratives. Children rely on the perceptions of others to define themselves and may incorporate into their own self-concepts the negative terms assigned to them by others.[50] Personal relationships with supportive others may help youth negotiate divergences between their perceived relation to social categories and social stereotypes. Some have suggested that positive role models are particularly important to the identity development of minority youth because they provide alternative models of identity.[51] For the East Side youth, their relationships with staff at the club stand in contrast to their experiences with some adults in other settings.

Although Charles and Cheryl are the staff who appear most frequently in these narratives, other staff also had strong relationships with youth. Diane (the former program director), an African American male art instructor, and an African American computer instructor (the latter two began during my last year at East Side) all bonded with youth. The impact of Charles and Cheryl is somewhat overrepresented in these youths' narratives because of the unprecedented number of years they were at East Side.

Highlighting the strength of the club relationships is not to suggest that these teens did not have supportive relationships with adults outside of East Side. Many of the teens spoke of family members, other youth group leaders, and school personnel as people who encouraged and nurtured them. But for many youth, East Side served as a uniquely supportive place, especially in relation to their experiences with authority figures outside of the club.

"Even the Black Teachers Are Racist": Race and Class as Defining Experiences

Nearly all the youth report being treated differently outside the club. They shift between attributing discrimination to their neighborhood or race, creating a fluidity of identity in which both class and race define their experiences. Peaches, a 16-year-old African American female, gives examples of negative treatment she and her peers receive from authority figures, both Black and White.

> Like one day we had a half day [at school] and we went to a park, a group of us, and [the police] were kind of picking on us cause we were the same color and there was a fight down the street and they thought we were involved. And this police, I don't know her color, I guess she was White,

she told us we had to leave the park. We were gonna leave anyway, but she called back-up and this policeman drove up and said, "Would all you Black niggas get out of the park" and he said he was gonna arrest us. And he took all our ID's and me and my friends got in trouble for nothing. And I don't really like my school cause people there are racist. Teachers too, even some of the Black ones. . . . But now I just do what I'm told and stay out of trouble.

In a prior interview Peaches talked about how a substitute teacher was "bringing down" all the "colored" people by saying things like "What are you going to be when you grow up? A drug dealer?" Peaches was also upset that the teacher used the phrase "*if* you go to college." Peaches said that she and her classmates stopped listening to the teacher, resisting her attitude.

Peaches' experiences affect her sense of self and behavior. Her passive resistance through disengagement from the teacher has not led to school success. Peaches has been held back in school. Such passive resistance may also increase her chances of engaging in other high-risk behaviors. Teen pregnancy has been linked to girls' academic and career expectations for themselves. Some have noted that girls who choose to have babies are often quieter girls who don't show active resistance. Not seeing academic or career success as a realistic possibility restricts the identities one sees as available and may also increase risk.[52] Furthermore, the "racism" of "even some of the Black [teachers]" may make it more difficult for Peaches to achieve a sense of positive racial identification. Research with African American youth from across socioeconomic classes has suggested that positive ethnic and racial identity, identification, and pride are linked to increased self-esteem, improved psychological adjustment, and academic achievement. These serve as a buffer against the effects of discrimination.[53] Unfortunately, by the end of the study period, the risk inherent in her experiences became reality; Peaches dropped out of school.

Kelly says that he and his friends are treated badly due to a combination of race and neighborhood.

It's like I be goin' into a library or something or into a store and it be a totally different race of people around and they be lookin' at me like what you doin' here? Why you shoppin' here? Or I be entering a chess competition and they say Black people don't play chess. [*Is it White people that say these things?*] Yea, or Mexican or any. There are certain places I feel I can't go cause it ain't my, what's that word, ethnicity. [*How often does that happen?*] Only when I go to certain places.

Although Kelly doesn't appear to allow these experiences to determine his daily activity, it is clear they wear on him. It is difficult to "get away and relax" when you are confronted by the presumption that you don't belong there.

A number of the boys discuss personal experiences of racism, all of which occurred outside of their neighborhood. Each of them also articulates their reactions and resistance to these incidents.

> We was at the pool and this boy was playing with a tennis ball and I asked if I could play and he said "No 'cause you're a nigga" and I said "Huh?" and he said "You heard. 'Cause you're a nigga," and I hit him in the eye. —Greg, age 12

> I was in the suburbs. We went to skate and swim thing. I saw a lady, she said she didn't but I asked for a root beer float and I saw her spit in it. I asked for the manager. She said she was the manager. I asked for my money back and she put up a sign that said no refunds. I just walked away. Haven't had a root beer float since. —Antonio, age 14

> Once when I was in 7th grade we had a substitute teacher and me and her exchanged words and she called me a nigger. [*Was she White?*] Yea. [*Did you tell anyone?*] I reacted. I was locked up. [*Did anything happen to her?*] She was fired. [*How did it make you feel?*] I was proud to be an African American. —Lorenzo, age 17

In each of these instances the boy reacts to discrimination by using his own agency to assert himself. Greg does so physically, Antonio economically, Lorenzo with pride and anger. In Greg's and Lorenzo's cases, race was the motivating factor for the incident. In Antonio's case, however, the motivation is less clear. He tells the story in response to a question about racial prejudice, but his explicit mention of the suburbs maps race onto class-based geography.

This type of fluidity, of being both from the inner city and Black, is common, as is shifting between linking experiences to one or the other of these categories. When I ask East Side teens how much prejudice people from their race face, eleven say none or a little, and only six say some or a lot. These numbers are reversed when I ask how much prejudice people from their neighborhood face. Twelve report some or a lot, and only five say none or a little. Yet when I ask about personal experiences of discrimination, ten youth say they have been treated differently because of their race and eight say they have been treated differently because of their neighborhood. The fact that youth perceive less prejudice against Blacks as a whole but report more personal experiences of racial discrimination may reflect an acknowledgment of their specific positioning within the racial system. They are seen as being urban, poor, and Black. A number of studies have demonstrated that personal experiences of discrimination, rather than perceptions of societal prejudice in general, influence adolescents' outcomes.[54] It may be that East Side teens do not think that Blacks in general face high levels of discrimination but view their own experiences of discrimination as stemming from the confluence of race and neighborhood.

The majority of boys report personal instances of both race-based and neighborhood-based discrimination. The majority of girls, in contrast, do not. In fact, all the boys except for the one White boy report personal experiences of racial prejudice. Again, the social marking of boys' bodies is evident.[55] For some youth, perceptions of prejudice against Blacks as a group and prejudice against people from their neighborhood mirror each other. This indicates that they perceive prejudice in these two realms similarly. Reports of personal experiences of racial and neighborhood-based discrimination are also correlated for some youth.[56] This is not true across the board. Although there is some overlap between these categories of perceived prejudice, they are not identical. It is not the case that some East Side youth are simply more prone to perceiving prejudice. Experiences of prejudice based on race and neighborhood are distinct yet linked. Race and neighborhood intertwine, complicating our notions of singular social categories and individual experience.

Here again, we see the importance of considering the context in which identities are developed. Much work on racial and ethnic identities has stemmed from an Eriksonian framework, privileging stages or statuses.[57] Measurement has focused on outcomes rather than process. This approach does not consider that the meaning of race or ethnicity may not be stable across contexts and relationships. Many East Side youth tell stories about neighborhood-based discrimination when responding to questions about racial discrimination and vice versa. This calls into question measures of racial and ethnic identity or prejudice that do not inquire into the meaning of these constructs to individuals. Whereas social class may influence the opportunities to which an individual has access, race may affect how those opportunities are negotiated. Carla O'Connor demonstrated this in her work with African American college students. Whereas social class affected students' abilities to take advantage of race-based opportunities, race shaped how they negotiated the constraints of completing college.[58] This is important for researchers to reflect on as we consider the developmental processes and settings of youth who are negotiating multiple, marginalized social categories.

African Americans' recognition of others' stereotypes of them have led theorists to examine Black identity through the notion of stigma management. This work suggests that when interacting with the White world, Blacks choose to display identities in reaction to stigma and are influenced in their behaviors by expected stereotypes.[59] The meaning of race and class is read by the East Side youth. They demonstrate various strategies for dealing with it, including managing stigma by shifting their presentation of self to outside authority figures.

The East Side teens' code-switching behaviors point out the way in which our identities are bound up with the geographic space that we inhabit and the ways in which others define that space. These are the lived realities of a debate that Margaret Mead and James Baldwin engaged in during their "rap on race" in 1970. In their voices we hear a return to John Donne, in an echo of the self in connection, in this case moving beyond the interpersonal. Mead, quoting Donne's "for whom the bell tolls" verse, insists that she will be concerned with everyone's suffering but will not accept responsibility for "what other people do because I happen to belong to that nation or that race or that religion." Baldwin counters:

> But, Margaret, I have to accept it. I have to accept it because I am a Black man in the world and I am not only in America. . . . It does not matter where I find myself . . . I am identified, whether I like it or not . . . with Senator McCarthy . . . with Vietnam. . . . According to the West I have no

history. . . . I have to wrest my identity out of the jaws of the West. . . . You are identified with the angels, and I'm identified with the devil.[60]

East Side members, too, recognize the ways in which their individual identities are circumscribed by others' recognition of them as "project kids." That recognition emerges from the intersection of gender, race, and class. Models of identity that attempt to parse out the effects of one of these social categories, therefore, do not adequately capture the ways in which it is their confluence that determines social positioning and daily interactions with the world. The East Side youths' shifting attributions of race and neighborhood as causal factors in their experiences demonstrate the fluid and complex nature of identity in a world in which singular social categories are not sufficient.

Gangbangers and Ho's: Separation of Self from Other

East Side youth use the construction of the Other urban teen as a way to define who they do not want to be. Bob, for example, says that he doesn't want to be like the "ghetto kids" in his neighborhood: "I see the violence that [gangs] cause and it gives me a negative opinion of what they do so it keeps me away from the whole gang scene." Daniel expresses a similar sentiment.

Because everyday you don't see people graduate high school or college and so [my mom] always enforced that I had to go farther and not be like the people in the neighborhood. . . . Now I know why: I had a curfew, I couldn't hang out, and all the kids I went to grammar school with, they're not in school, have kids. And my mom always pushed me. A "B" wasn't good enough—"a 'B' is good but an 'A' is better."

Daniel goes on to say that he does not want to be like drug addicts or "people who aren't doing anything for themselves. 'Cause . . . that's not living life. They're just living." He sees teens who drop out of school and gangbang as examples of things he does not want to be. The gangs and violence in his neighborhood have affected him because "they made me want more than to just be hanging out gangbanging and going to jail and stuff. Shows you what *not* to do." Antonio echoes Daniel, stating that he also does not want to be like "the teenagers that be out here selling drugs and stuff, fighting and stuff."

Like Bob, Daniel and Antonio use the construction of the Other urban teen as an image against which they can define their own sense of self. That image motivates them to move beyond what they see their peers doing. The construction of the Other as an oppositional mirror for the self stereotypes other youth in the same way that the East Side teens are stereotyped. Yet it also serves an important developmental function. The presence of both positive and negative possible selves provides motivation for achieving the positive self. Thus, having an image of what we want to be is not sufficient. Understanding the possible negative outcomes of not achieving that positive self also motivates us to work toward our goals.[61]

Images of gangbangers, drug dealers, and school dropouts dominate club members' descriptions of teens who they do not want to be. Many of the youth took photographs of local drug dealers and gang members as part of the photography assignment for this research project. They took these photos of neighborhood youth to provide examples of what they do not want to be in the future. Other kids say that they wanted to take such pictures but that "no hype [crackhead] would let me take a picture of him." These individuals pepper the streets around the neighborhood but do not appear inside the club. A couple of the girls say they do not want to be like "ho's" or "the girls around here they having babies and whatever." Although some teen mothers were club members, the girls did not refer to them in negative terms. Nicole says that she looks up to a young female staff person, "even though she has a daughter she goes to school, works, has a car. Some people when they have a kid fall back but she does everything." Only one girl names a club member as an example of something she does not want to be, noting that she is still friends with the girl but sees her "going down the wrong road." Thus, East Side serves as a convenient demarcation point for self and Other. The club keeps the youth off the streets and out of trouble. Most of youths' constructions of Others use East Side as a site for keeping oneself out of trouble and on the road to a successful future. In this case, East Side serves not just as a site for positive, discursive resistance, a more abstract form of self-construction, but also as an actual physical location in which to escape negative possible identities.

"She Doesn't Even Look Black": Race as a Shared Identity

East Side youth use race and class discourse to construct their own senses of self and Other. They divide themselves from other teens using the same boundaries used against them. They use club membership as a key demarcation. But they also rely on race and neighborhood stereotypes. These constructions of the Other are seen in the youths' daily activities as well as in their narratives of self.

One afternoon in the computer room, Jade remarks that one of the girls on the regional Boys and Girls Club web site "doesn't even look Black." Her comment reflects an assumption that members of these inner-city clubs, "urban teens," are all of the same racial background. This is particularly interesting coming from Jade. As noted earlier, Jade sees herself as "better than" the other girls at East Side because she does not live in the projects. Her mother does not allow her to date Black boys, a rule that Jade seems determined to violate. Her observation of the girl's race may have been an attempt to ensure her own place at East Side despite her issues with her peers. Her actions channel an idea of "racial authenticity" that privileges pigmentation over other aspects of social experience.[62] Creating a shared sense of experience with ones' peers can help adolescents negotiate situations that may otherwise be confusing. In doing so, they construct a sense of mutuality that defines experiences as "ours" rather than as different.[63] Given Jade's troubled history with the girls at East Side, it seems likely that her racial policing was such an attempt.

There were numerous incidents at East Side when assumptions were made about what White, Black, and Hispanic people did or did not know or do. I was asked why all White people "talk so perfectly" on television. Kids were surprised that I knew local gangs, could sing along with the hip-hop videos on BET, and let's not get into the night when the teen girls convinced me to get up and dance with them. In her interview, Carla, a 14-year-old African American girl, remarked on the ways in which people of different races try to "act like" each other.

> For instance but say, not to be racist or anything, but if they're a different color than us and they try to act like us. It geeks me up and I just laugh. They act like they want to be Black or some Blacks act like they want to be Puerto Rican or White.

Carla reveals a belief in behavioral markers that are appropriate for people of different races. Thus, although their own construction of self fluidly combines race and class, they use race alone as an indicator for other people's identities, assuming knowledge or behavior based around essentialized racial lines.

Boundaries of racially appropriate behavior within the club were illuminated when a Hispanic staff member began a cotillion group. An earlier dance group, led by Cheryl, had been popular with the Black teens. All the youth who participated in the cotillion, at least at first, were Hispanic. When asked if she was going to join, one Black teenage girl responded, "Please, girl, . . . whatever. I'm Black, I'm not going to that." The research assistant who observed the interaction, who herself is Black, chronicles the way in which a Black staff member responded to the girl's remark. The staff attempted to break down the girl's construction of activity preferences by race. The research assistant's analytical notes provide a glimpse into her reading of the situation and the questions it raised for her about race at the club.

> Annie then frowned and commented back at the girl, "What do you mean, 'you Black' . . . girl, please. And Black people dance too, that don't mean nothing." The girl just smiled and rolled her eyes at Annie. [*The exchange between Annie and the younger girl revealed a lot about the possible feelings by many of the Black kids in the club regarding the cotillion dance. Like I noticed earlier, there were no African American kids in the room participating in the activity, let alone old members of the club. I had only seen new faces in the room, which all happened to be Hispanic. I wondered if maybe some of the Black kids felt out of place joining in or that the cotillion was "not a Black thing" like the girl had joked.*]

The teen girl in the interaction dismisses the question of whether or not she will participate in the cotillion as absurd. Annie, a young staff person, attempts to dissuade her, but the girl upholds the barrier between herself and the Hispanic youth at East Side.

Over my four years at East Side, the club became slightly more mixed racially. Although it was still predominantly African American, there were more Hispanic and White youth by the end of the study period. Yet many of the Hispanic youth gravitated toward specific activities, particularly dance groups led by a Hispanic staff member. They were not as integrated into the overall culture of East Side through hanging out and playing informal games in common areas. By upholding these boundaries, members are both maintaining racial lines and demonstrating their social position in the East Side community. This fieldwork was done before immigration took center stage on the streets and in political discourse. Looking back, the seeds of current racial divisions are apparent. Despite shared economic positioning, cementing race-based identities that confirm the legitimacy of one's own group appears important to the East Side teens. This discourse has been reiterated by many adults, Black and White alike, in the current debates about the place of immigrants in American society.

During focus groups, youth did not discuss race as relevant to their experiences at the club. When asked if race was an issue at East Side, the participants instantly said "no." Bob, the only White boy in the focus group, said that if race were an issue other kids wouldn't be his friend. Other kids also equated race with racism. They noted that race was not an issue because everyone at the club is "the same." The youth don't seem to ascribe any meaning to race outside of its association with discrimination. This may be in part because I am White, a racial outsider. It may be that youth do not feel comfortable talking to me about what being Black means to them outside of prejudice. But it may also be due to the discrimination that youth attribute to the mixture of race and neighborhood. Such discrimination may make association with African American culture at large less salient. This conflation of race and racism evokes Cornel West's observation that race has no meaning outside of a social system that ascribes meaning to it. He suggests, therefore, that the only true essential "Blackness" is the shared possibility of being an object of racism.[64] The youths' ascriptions of appropriate behavior based on race in their daily activities suggest that they do have an idea of a common culture. Yet in the focus groups and interviews they do not articulate this culture as being based on race. The influence of the discourse of Black culture, therefore, may be more subconscious than deliberate in their self-constructions.

Conclusion

In the process of their self-construction, teens at East Side have to engage with others' images of them. They both resist and reconstruct the image of the "urban teen" in their own activities and discourse. These youth are aware of society's stereotypes and confront them in their daily lives. Rather than incorporate them into their own identities, most resist such definitions, creating a self that is in relation to, but not in accordance with, social stereotypes. Prior research supports this observation, finding that youth are aware of negative stereotypes of their ethnic groups yet resist racism, sexism, and classism and maintain optimistic views of their chances for success.[65]

The teens at East Side demonstrate the ways in which race and class work together to shape experience. These social categories, often talked about as being correlated, cannot necessarily be separated into singular factors with independent effects. They have both shared and unique influences on youths' experiences. Given the ways in which youth talk about their lives and identities, attempting to control for a single category or to examine its "true" effect on development seems disconnected from real-world experiences. Furthermore, gender also shapes youths' experiences of the race/class system, creating yet another axis of power around which their lives revolve.

These youths' stories call for a deeper understanding of the processes of identity in relation to the social structure. We need a consideration of identity that goes beyond measuring stages or outcomes. It is seldom one social category alone that shapes experience and identity. Rather, it is the confluence of multiple categories that determines social positioning. Furthermore, youth need spaces in which they can safely and constructively confront and engage with cultural discourses of race and class in the process of forming their own shared and individual identities. What is clear from these teens' narratives are the ways in which social identities are negotiated within and through their interpersonal relationships. Thus, it is important to carve out spaces for relationships that are supportive of this process and which allow youth to resist stereotypes and categories in positive and proactive ways.

5

■　■　■　■　■　■　■　■　■

"I've Never Seen Any Dark-Skinned Girls in Videos"

Nicole's Story

Everyone says that race don't matter no more but then they all ask us like what it means to be Black, and if it don't matter then why does everyone want to know?　　　　　　　　　　　　　—Nicole

Nicole is a 15-year-old Black female who has been coming to the club for eleven years. She has a dark complexion, curvaceous frame, and long legs that place her a head above her peers. Her smile is wide and bright, her eyes sparkling. Nicole is attractive with a serious side she is not afraid to display. She is engaging and energetic, frequently greets me with a hug, yet can be moody. She says her, "feelings change in the midst of a second." While often talkative and friendly, Nicole withdraws at times. She has a strong presence and is not afraid to speak her mind.

Nicole lives with her mom and a number of siblings in the housing project near the club. She is the oldest child living at home and has a clear "older sister" air about her, which she demonstrates around younger kids at the club. Nicole's favorite places to be are in the front room of her house and her bedroom "because it is so comfortable." She likes to play sports and go shopping, although she says that she doesn't really have the money to go shopping.

Nicole usually keeps her hair short, often worn straightened or in braids. During her first year in high school, she experimented with elaborate longer styles and dyes. Nicole is stylish and wears brightly colored clothes and jewelry that compliment her figure. She is also athletic and puts on t-shirts and shorts for her team practices.

Nicole reveals the ways in which race can be both an issue, shaping experiences, and a non-issue, downplayed in one's overall sense of self. Her narrative turns attention to the intersection of race and gender, as well as the role of gender stereotyping in constricting identity choices. Yet Nicole also demonstrates how personal agency can challenge such stereotypes. She shows us how a youth organization, and the relationships developed within it, can serve as a supportive environment for teens attempting to find a niche in the adult world.

Nicole's Role at East Side

Nicole worked at the club during my final year at East Side. Throughout the earlier years, she was involved in many groups there, including Cheryl's girls' groups and the girls' sports teams. She often took leadership roles within these activities. Nicole participated in a number of pilot interviews and activities with me over the years. Although the level of her participation at East Side varied, especially after Cheryl's departure, she always returned to the club, especially to work or play sports. Nicole helps out staff in a variety of ways, such as making bulletin boards, staffing the front desk, and assisting with administrative paperwork. She is a good student and attends one of the best public schools in the city. Nicole is extremely introspective, both about herself and the social world. She is very aware of her problematic relationship to gender norms and is articulate on that subject. She sees discrepancies in many areas of the gender system, and she seemed to enjoy discussing her observations with me.

Nicole became the seventeenth youth in my study in the spring of my final year at East Side. She asked me if I was still planning on interviewing kids and, if so, could she be part of the project. Although I did not need more participants, I decided to include Nicole because of her enthusiasm and active presence over the years.

Nicole's Sense of Self

Nicole describes herself as "smart, nice, outgoing, shy." Her definition of outgoing is "if there's something that's gonna help me I'll try it. I'm not afraid to try new things." In her choice of such descriptors as "smart" and "nice," she splits her self-definition between individuated and connected words.[1] In an interview a year earlier, Nicole had described herself as "athletic, tall, talented, dark, goofy." Over the course of a year, in line with cognitive changes associated with adolescence, Nicole began to describe herself with more personality characteristics (nice, outgoing) than physical traits (tall, dark). Yet her racial positioning, as suggested by use of the word "dark" in the earlier interview, remains a salient issue.

Nicole considers shyness her most important quality and says that she "doesn't like to say some things in front of people I don't really know so I'll stay quiet." When she is working at the club, however, she notes that she cannot be shy. If someone is doing something wrong "if you're working . . . you have to let them know, you can't sugarcoat it even if they're your friends you have to let them know, but in a nice way." Through working at the club, she has learned to conquer her shyness as needed for professional purposes. This position of authority, and her view of herself as a "worker," is an important part of her self-concept.

While Nicole's worker personality comes up repeatedly in her descriptions of herself, she also says that when she is not at work she will act less mature if she is with "people . . . who aren't as mature as me. . . . I'll act how they would act so they won't think I think I'm better than them." Like most teenagers, Nicole is somewhat conflicted about this "acting."[2] On the one hand, Nicole says that she is still being herself, because she has different personalities. But she also feels like it is putting on an act " 'cause people . . . know it's not me. But I don't mind as long as I'm not hurting anybody." Rather than seeing these different displays as different selves, she integrates these "acts" into a singular identity trait: having different personalities. Nicole says that her personality is appreciated and encouraged at the club because she knows "when to act my age and when to act older." Her ability to "change her personality" is one of her favorite things about herself. This suggests that she is aware of the necessity and appropriateness of displaying different sides of oneself in different situations. Nicole's comfort with this type of shifting self calls to mind theories of postmodern subjectivities. Her use of the phrase "it's not *me*" (emphasis added) also suggests that she carries with her a notion of a stable identity that is sustained across contexts, one that she seeks to integrate with her various outward "personalities" or "acts." Her remark that her personality is encouraged and appreciated at the club suggests that East Side serves as a space in which she can negotiate the integration of these various aspects of her identity.

Nicole likes to spend time with her mom but doesn't feel that she can really talk to her. Nicole took a picture of her mother and some siblings in her kitchen to "show how I don't get along. I'd like to but I don't. . . . They don't see the goofy, like to have fun. . . . I don't like to be yelled at or disrespected, and that's all I get at home." She does, however, make a point of showing me the scarf and shoes that her mother is wearing in the photo. Nicole proudly tells me she bought these items with her first paycheck from the club as a surprise for her mother. Thus, despite some conflicted feelings about her family, she emphasizes things that she has done for her mother as part of her narrative of self. She highlights a sense of self in connection with her family and, particularly, as an adult-like figure who can provide things for her mother.

When asked if she changes at all depending on where she is, Nicole responds that at her house she acts "the way everybody else act. I don't wanna say ghetto but you know, relaxed, whatever. But when I'm at work [at the club] I act more professional, less like a kid. . . . When I wasn't working here I played and didn't take stuff seriously, but when I started working here I take stuff seriously." As we saw earlier, "ghetto" is a term youth play with and use as a marker for certain types of behavior. Here, Nicole juxtaposes "ghetto" behavior with "professional" behavior. Although her qualification "I don't wanna say ghetto" suggests that she sees "ghetto" as having negative connotations, her overall statement seems to acknowledge a comfort with different types of behavior, including "ghetto" behavior, at home and in the workplace. I can't help but wonder if her distancing of herself from "ghetto" behavior is related more to my position as an outsider than to her actual feelings about "acting ghetto."

Nicole says that when she was younger she was "bad, hard-headed, goofy, and confused." She says that she is no longer confused and "always find[s] a way to understand something." She also says that "I'm not a bad child. I might be mean, but I'm not a bad child . . . I don't have time to be bad." She says that she is no longer bad because of her participation in the club: "Because if I wasn't at the club I'd be out running around doing something I ain't got no business doing, but the club keeps me busy." Nicole reports that when she first came to East Side "if I saw something I liked I'd try and then quit when I saw something else. I didn't stick to anything." She says that she would not be the same person that she is today if she didn't come to the club "because I have a bad attitude. I think my attitude would be worse than it is. I think I wouldn't believe in myself. . . . [I] used to be serious and mean, still am at times, but learned to get along here and smile." Like Lorenzo and other youth, she discusses a transformation of self that occurs through her participation at East Side.

Nicole's model of success revolves around being a successful employee. She admires one of her older female cousins because she is "never without a job. If she gets laid off one day she has one the next. . . . She's totally successful, depends on herself." Nicole mentions another cousin as an adult whom she admires because, "even though we don't really talk, she is in school, works, has no kids. Even though she lives with her mom 'cause she's a mother's girl, she has money to go buy a house. She goes out and parties but still gets 'A's' and 'B's' in college. That's really cool." Nicole's goal for the future is to be successful. She defines success as being able "to depend on myself. If I can depend on myself I'm successful. If I have a job, can depend on myself. I don't have to ask you for nothing." The theme of Nicole as a "worker" is a common one in her story.

"If I Wasn't Working Here I'd Still Be Goofy": East Side as a Developmental Context

Nicole's relationship to the club, especially during the study year, is closely linked to her sense of self as a responsible employee. At the club, she is building an adult self. Her role as a leader and worker began well before she was working at East Side for money. According to my field notes, three years earlier, I talked with Nicole while she was staffing a candy store to raise money for a club group in which she was involved.

[*Do you think you will keep coming to the club?*] . . . Oh yeah, I'll keep coming. Because it gives you something to do. And then I can work here, like when I get to be a teenager, 'cause I will have been around so long.

[*Interestingly, during the beginning of our conversation Shonda, an older teen girl, had come over and bought a couple pieces of candy and gone back to sit down at the front desk. Having her working about 25 feet from where we were having this conversation was sort of proof of what Nicole was saying.*]

Three years later, Nicole had taken up the position at the front desk. Not only does this demonstrate that East Side encourages responsible adult roles, but it is also an example of how older teens can be role models for the younger members. Shonda and another older girl both worked at the club and helped coach the girls' sports teams on which Nicole played. Nicole saw girls' social roles at East Side develop and change as they grew older. The older teens modeled a career path at the club, which Nicole took in and incorporated into her future identity. Like Lorenzo, she benefited from the tri-level role modeling available at East Side. Nicole had both the older teens and the adult staff to look up to for models of job success. As she aged, she took on the role of the responsible older teen, modeling a more adult-like self. Nicole acknowledges this changing role. She says that she does not play around as much as she used to at the club and feels that she does not act as "goofy" as she would if she were not working there.

Alyiah, a 15-year-old African American girl who is a close friend of Nicole's, also talks about how her role at the club has changed since she began working at East Side. She says that she no longer has time to play at the club. Yet this has not diminished the place of East Side in her life. In fact, it seems to have enhanced it. Alyiah names the club as the most influential place in her life. She says she would not be the same person she is today without it. Alyiah and Nicole often work together at the club, combining friendship with career development. As part of her photo project Nicole took a picture of Alyiah and herself next to the front desk of the club.

Alyiah has a strong sense of the club as a place that supports her future self. She takes her job at the club seriously. Like Nicole, even in the years before she worked there, she was called on by staff to help out with various tasks and events. Alyiah was often seen doing her homework at the club and using the club computers to complete school projects. Her goal is to be a lawyer, and she uses the club to support her academic and adult worker roles, both of which are linked to her image of herself as an adult.

She also says that club staff have directly influenced her by helping her think about her future; they talk about it together and "they ask us what we want to do in the future."

Part of constructing an individual identity is finding a position for oneself in the adult social world. An important part of the process of finding a space for oneself in the future is having adults who are willing to share their own knowledge and experiences.[3] As employment opportunities have become scarcer in the inner city, it has become more and more difficult for teens to see productive roles for themselves in the adult job market. Club staff sometimes address future employment issues directly. Asked if he thought that working at the club had influenced Nicole, Sean says that he hopes that it has put her into the workforce and taught her "work responsibilities in general, coming to work on time, reporting to a supervisor." He sees this first job as laying the groundwork for her future experiences in the workplace. Judging by Nicole's narrative of self, especially in relation to the club, it does seem that these experiences at East Side help to support her emerging adult self.

A conversation I had with Cheryl, to whom Nicole was very close, indicated her awareness of being a model for youth of appropriate modes of adult interactions. She says that when the teen girls hear her talking on the phone to other adults, organizing interclub events or trying to get donations or volunteers for East Side, they tease her about her "adult voice." "But what am I supposed to be like 'Yo! What up?!' to adults?" Cheryl asks, laughing. Cheryl demonstrates the types of interactions that are expected between working adults. By being able to switch back and forth between informal conversations with the teens and formal interactions with colleagues, she models a construction of self that comfortably encompasses a variety of adult roles. Because the girls like and respect Cheryl, they can use her example to help themselves feel more comfortable about their own changes in behavior.

Many staff explicitly address career issues in their programs. When Cheryl planned a beauty pageant with one of her girls' groups, she made sure that the pageant included some attention to careers along with traditional fashion wear.

"We need to come up with categories," Cheryl said. [One of the girls] read the list she had made of categories, including casual/hip-hop, evening wear, and athletic wear, as well as a talent category. "And career wear," said Cheryl. "We need career." "Yeah, but that's just suits," said Janet. "No —I need to be able to tell what you want to be. If you want to be an architect, you have to have one of those triangle things they use. If you want to be a nurse, you should be wearing a uniform, not just a suit but something that people can look at you and say, oh that's what she wants to be." Cheryl said that the girls would also have to read an essay. "That would be boring!" [one girl] said. "Who wants to sit and listen to someone read?" "No, you'd have to learn to make it interesting, not to just read it. We could make it so you write about your career and then you read it while you're dressed for that so it's more interesting" [Cheryl said].

Thus, Cheryl encourages the girls to explicitly think about their careers. By incorporating an essay and tools of the trade, she forces them to conduct research into their chosen field.

Staff at East Side are realistic about the teens' job options. Many attempt to help youth negotiate the labor market. Staff members and youth alike discuss how local businesses won't hire kids from the projects. East Side staff serve as "sharers of experience."[4] One afternoon while hanging out with the girls, Cheryl encourages Janet, an older teen girl, to get a job. She also acknowledges that stores are prejudiced against the local teens.

"Go out and get a job! [Store A] is hiring" [Cheryl said]. "Not nobody from [the housing project], they ain't hiring," Janet replies. "Not no 16-year-old, either," Shelby adds. "What about [Store B]?" offers [another girl]. "Oh no," Cheryl replies, "Not [Store B]. They're no good." The girls stare at her with bewilderment on their faces. "[Store B's] prejudiced, you don't gotta whisper it," she explains. "They have not hired *one* of my girls that I have referred to them. Five years. Not *one*." Cheryl goes on to talk about the importance of impressing a prospective employer by creating a resume that "sells you" and by giving back the job application promptly with references.

Janet was a leader in many of the girls' groups in which Nicole was involved. Nicole was also close to Cheryl and was usually part of these informal, hanging-out sessions. She therefore witnessed many of Janet and Cheryl's conversations about work over the years. Given Nicole's strong sense of herself as an employee at East Side, and her expectations for future career success, such interactions likely helped support her own development. Nicole, who acted as a big sister to younger kids at the club, slowly began to identify herself more and more with adult staff. She became comfortable acting "more mature" and saw herself as a reliable employee. In using East Side as a staging ground for this more responsible, mature, adult self, she gained important work experience and became comfortable with the roles and behaviors that will be required of her as she moves into the job market.

Schools have historically not been successful in linking students with jobs.[5] East Side, however, is able to validate and reward youths' abilities while showing that their talents can be transformed into productive job skills. In addition to Nicole and Lorenzo, other youth also talked about how staff at East Side made them think about their futures by asking them where they expected to be in five or ten years. Daniel believes that the club has helped him "get mature." He feels that the staff in particular assist him in striving toward his future goals.

> The people here inspire you to do what you can, reach for higher goals so you can be a success when you get older. Always encourage you to do positive things with your life. . . . They motivate you to do whatever you want to do in the future. And a lot of staff help you find scholarships and whatever that fit you. . . . They let you know that it's alright to be different, everybody's not the same and you have to change your attitude in different places . . . like Sean said about me and [my friend]. That we can turn our professionalism on and off in different situations. You can act more proper.

As it does for Nicole and Alyiah, East Side helps Daniel cultivate a sense of himself as an emerging adult and inspires him to reach for his goals. Along with simple encouragement, the club provides formal support and assistance in meeting his goals. For Nicole, this support allows her to cultivate a sense of herself as a developing adult, an identity that became paramount in her own self-concept.

East Side holds special events geared to helping youth achieve educational and career goals. They take youth to college fairs, hold ACT preparation classes, and help youth obtain work permits. Many staff actively assist teens in looking for jobs and filling out job applications. Bob talks specifically about the resources of East Side as beneficial for the teens in his neighborhood, saying that the most important part of the club is "the opportunities they provide to low-income children. They take us to different parts of the state. . . . Sean has taken several club members to different events where goals in life are thought about, analyzed. They try to help you."

It is not just the specific events and resources that Bob cites as important, however. Bob, like Nicole, refers to the staff's overall attitudes as encouraging him and providing him with needed support. He feels that he can talk to staff comfortably, especially because some of them grew up in housing projects themselves and have an understanding of what Bob and his peers are going through. Bob notes that Rick, the club director, doesn't do his job for the money. Rather, Bob says, "he deeply cares about the people he works with." Bob and Nicole both attend top academic high schools in the city. Yet both of them supplement the resources at their schools with those at the club. They draw on the staff and resources at East Side to expand their options for out-of-school opportunities. They use their relationships as well as activities at the club to shape and support their identities.

Dark-Skinned Girls: The Intersection of Race and Gender

Nicole defines her race/ethnicity as "Black, African American." But she continues on to explain that her grandparents are "Indian and Hispanic."[6] Although she lists the specific ethnic background of her family members as part of her self-definition, Nicole also tells me that she calls herself Black because she knows that is how people see her. Thus, she defines her ethnic background in part by the biologic roots of her family; yet she also acknowledges her "perceived race," demonstrating an awareness of the social nature of race and ethnicity. Her description of a trip to the Puerto Rican Day parade with her grandfather highlights this duality.

> Once I was at the Puerto Rican parade with my grandfather, and they said you have a Puerto Rican flag and there's nothing wrong with that but

are you really Puerto Rican? And I said, yeah, that's my grandfather. . . . I
look Black so I just say I'm African American.

Nicole is aware of the difference between biologic and socially constructed
race; she negotiates those meanings in her interactions with the world.
Other East Side youth, especially those who are biracial, recognize the
constructed nature of racial boundaries. They are frustrated by what they
see as arbitrary rules regarding racial categorization.

Daniel, a 16-year-old biracial boy, notes that he is forced to think about
his race and ethnicity whenever he fills out a form for school: "Well, sometimes I think about it because we have to fill in on a test or something it
says you have to choose one and I just choose 'other.' I had a teacher tell
me I had to pick one. You don't have to pick one." Daniel resists having
to choose just one ethnicity. As a biracial individual, he feels that such a
choice does not reflect his true identity. The language society provides
him is inadequate to define himself.[7] Te Te, a 14-year-old girl, expands
her view of ethnicity beyond what the outside world sees. She says that
because she is "multiracial" she "has a lot of ethnicity in my family." Although she is not Puerto Rican, she often refers to herself as Puerto Rican
because her half-siblings are. She likes to "represent" on their behalf. Te Te
expands her sense of herself as an individual to include her family members. She melds their ethnic backgrounds with hers in her self-construction. For both Te Te and Nicole, relationships with family members shape
their racial identifications, pushing the definition of race in our culture.

The choice of a racial reference group for biracial individuals is often
informed by knowledge of how one is perceived by others. Our current
definitions of race fail to capture the distinction between one's self-concept and one's social identity. To avoid using biologic phenotype as the
defining factor, the biracial individual must choose between self-acknowl-
edgment and social recognition. To be put in such a position complicates
the process of identity development. Revisions to self-concept are made as
people interact with the social world and see themselves through the eyes
of others. Nicole's decision to self-identify as Black because "that's how
others see me" reflects this process. She has to choose a static identity. She
is not afforded opportunities to define her ethnic and racial background as
fluid, informing her in different ways in different situations. This reflects

our culture's insistence on a biologic model of race, as well as our predominant definition of identity as unified and constant.[8]

Nicole and her peers present a challenge to researchers to push our definitions of race and ethnicity beyond either phenotype or biology alone. Rather than identifying based on either bloodlines or social recognition, many East Side members attempt to create fluid identities that incorporate a variety of ethnic and racial connections. These connections include family relationships, as well as relations to social structure. They also include other people in youths' daily environments with whom they may be seeking common ground or from whom they may wish to separate. Sometimes the East Side teens even challenge each other's rigid notions of race. The club can be a safe space for such activity and discussion.

Although we saw earlier that youth within the club use race as a category around which to construct self and Others, one incident demonstrates how youth may reject race as a rigid, defining category. The following are excerpts from my field notes from October 30, 2001.

Alyiah and Tyrone had started to talk about Halloween and the fears of terrorism and trick or treating. Alyiah said they had arrested a guy buying a whole bunch of candy at Costco. Tyrone asked why they did that, and Alyiah said he was Pakistani. "Oh, okay," Tyrone said. . . . Tyrone said that he would not take candy from any Pakistani. Alyiah looked up at him with her eyes widened. "What?!? How you going to know if they Pakistani?" she asked him. "Because, you know, I'll look at them." Alyiah shook her head with a disgusted expression on her face. "And how you gonna know that? You gonna know just by looking at them? You can't tell that. I mean that's just race and there's all different races and you don't know just by looking at someone." I nodded. "Yeah, and you know, India and Pakistan used to be one country, and so if you look at someone from India and someone from Pakistan they look really the same but they are different religions and from different countries, so you can't tell just by looking." "Yeah, and I have some Indian in me, and look at me," Alyiah said. Tyrone shrugged. "Yeah, me too." "So that's just stupid. I mean that's just race," Alyiah said.

This incident is particularly notable because Nicole's best friend, Alyiah, challenges not only her friend but also the national discourse around self and Other that was prevalent at the time. September 11, 2001, shifted America's constructions of self and Other. The discourse of "us versus them" that prevailed in the height of the country's shared grief led to a crystallization of an American identity. This hid the very real divisions that still existed and which a hurricane named Katrina would bring to our attention four years later. The idea of a shared American identity, which rejected particular other ethnicities, filtered down to the East Side youth. Tyrone had clearly been influenced by the discourse of "us versus them" that became prevalent in the post-9/11 United States.

What was notable to me, as a participant-observer in this situation, was Tyrone's willingness to racially profile the Other, something which his Black, male peers at East Side often experienced being done to them. All of us partake in such Othering, both consciously and unconsciously. Such activity has historically served as a powerful identity-building tool. As such, it is all the more difficult to resist and deconstruct in our daily lives. Having a space in which such reconstructions can be safely challenged by both peers and adults is important. East Side did not always serve as a radical space for deconstruction of social norms. Statements such as Tyrone's often went unchallenged, either missed or ignored by staff. Opportunities for deeper discussion were not always realized, perhaps due to staff discomfort with taking on such issues or the daily grind of managing activities and youth. But youth did at times engage in such discourse, sometimes resisting and sometimes reconstructing it.

Nicole was also quite willing to speak up about her feelings on race and ethnicity. During an interview the year prior to the study, she said it was not a good idea to ask questions about race and ethnicity.[9] My notes from that interview present my reflections on our interaction.

> Nicole had an interesting response to the question about what she thinks it means to be Black (which was how she identified her race/ethnicity). "I don't think that's a good question," she said, shaking her head. "Okay, why not?" I asked. "'Cause you know, everyone says that race don't matter no more, but then they all ask us like what it means to be Black and if it don't matter then why does everyone want to know?" "That's a good question," I said. "I can tell you why I am interested in it. I think that we like to pretend that race doesn't matter anymore, but unfortunately I think that racism still exists. And White people a lot of time think that race

doesn't mean them. You know, like people think that race only applies to people who are Black. And so I am interested in what race means to different people, you know? Like for some people it seems to be important to have a sort of connection to their culture. And for others that doesn't seem to matter as much." Nicole nodded. "Yeah, yeah, nah, I know what you mean . . ."

Nicole's response to my question demonstrates a keen awareness of racial positioning and power issues. She clearly implicates me in the racial power structure, as I am obviously part of the "everyone" who comes around asking her what it means to be Black. She forces me to acknowledge my positioning, and the fact that I, a White female, am asking Nicole and her Black peers how they feel about their own race and ethnicity without having to answer for myself. Furthermore, she challenges American society's hypocrisy surrounding issues of race. On the one hand, we claim that race is no longer an issue. On the other hand, we continually place racial minorities in the position of having to speak for their peers or serve as examples of their group. Thus, Nicole's question: If it's not an issue, why are you asking me about it?

In Nicole's interviews we hear that her response to my question does not suggest that she feels race doesn't matter. Rather, she is demonstrating the way in which her own self-construction has been influenced by society's construction of race and thereby of her as an African American teen. This becomes apparent when Nicole describes herself. One of the five words that she uses to describe herself in an early interview is "dark." During that interview she defines herself solely as Black, whereas a year later she includes her grandparents' heritage in her racial and ethnic self-definition and does not use skin tone to describe herself. Nicole's identity as a dark-skinned African American female is salient to her at some times more than others. Her self-description becomes more complex and fluid in the final year of the study, reflecting her developmental stage and growth.

Although Nicole reports that in general she does not think Blacks face prejudice, she does feel that women face a little prejudice and people from her neighborhood face some prejudice. Yet for Nicole, as for other youth, race and class in lived experience are often enmeshed. When asked if she has ever been treated differently because of her race, she says yes:

"[People say] oh, you're from the projects; what you gonna do, beat me up or something?" Asked about racial discrimination, she talks about being treated as a kid from "the projects." Nicole perceives the incident as racially motivated, even though the dialogue refers not to race but to neighborhood. Thus, she demonstrates how the two can be intertwined in lived identity.

"All Those Red-Boned Girls in Videos"

Whereas the influence of the media on girls' self-esteem has been widely discussed, less work has been done on racial differences in the effects of media on gender identity. Nicole talks openly about the role of skin color in defining femininity for African American females and the ways in which media affects her as a dark-skinned female.

"I was just thinkin'—like videos—light-skinned girls. I've never seen any dark-skinned girls in videos or movies. I mean, it's like whenever there is someone dark they are bad and the light-skinned people are all good. But in my life . . . I don't know. I think they got it wrong." She talked a fair amount about how frustrating it was and how there is no one who looks like her. "You know, I have noticed that, too [I said]. "I mean, it's great that Halle Berry won the Academy Award and was the first African American to win Best Actress and the same year as Denzel and all that, but I was sitting there thinking, Does anyone else notice that she is about the lightest Black woman you can get?" "Yeah!" Nicole said, her face lighting up and nodding. "I thought I was just crazy and that I was the only one who noticed this and was just crazy. I mean, I love videos and I get so angry when I watch videos cause its all them red-bone girls." "What's red-bone?" I asked. "Red-bone like," Nicole pointed at her arm. "Like, it just means light skinned. I guess, I don't know why, I guess cause you can see the red. Like light-skinned people and White people get red, you know. Like you'd be red-boned. But you know I get red, too. That's why I like rock. I love rock videos cause they don't have any of those color issues where —— you know it's all red-boned girls . . . I had long hair, but I cut it. And I hate it when they say, "Oh you bald headed." I say, no, I just have short hair. And my marks all over." [*Shows me her arm with dark marks on it, and I show her my own moles and freckles.*]

Nicole expresses an awareness of the gendered expectations for female appearance and the ways in which she herself does not fit those expectations. She also demonstrates that gender is braided with race, placing her in a specific position within the gender system.[10] It is not merely that there are certain assumptions about what a female should look like, such as having long hair or skin free of marks. The color and tone of a woman's skin, particularly an African American woman's skin, is also used in the media as a signifier for other characteristics, attributes that Nicole does not feel describe who she is as a dark-skinned woman. Nicole is not alone in her thoughts, despite her feelings of "craziness."

Skin tone has long been an issue in the African American community.[11] Nicole picks up on this in her construction of herself as a Black female. The association of Whiteness with power has infiltrated postcolonial discourses of race and skin color, in both White and Black communities.[12] Satisfaction with skin color has been linked to self-esteem for Black youth. Researchers have consistently found that youth who perceive themselves as being either very light or very dark—that is, at either end of the skin-color spectrum—are least satisfied with their appearance.[13] Black women in particular are subject to evaluation based on skin color, in part because of the "cult of true womanhood," which associated Whiteness with femininity.[14] Nicole's discourse surrounding these issues demonstrates her "body-smarts," a distinct self-awareness combined with a vivid social awareness.[15] Nicole's willingness to discuss these issues with me may be due to my Whiteness, which reduces the tensions she feels around these issues within the Black community. Thus, our personal relationship, as a White woman and a Black teen, gives her a space in which to work out some of these identity issues.

"Now It's Coming around to Women": East Side as a Site for Gender Construction

Despite her consciousness of the expectations for females in terms of physicality, Nicole reports taking pleasure in confronting gender norms. In her pilot interview she talks about a significant event in her life: when she played basketball with a group of guys and proved to them that a girl could play: "I had no gym shoes, and I was wearing sandals. This boy went up to shoot, and I smacked the ball down. I kind of liked that." She also mentions that people sometimes tell her that she acts like a boy.

> Certain boys say you can't play basketball. Some boys I can play basketball with but others come up and say, "You're a girl; you're not supposed to be playing that." When I do play, I have a boy part and a girl part of me. I like rap. and other girls like slow songs. Girls will "ah, Nicole, you act like a boy" or "look at that man."

Thus, Nicole confronts stereotypes of feminine behavior in sports and music. East Side becomes a site in which she can express and experiment with the "boy part" of herself. Nicole is actively involved in the girls' sports teams and sometimes also plays with the boys. She expresses the type of split self that has been described by teen girls participating in sports, wherein the "athletic self" and the "feminine self" are divided and maintained separately.[16] Rather than seeing sports as part of her femininity, Nicole has "a boy part and a girl part" of herself. Her athleticism appears to exist in spite of, rather than as part of, her feminine self. Yet both are parts of who she is, and Nicole does not express a conflicted relationship to this split self. Rather, her narrative is suggestive of a split subjectivity, whereby both the boy and girl are valid parts of her self that are enacted in different contexts.[17] East Side becomes a context in which she can enact, and receive support and validation for, both parts.

When asked in the first interview if there was ever an activity she felt she couldn't do because she is a girl, Nicole responded:

> Baseball. . . . Like before I told this guy who's like my brother, I told him I wanted to try out for the baseball team, and he was kidding around and saying I couldn't try out 'cause I'm female and was teasing me, but I took it seriously and said I'd stick with softball.

She says that if she had seen a girl on a baseball team, she would have changed her mind. Thus, what she sees around her as possible for her own gender influences her activity. The fact that East Side has active girls' softball and basketball teams may have helped her overcome the stereotypes in those sports.

In line with her mixed relationship to feminine norms, Nicole says, "I don't even know [what it means to be feminine]. I like, just say acting like a female. I don't even use it unless I'm talking to a boy, if they're acting real sweet, in a bad way, acting like a girl. Like, acting, wearing tight pants, doing stuff like that." Femininity, to Nicole, is something that is put on, defined by what it means if a boy dons it. Nicole says that she doesn't know whether or not she is feminine but would like to be, "sort of, sometimes. I just like to have a good time and act like I want to." Thus, Nicole is more concerned about being able to do what she wants to do than about subscribing to any particular gender norms.

Nicole's definition of masculine is "strong and buff." She does not think of herself as masculine in a "strong and buff way." But she believes that she is, and wants to be, brave, which she associates with masculinity. Nicole also likes to have "muscles in your legs and arms. I like that. It's cute to me." In defining her relationship to masculinity, Nicole voices common themes that appear among her peers: strength/independence as desirable for girls, as well as a focus on physical appearance. She wants to be brave, a traditional masculine trait but one with ties to qualities that have been emphasized by African American women. She sees having muscles as "cute" for girls, thus linking physical appearance to traditional gender identity.

In line with this focus on physicality, Nicole displays her femininity through changes in her hair and clothes. Although she was wearing her hair short at the time of her interviews, earlier in the year she experimented with longer and more elaborately feminine styles. Even her shorter cut was stylish and straightened. Frequent hairstyle changes and elaborate fake nails were common displays of femininity by the teen girls, as well as by some of the younger African American female staff at East Side. Girls' hair and bodies were topics of conversation and often generated praise or criticism. Nicole added to this by linking masculinity in the form of musculature to girls' physical attractiveness.

Nicole finds strength in womanhood and in her relationships with other women. She says that the former young women's group at the club, which disbanded when Cheryl left, influenced her: "I don't have a big sister, [but] within the group everyone had a big sister and Cheryl was like the mom. With Cheryl you could talk to her about anything and she always had an answer." Nicole says that the club has made her appreciate life as a woman.

'Cause I see men who really want to be female. It's good to be a woman. You've got much more advantages. . . . [In the young women's group, Cheryl would] tell us stories about when she was younger and like she and her boyfriend got in an argument and I'm not saying it's good to lie, but women get away with more. Men have always had the upper hand, and now it's coming around to women.

Black feminist scholars and researchers have pointed to the strength that Black women have drawn from each other and the ways in which teen girls as well as adult women construct strong identities within communities of their African American sisters.[18] Nicole, too, finds strength and comfort from these networks, especially at East Side.

Despite her attachment to the girls' groups, Nicole claims to have more male friends than female. With girls, she says, there is "too much emotion." Yet Nicole mentions a number of girls to whom she is close. She also took pictures of quite a few female friends, both from school and from the club. Nicole mentions Anita [another club member] as her best friend and says that they used "to own" the park across the street.

> "That was our park. We were little tomboys, always climbing trees and stuff." She grinned and shook her head. I mentioned that I was surprised when I saw Anita this year because I always think of them from a few years ago, as being sort of tough and playing a lot of sports and running around the club. "And when I saw her she looked so much like a young woman, all done up and what not," I said. Nicole laughed. "Yeah, we used to run around here and be tomboys and stuff. We grew up together."

As I reread my field notes, I noticed that I had fallen back on gendered stereotypes in describing the change in Anita over the years. By remarking that she now looked like a "young woman, all done up," I was subscribing to the stereotype of females as being made up, dressed up, of womanhood as dependent on a particular physical appearance. This appearance, I was clearly implying, contrasted with the girls' "tomboyish" demeanor of prior years. Anita's physically developing physique was also commented on by a staff member a few years before: "Cheryl saw Anita and Nicole across the street and yelled something to them, teasing Anita, saying something about her chest. Anita said something back that I couldn't hear, laughing and sticking her chest further out." Despite Cheryl's support of the girls' athleticism, and my own commitment to breaking down the dichotomy of gender, when faced with developing teenage girls, we both fell back on looking to girls' bodies and appearance as signs of femininity.

In addition to providing a community of supportive female peers and adults, East Side also serves as a place where Nicole can partake in cross-gender activities. Nicole reports that she wouldn't have played football if she hadn't been able to do so at the club. Nicole was observed participating in a variety of activities in the gym, with both boys and girls. In my second year at East Side, for example, I observed Nicole taking over for another girl during a floor hockey game that was otherwise all boys. Nicole also reports adult support for her athleticism, saying staff members tell her that athletics can get you anywhere and that she should look at successful female athletes as examples. Thus, East Side is a place where Nicole can resist the gendered norms surrounding athletics and participate in sports that otherwise may be unavailable to her.

The girls at East Side recognize that their identities are influenced and circumscribed by the gender system. On a local level, this often comes in the form of limited access to different activities. As Nicole indicates, the girls feel that they do not always have the same opportunities as boys in sports. Te Te presents a common theme in the girls' narratives when she says that the boys and the girls participate in different activities at the club. She states that this is not just by choice.

> The boys get more activities than the girls. For instance, basketball teams, they really don't have a basketball or hockey team for girls here. They want it mixed, but they have boys on the team, and I don't think it's right 'cause there's a lot of talent out here. I love hockey, but they don't give little girls a chance, just girls' sports like volleyball or softball. Girls play volleyball, softball, tennis. [*Why do you not feel comfortable playing on mixed teams?*] Because they want it their way. If you mess up it's . . . they're so perfect like they know every sport in the world. They're aggressive, especially in football. [*What about outside the gym?*] It's like together—have something for the girls, not the boys. They used to be when Cheryl was here, a lot of activities, like girls to women group, cheerleading team, more volleyball, more.

Te Te does not think that the girls lack athletic talent, only that they are not provided with opportunity to develop their talents. Te Te also recognizes the limitations of coed sports for many girls. The combination of aggression and pressure to play well keeps Te Te from enjoying such coed interactions.

Some researchers have suggested that expecting girls to contradict hegemonic femininity by participating in sports, without allowing for the melding of femininity with athleticism, is unrealistic for many girls.[19] Nicole and other girls describe the feminine parts of themselves as separate from the athletic parts. The ability to join the "boy and girl" parts of themselves may require more than just opportunity. It entails reenvisioning athleticism as part of femininity rather than as separate from it. Many of the girls talk about sports as masculine, saying that they aren't feminine when they play sports. Some, like Nicole, describe having a masculine part of themselves that accounts for their athleticism. Girls describe wearing skirts and playing sports as two separate sides of themselves, two different subjectivities. This is similar to research on androgyny, which conceptualizes femininity and masculinity as independent dimensions. This allows androgyny to be a separate domain consisting of either the presence or absence of both masculine and feminine traits.[20] Girls revert to certain feminine stereotypes most often in the realm of sexuality and physicality, suggesting that acceptance of "masculine" traits is limited to particular domains.

Nicole recognizes the social nature of unequal behavioral expectations for girls and boys. She says that "[boys] can do something and they'll be called a different name from girls. Like if boys go with a lot of girls they're called a pimp, but if a girl goes with a lot of guys she's called a slut or something." The conflation of gender and sexuality, as well as the unequal sexual expectations based on gender, is consistently pointed out by teen girls. Prior studies with diverse populations of girls have documented the time and energy devoted by girls to portraying oneself as the "right kind" of girl. Such a girl is neither too "prudish" nor too "slutty." Such research also notes that while engaging in this activity, the girls are aware that they are working within a system of double standards.[21] This system is maintained through their relationships with boys as well as other girls.

Conclusion

Nicole is aware of gender norms and expectations. She identifies the structure of gender in some areas of her life and discusses it openly. In this way, she may be developmentally ahead of some of her peers. Although she confronts many stereotypes through her own activity, she is not immune to societal messages. She is particularly cognizant of the discourse of skin tone and its relation to African American femininity as well as to racial and ethnic identification overall.

Nicole demonstrates the role of a site such as East Side in allowing for both confronting stereotypes and developing a productive possible self. Through her relationships and job at East Side, Nicole fosters an adult self, taking on responsibility in work roles and relationships with younger club members. Through her involvement in sports at the club, she struggles against, resists, and reconstructs certain gender structures.

6

. . . .

"I Can't Lose to No Girl, Man"
The Gendered Self

This is the place.
And I am here, the mermaid whose dark hair
Streams black, the merman in his armored body
We circle silently
About the wreck
We dive into the hold.
I am she: I am he.

—Adrienne Rich, "Diving into the Wreck" (1984)

Gender organizes our lives on multiple levels, from the individual to the institutional, in ways that are both explicit and invisible.[1] The salience of gender is so ubiquitous, it's often unnoticeable. Not only do we quickly encode and cognitively process the gender of people we see,[2] but also the landscapes of our lives are marked by gender, from public bathrooms to the shoe aisles of department stores. Gender is a powerful, organizing social category. Yet the assumption of gender as a natural binary ignores the fact that our culture's conception of what is natural is itself a cultural construct.[3]

We often ignore the fact that gender is but one location on our social maps.[4] I challenge our culture's treatment of gender as a static, dichotomous category by exploring the ways in which other social positions influence our constructions of gendered identities. Gender is constructed and maintained through two interacting processes: activity and structure. The social activity within East Side allows for both re-creation of and resistance to gender norms, but only within certain social and structural constraints. As with race and class, the construction of gendered identity rests on an image of the Other. I examine the ways in which social structures determine who our Others will be and how youth actively construct gendered selves in relation to gendered Others.

The East Side teens' experiences and constructions of gendered selves are influenced not only by the dichotomous gender system but also by the larger rubric of race and class relations. The teens' positioning within the social structure influences their relationships with gender. In some ways East Side youth are removed from the traditional gender system. Yet they re-create certain gender stereotypes in their daily activities and relationships with others. This is particularly true in the realms of sexuality and physical appearance. Youth both challenge and affirm gender norms, negotiating social structures through their activities and interactions with each other in the club.

The Social Construction of Gender

Gender can be thought of in three ways: (1) as activity, (2) as structure, and (3) as an interaction of activity and structure. I privilege this last view of gender, as it centralizes human action while acknowledging the power of social structures. Before turning to the East Side teens, I will discuss these three views of gender as a frame for considering their experiences.

Gender as activity focuses on how individuals "do" and "perform" gender in interaction with others.[5] Wearing a necklace, putting on lipstick, and crossing my legs are natural parts of my day. I don't consciously think about them as constructing my gender. Yet it is these small acts that provide others with the markers by which to read my gender. By enacting gender, I am bringing it into existence.

Our discomfort with individuals who do not enact gender in "appropriate" or readable ways attests to gender's power as an organizing social category. The use of "mixed-up" or confused gender signals as a humoristic device, such as the androgynous character Pat on *Saturday Night Live*, and the prevalence of tropes of cross-gender acting as the basis for comedy—from Shakespeare's *As You Like It* to *Mrs. Doubtfire*—highlights the work of gender. Yet this labor is actually done by all of us who choose to identify as male or female.[6] In the classic comedy *Some Like It Hot*, we focus on the effort exerted by Jack Lemmon to disguise himself as a female without considering the work done by Norma Jean Baker to become Marilyn Monroe. The great pain we take to mark our gender differences suggests to some that males and females are actually more alike than we are different.[7]

Children learn early on to participate in and reconstruct gender.[8] Young children are socialized through their interactions with the adult world, but they also construct gender in their own activities with peers.[9] During adolescence, gender's salience increases as budding breasts and sprouting hair mark our bodies with our biologic sex. The enacting of gender becomes more prevalent as teens engage in fewer activities that cross gender norms and as coed interactions privilege heterosexual dating. An example of such a transition can be seen in BJ, a tomboy at East Side who begins to wear tighter jeans and more feminine clothing after turning 13. She is "doing" femininity. This is especially noticeable in contrast to her earlier androgynous appearance and participation on boys' sports teams.

Yet gender can also be considered as a structure, a set of rules and norms that both govern and confine human behavior. As such, gender "refers to the social institutionalization of sexual difference."[10] Gender has become crystallized into a social category that structures our lives. Social policies underlie as well as reproduce different experiences by gender.[11] These experiences are further influenced by our race and class positioning; gender operates differently across social categories. This problematizes the concept of gender as a static category that influences lives and identities in a universally predictable manner.

On a local level, gender structure is obvious in gender-based rules and norms. For example, an effort to privilege girls' sports by a regional Boys and Girls Club branch challenged the structural norm of females as less athletic and attempted to rebuild its institutional structure to reflect this. The fact that this took much effort and time and only succeeded in part at select clubs highlights the strength of gender as an entrenched social structure.[12]

I consider gender as an interaction between individual behavior and the structures and discourses of society.[13] We constantly enact our gender in and through our relationships with other people. In doing so, we create and re-create beliefs and stereotypes, all within the framework of our society's gender structure. Because gender systems are constructed by and within particular societies, they are constrained by and built to support society's power structures.[14] Cross-cultural research, however, does not demonstrate any absolute personality differences between men and women; there is nothing innate about femininity or masculinity.[15] But the social organization of gender is built into the heads of children early on, ensuring that their activity will support the present gender structure.

Most research examines gender as an independent variable, studying the ways in which gender influences individual outcomes. In reality, it is seldom gender alone that determines our experiences. A deeper understanding of the interaction of the gender system with other axes of power is needed to understand gender's influence on individual lives and to create an equitable social structure. The East Side teens' narratives describe complex interactions of race and class influencing both the structure and activity of gender in their lives. Furthermore, their experiences demonstrate how gender is enacted and gendered identities are constructed within the context of local settings and relationships.

"She Has a Good Record for Herself": Gender, Role Models, and Expectations

During the first interview I asked youth to name someone whom they admire. After they described that person, I asked, "The person you just named is a male/female. Is there a (opposite gender) person that you admire?" The youth ascribe similar traits to the men and women they admire. They list independence, responsibility, and goal achievement as desirable for both men and women. Yet, as noted in chapter 2, boys and girls both prize relational traits as part of their own identities.

Alyiah, a 15-year-old female, says that she admires her female cousin because she is "respectful, honest, funny, determined, a good dresser" and "has a good record for herself."[16] When asked if there are any males that she admires, she names Charles, East Side's physical education director: "He is very respectful and honest. He has a good record for himself also." She does not distinguish between the female and male she admires. She refers to her female cousin as dressing nicely and does not make any comments about Charles's physical appearance. Yet the key traits—respectful, honest, and "having a good record"—apply to both her role models.

Rashad, a 13-year-old boy, reverses stereotypical gender roles in describing who he admires. He first names his brother, saying that he "has a nice personality. He's kind to others." Rashad then says his mother because of "the fight in her. She is very independent." Notably, it is his brother's interpersonal skills and his mother's independence that Rashad admires. This contrasts with the popular idea of relational traits as feminine. In a neighborhood in which rates of single motherhood are high, Rashad may be reflecting qualities that are needed in the community. During focus groups, boys talk about how Charles expresses disdain for men who father and abandon children. This may be one factor in increasing the importance of relational traits to males. Rashad's admiration of his mother's "fight" is also in line with African American women's traditional image as strong and independent. Both these issues, which highlight the contextual nature of gender construction, are explored below.

Two banners made by girls' groups at the club indicate the importance girls place on independence and responsibility. They also point out that the club becomes a site in which these traits are enacted and validated. One banner, made to show what women should be, includes the words "strong, independent, patience, pretty." Agentic traits are combined with empathy (patience) and physical appearance (pretty), two more traditionally feminine expectations. Another banner, made by a different girls' group, is emblazoned with the phrase "show me the money" because the girls feel that they are the most successful fund-raising group at the club. Being successful, achieving educational and career goals, and treating other people well are traits that the teens admire in both males and females. Bob, a 14-year-old male, sums it up by saying, "When I think of things or characteristics to admire, I don't try to categorize it as boys or girls. . . . I admire virtues like honesty."

One of the ways in which the gender system influences individual identity is by setting up gender-based behavioral expectations. Within those sets of expectations we mold our identities. Whereas masculinity is typically described by "agentic and instrumental traits," such as assertiveness, femininity is most often related to "communal and expressive attributes," such as empathy.[17] These traits map onto and help support our society's traditional, gendered division of labor into public (the market) and private (the family). Yet the gendered division of labor has not been the norm for working-class or African American women, who have a history of working outside of the home. In contrast to the idea of feminine dependence, African American women have been considered independent in relation to African American men.[18] This sets up a different relationship with the gender structure. This structural relationship is distinctly rooted in the relations between individual men and women.

The salience of gender in forming behavioral expectations may depend on how important gender is in that context. Gender shapes behavioral expectations over and above other social categories when gender is relevant to the interaction. Yet gender can mediate other social categories even in seemingly gender-neutral situations.[19] Because of their social positioning by class and race, the East Side youth may be less subject to the constraints of certain gender norms in setting their expectations for themselves.

The Strong Black Woman: Mothers and Others

Kelly, a 16-year-old male, expresses feelings that are fairly typical of East Side boys when talking about their mothers. What Kelly likes best about himself is that he is determined, independent, very social, smart, and a nice person. He says that he looks up to his mother for those things because "she's a really strong Black woman. She took care of three kids and still went to school and took care of her mom. . . . We don't want for nothing."

Only one girl, as compared with four boys, names her mother as someone whom she admires. All four boys list their mother second, after first naming a male. Thus, I cannot rule out that the greater presence of mothers in the boys' narratives may be related to the order of my questions.[20] Five of the nine girls name a female first, but none name their mother. The only girl to name her mother does so after first naming a male. Yet girls did name other female relatives as influential, especially in modeling independence, strength, academic achievement, and career success. It may be that East Side girls do not see their mothers as exemplifying the type of achievement that they emphasize as their own goals. Many of them live in public housing with single mothers. It is possible that the girls do not view their mothers as role models in terms of their expectations for themselves as women, even while they admire their strength in raising them.[21] In her work with racial and ethnic minority teens, Niobe Way found that mothers were frequently named as the most important person in teens' lives. Youth admired their mothers' strength and independence. Whereas this was true for both boys and girls, the boys in her study appeared to idealize their mothers more, whereas girls were more open to discussing their disagreements and to challenging their mothers.[22]

The image of the strong, independent African American woman has been written about extensively.[23] Given the sociohistorical and cultural positioning of East Side teens, it is not surprising that they do not use stereotypical gendered traits to describe people they admire. The prominence of independence as an admired trait for women may reflect resistance to the "welfare queen" image. This cultural icon, created by conservative political regimes in the 1980s to divert attention away from deteriorating social programs, paints a picture of African American women as dependent on the state and as the source of society's ills.[24] Yet this image of female dependence has its roots in the institutionalization of gender difference in the United States. Gender differences became institutionalized in industrialized nations through the movement from household economies to a market-based, nonagrarian society. Women's labor became less visible, centered in the private sphere, leading to a view of women as dependent on men's public labor.[25] The rise of the Protestant work ethic and the ideology of individualism contributed to the pathologizing and feminizing of dependence.[26] The linking of African American women to dependence, and the construction of dependence as "bad" and "feminine," is a discursive trick that draws attention away from the ways in which all humans are dependent on our relationships with other people and the state for survival.[27] It is also the opposite of the image of the Black matriarch, popularized in the 1960s by Senator Patrick Moynihan's report on the Black family.[28]

Some have questioned the effect of the "strong Black woman" on individual African American females.[29] Author bell hooks has observed that the valuing of strength and independence in Black women, especially in relation to economic independence, has not dismantled patriarchy. In fact, it has sometimes made things more difficult for Black women, as they have been expected to move into the "masculine" role of worker with no corresponding shift by men into "feminine" roles as either caretakers or domestic helpers.[30] The economic independence is not matched by interdependence within interpersonal relationships. Furthermore, Black women were historically shuttled into "mammified" jobs that were low in both wage and prestige. Their economic independence, therefore, is still predicated on a subservient position in larger society.[31]

The East Side teens are aware of the "welfare queen" as one of our cultural images of Black mothers. It is not uncommon to hear kids at East Side insisting that their families are not on welfare, thereby defending their social status. Independence and strength are qualities antithetical to social constructions of welfare recipients and, therefore, the association of such traits with women may be in direct dialogue with cultural discourses of both poverty and race.

"All the Boys Get Stopped by the Cops": On Being Black and Male

East Side boys talk more often than the girls about escaping the projects. This appears to be in part because they are frequently targets of police harassment. Their bodies are socially marked by their gender and race. A number of the boys talk about how they are treated differently by authority figures, especially the police and teachers, because they are male.

[You] get treated differently all the time cause you're a boy, outside, all the boys get stopped by the cops. —John, 16-year-old Black male

At school, I feel as if the teachers give the girls more attention than the boys. —Lorenzo, 17-year-old African American male

Rashad says that he sometimes gets harsher punishments than girls at school. He feels that males face "a lot" of prejudice. Blacks and people from his neighborhood, according to Rashad, only face "some" prejudice. Local adults recognize and validate these views. Rashad says that Charles talks with the boys about how males get harassed by the police. Club staff tell him to stay in school "to try to get an education cause it's hard for a Black man to make it in this world." Kelly, who is a few years older than

Rashad, belongs to a local church group that "teaches you how to become a man, grow up, realize cards are already stacked against you and you shouldn't do things to make it worse for yourself." Being male is traditionally thought of as carrying advantage in our society; being a Black male poses specific challenges in East Side boys' daily lives and futures. The boys are confronted with threats of bodily harm from police and gangs. Yet they also face other people's perceptions of them as potential perpetrators of violence. The construction of the Black male body as threatening forces Black males to negotiate interactions in which Whites' first responses to them are often colored by fear.[32] The boys' relationships with other people, from teachers to shopkeepers to peers, are influenced by the intersection of race and gender. From their experiences they develop expectations of how they will be treated in the future, which then shapes their future interactions.[33]

As we heard earlier, East Side seems to be a safe space for the boys. They can escape from these negotiations of stereotypes because the adults and kids are "like them." Their relationships at East Side are not colored, literally and figuratively, by their social positioning. Furthermore, club staff acknowledge the challenges the boys face, give them advice, and model modes of behavior to help them handle these issues.

Despite their distance from White, middle-class male experience in many areas, the East Side boys retain certain traditionally masculine goals and expectations. Financially supporting a family and being a husband and father are important to some boys. Kelly, for example, says that one of the things he plans to be is a homemaker. His goals are "to be financially stable, have a nice job, a house, be able to take care of my kids, be a good father, a good husband."

Overall, the youths' expectations for themselves and others reflect their social positioning. Because of different relationships with the labor market and authority structures, African American and low-income men and women have had to remove themselves from certain middle-class, White American gender norms. This leaves youth to reconstruct masculinity and femininity within a system that often blocks them from routes to traditional gender identities. Sites such as East Side become spaces in which to explore and enact gender constructions in relationships with people who share their experiences.

"Boys and Girls Are Just So Different": Defining the Masculine and Feminine

Despite the absence of gender differences in admired traits and goals, youths' narratives in other areas are peppered with what they report as intrinsic gender differences. This is especially notable in their discussions of boys' and girls' activities at East Side.

> Guys tend to be more athletic than women. . . . Other activities it's the same . . . but in the gym it's like, majority of guys who come in go to the gym. —Daniel, 16-year-old male

> Boys and girls are just so different from each other. They have their own minds, and we have our own minds. —Alyiah, 15-year-old female

> You get more feminine genes when you get older and into talking and stuff and then into sports like boys would. Most girls like playing on the computers. Boys like going in the game room, weight room, running around, chasing each other. Girls will sit on the computer and just type shit. —Antonio, 14-year-old male

Youth mostly attribute gender differences in activity preferences to intrinsic differences between boys and girls. This is not unusual. A study of an urban Canadian youth center found that although girls sometimes resisted exclusion from "masculine" realms of activity in the center, overall they accepted male domination of sports as "natural and normal."[34] Likewise, the East Side youth admire gender-neutral traits. Yet they witness gender differences in daily activity; rather than challenge the status quo, they make sense of these differences by ascribing them to nature rather than structure.

The traits that youth list as typical for boys and girls map onto these activity differences. They associate athleticism with boys, and talking, especially emotional talk and gossip, with girls. Many youth, both boys and girls, express a dislike of hanging around with large groups of girls because there is "too much emotion" and the girls "just talk about themselves." Among the girls this is related to a need to manage their reputations by not getting involved in any drama, an issue I return to later.

Asked to define masculine and feminine, youth frequently fall back on stereotypes. The traditional gender system emerges in their abstract discussions of gender, as well as in descriptions of daily activity. Yet how they talk about themselves in relation to those traits reflects a complex relationship to gender norms. Girls in particular distance themselves from stereotypical femininity, reflecting both knowledge of and resistance to traditional gender norms.

"I Can Play Any Sport a Boy Can": Gender as Acting

The teens' definitions of feminine and masculine reflect the idea of gender as an activity that people perform. The word "act" comes up repeatedly, especially in discussing what it means to be feminine.

> Acting like a female. I don't even use it unless I'm talking to a boy, if they're acting real sweet, in a bad way, acting like a girl. Like, acting, wearing tight pants, doing stuff like that . . . —Nicole, 15-year-old female

> Act like a girl . . . acting like you don't want to be bothered. —Rashad, 13-year-old male

> [Feminine is] like girly like . . . like dressy, real fashionable, and prissy, like acting ladylike. . . . If I'm at a fancy dinner then I act feminine, but when I'm around here I'm gonna be who I am. . . . Like for some sports, like softball, you can't act feminine for that. . . . [Masculine is] like to be like boyly, act like a tomboy, do boys stuff, act like a gentleman. —Alyiah, 15-year-old female

> Feminine is too girly . . . like a model. . . . Like they don't ever play basketball. . . . I have some feminine in me. Like in the summertime I wear skirts and don't wear jeans and shorts. But I do play softball. —BJ, 16-year-old female

"Acting" feminine is seen by some girls as appropriate and expected in certain situations. Yet it retains the characteristic of something that is "put on" rather than an intrinsic trait. Most of these girls do in fact play sports at East Side, an activity that they define as not feminine. Thus, the club becomes a site in which they can safely "act masculine." In fact, Alyiah explicitly says that, although she acts feminine sometimes, when at East Side she is "gonna be who I am." Thus, she highlights how femininity is, for her, as much an activity, or an act, as is masculinity. These activities occur in relationship to other people, either as social activities (e.g., playing sports) or as performances for audiences (e.g., wearing makeup).

In line with this, many of the teens' definitions of femininity and masculinity rest on images of people who cross gender norms. Nicole, for example, talks about using feminine to describe boys who are "acting real sweet, in a bad way." Alyiah defines masculine as "a tomboy." Other youth echo this.

[Masculine is] like dress casually, wear makeup only on special occasions. —Peaches, 16-year-old female

In some ways [I am feminine], like crying. Everyone cries. Everyone has a feminine side to them. Like whining and stuff. My grandma will say stop acting like a little girl. —Daniel, 16-year-old male

[Sometimes I am masculine] because I can play any sport a boy can play. —Alyiah, 15-year-old female

Femininity and masculinity are determined by activity; femininity in particular is "acting." It can, therefore, be enacted by both girls and boys.

As we see above, femininity is not associated with the positive traits that youth ascribe to their female role models. Eight of the thirteen youth (four girls) who give definitions of feminine imply that such traits are not desirable. Whereas "acting like a girl" is always bad for boys, it is sometimes undesirable for girls, too.

[*Do you wanna be feminine?*] Not all the time 'cause feminine, like when you think you're too pretty. —Alyiah, 15-year-old female

[Feminine is] like choosy, sassy, complain a lot, don't like to be touched a lot, stuff like that. [*Are you feminine?*] Uh uh. [*Do you want to be?*] Nope. —Peaches, 16-year-old female

Only four of the girls say they want to be feminine, and three of those say they only want to be feminine some of the time. Adolescent girls and women sometimes look toward masculine attributes to make themselves more powerful.[35] Such resistance to femininity supports the traditional gender system, maintaining femininity's inferiority to masculinity. This speaks to the heart of one of the major debates in feminism: sameness versus difference. If women are only granted equal rights if we emulate "male" behavior, have we achieved equity? By upholding the gender hierarchy in our own activities and relationships, are we moving women forward?

The East Side girls' rejection of traditional femininity may be related to their race and class positioning. In postcolonial discourses, femininity and power are both associated with Whiteness.[36] African American women did not historically have much to gain within White society from engaging in a femininity rooted in dependence on men and perceived physical attractiveness. Their position in the labor market and the legacy of slavery also change Black women's relationships to White, middle-class feminine norms.

Unlike femininity, the East Side youth tend to associate masculinity with positive and agentic traits. Seven of the thirteen youth refer to positive strength or activity in their definitions.

A person that believes in themselves. —Moonie, 12-year-old female

It means strong. The way a person choose to be. —Lorenzo, 17-year-old male

Strong and buff. [*Are you?*] Not in a strong and buff way, but I'm brave. [*Do you want to be masculine?*] Not strong and buff way, but brave. —Nicole, 15-year-old female

Peaches, a 16-year-old girl, admires that boys don't cry. "Like if their mother pass or something they're strong. They just go on with life as if it was yesterday." Strength, personal agency, and courage are emphasized in these definitions. Both girls and boys admire and emulate these "masculine" characteristics. These are qualities that, historically, African Americans have had to rely on to succeed and survive.

The Activity of Gender

I now move from the teens' discussions of gender to their activity. In this activity, they both reconstruct and challenge gender norms and expectations within the context of their relationships and activities at East Side.

Boys

Overall, whereas boys report admiration for similar traits in men and women, they hold traditional gendered beliefs in the abstract. All the East Side boys say they want to be masculine. Masculinity is still prized in America. Power and strength are characteristics that the government flexes. This is filtered down into individual lives. Only one boy says he wants to be feminine, and then only with regard to being nonviolent.

> I was going to say that girls tend to be less violent than the whole male "uh uh" thing. But it's not actually true. [*Are you feminine?*] I don't know. [*Do you want to be?*] Depends on what feminine means. If it means non-violent, yes. —Bob, 14-year-old White male

Given the violence that is prevalent in his neighborhood, and which he talks about in length at other points in his interviews, Bob's desire for non-violent femininity appears tied to his location in this urban public housing project. This desire may be made safe by his involvement in East Side, which privileges alternative identities to those emphasized by teen gang-bangers in his neighborhood. Bob is also the only White boy in the study. He is thus positioned differently in the gender system than his Black peers at the club.

When asked what defines a successful man, East Side boys respond in terms that echo traditional gender norms. All the boys use at least one of the following words or phrases in their definitions: works, takes care of responsibilities, takes care of family, achieves his goals. The idea that being a man includes taking care of your business and not having kids you can't care for is reinforced by East Side staff. During one of the focus groups, a teen boy talks about how Charles tells the boys that they should not be running around having kids. Rather, they should wait until they find a woman they can see themselves with in the future. The boys emphasize that Charles shares his own life experiences with them, helping them to identify with him as an adult male role model.

Boys define themselves as male in part by rejecting behavior they view as feminine. The boys discuss fatherhood and caretaking but do so in ways that reflect traditional norms of the male as financial provider. Boys still reject the more empathic feminine traits. Greg, a 12-year-old male, says that he admires when boys can keep from crying, especially when they are playing rough sports. To him this appears to be associated with becoming a man from a boy. He says that older males "don't cry a lot like little brothers do." Antonio, a 14-year-old boy, makes it clear that certain behaviors are not appropriate for males. While telling me a story about his friendship with a female cousin, he mentions that he used to play with her Barbie dolls.

> We used to play together all the time. There was a time I played with her Barbies all the time and I could braid hair. Good thing I lost that ability. [*Why?*] 'Cause I don't need to know how to braid hair. Don't know how that happened that I played with her Barbies. But I grew out of that and started playing GI Joes and cars.

Antonio's adolescent male identity relies on losing traits he associates with the female Other. Expelling the feminine is part of the construction of the masculine.[37] Antonio "grew out of" that behavior, moving on to more traditional masculine toys, such as cars and GI Joes. GI Joes are still dolls. But as dolls that represent violence, they are seen as acceptable; they socialize boys into a condoned male realm.[38]

Boys police gender norms through their activity and discourse within East Side. One afternoon, a boy became upset after losing a game of air hockey to a female researcher. He immediately demanded a rematch, declaring "I can't lose to no girl, man!" The linguistic juxtaposition of "girl" and "man" recalls the lyrical refrain "don't call me nigger, whitey." Gender, like race, is oppositional. Asserting oneself is in part disparaging the Other.

The policing of gender also occurs through group socialization. One night a group of teen boys attempted to bring one of the younger boys "into the fold" of the male peer group.

A small boy who the kids called Jay (I would guess he was about 6) came in and sat down on the couch with John . . . and the boys. The little boy had a soda and the older boys were trying to get him to share it. "Come on, man, you know, we all brothers. We share everything," John was saying. Alyiah looked over and yelled at them. "Hey, Jay, come over here," she said in a softer voice. "Would y'all leave him alone?" she said. Jay got off the couch and began to walk toward Alyiah at the table. "Give him back his pick, y'all," she said. John had taken the boy's pick and was picking his hair with it. John handed the pick to Jay, and Jay sat down with them again. "Yeah, come here, boy. You be one of us. You wanna be a rapper? Yeah, you hang with us. You one of the boys. You're a brother. We're all brothers."

This type of socialization of young boys by older males is part of how males "attain and maintain masculinity." Through this bonding, men recognize and reinforce each other's patriarchal power.[39] Author bell hooks notes that through such activity Black men internalize sexism and the myth of inherent male power as they seek recognition of their manhood.[40] This type of policing is discussed further in chapter 7, where John's narrative brings the construction of masculinity to the fore.

Girls

Despite distancing themselves from femininity, girls often uphold gender norms through their activity and relationships with each other. This is especially true in the realm of appearance. The daily enactment of gender is reflected in field notes from one of my first visits to East Side.

I sat down on the bleachers near Dynasty and . . . Jade. . . . I asked Jade how the volleyball game had gone last week, and she told me that they had lost by one point. "Isn't City Center supposed to be a tough team? So that's great that you only lost by one!" I said. "Yeah—they're all really big and they play like guys," Jade responded. I asked her what she meant, and she said, "They whack the ball like this [demonstrating a hard slap with her hand in the air], and it goes flying all the way across the room." I nodded. "Are they bigger because they're older or just because they're

bigger?" "Both." . . . Dynasty then started to talk about how Jade had gotten her hair cut off. Jade's hair was pulled back into a ponytail so I could
not see how short it really was. Dynasty told Jade to show me. Jade took
her hair out of the elastic and turned to show me the length, which was
just below her ears. "See, she got it all cut off. Why would you do that,
cut it all off? You need to grow it back," Dynasty went on. Jade shrugged
and rolled her eyes. "I think it looks nice," I said. Jade thanked me. "Nah,
why would you cut it, boys liked you, and now . . ." "I don't care if they
like me," Jade said. At this point, two or three boys the same age came
over from the football game, and Dynasty started talking to them. The
boys were climbing on the bleachers around Dynasty and Jade. I think
Dynasty was still talking about Jade's hair. One of the boys looked at Dynasty and said, "Yeah, you need to go on a diet!"

Dynasty is extremely concerned with Jade's hair as a feminine magnet
for boys. Dynasty herself is overweight, and other kids occasionally comment on her body. Jade, meanwhile, expresses no interest in boys' attrac-
tion to her. Yet gender is important to her in its implications for East Side's
girls' sports teams. Dynasty, too, feels that boys and girls are different. She
later tells me: "Girls at this club aren't athletic. They're into computers and
stuff. The boys are athletic and into sports." Appearance and activity work
together in these teens' construction of gender, especially femininity. In
this case, the club becomes a site in which the girls see gender norms as
innate and reinforced. Even though girls at other times report a lack of
sports opportunity for girls at the club, their daily conversations tend to
put the onus on themselves. This erases the role of structure in constrain-
ing and defining activity preferences. Attitudes of club staff and leaders
sometimes support the girls' beliefs.

Yet adult staff at the club could be helpful in creating a space that allows youth to resist the stereotypical gender structure. In the field notes
below, Rick leads a successful coed football game, despite Te Te's earlier
complaints that coed games don't work because the boys always want it
"their way."

There are 25 or so kids running around the gym, some on the bleachers
and most running around the court. Rick is playing football with a group

of about 12, including 3 girls. . . . The girls appear well integrated into the game, running and catching and throwing the ball. A couple of times I see Rick purposely throw the ball to a girl, and the girls score touchdowns as well as the boys. There is a lot of running, laughter, and talking.

Thus, with proper leadership, girls and boys could participate in sports together. Coed sports participation did become increasingly rare with age, however, a phenomenon that has been found in other studies of girls' athletic participation.[41]

In answer to the call for an all-girls' athletic venue, Cheryl developed and coordinated an organization-wide girls' sports league. This was extremely popular with the girls, who enjoyed the opportunity to have time in the gym and compete against teams from other clubs. The boys became involved by coming to games, practicing with the girls on occasion, and playing informal games against them. After Cheryl left, even though Charles gave the girls gym time, the teams dissipated, and the boys began to use the gym more than the girls. Nicole feels mixed about the reasons for this, indicating both the girls' own attitudes and structure that allows them to remain complacent.

[Charles is] cool and he'll let us use the gym, but we don't really have the spirit for it anymore. We just hang around and talk more. When Cheryl was here we had cheerleading practice, pom pom practice, softball, volleyball practice, we always had a practice. . . . Now there's cheerleading for young girls . . . but now it's all guys in the gym. . . . Having someone there to say it's our turn, who cares how we feel [makes a difference].

Nicole acknowledges the importance of a female staff person. Without Cheryl there to push them and help them negotiate the gendered space of the gym, the girls don't do it. Many girls appreciate Charles and express close relationships with him. But his presence is not the same as a female, who can serve as both a role model and an advocate for girls' athletic identities. Cheryl was a proactive advocate for the girls. When she left East Side, there was no one there to fill that void. This silence was one of the club's biggest negatives, and one that never seemed to be fully overcome despite various attempts to address issues of gender equity.

Acting feminine is seen by some girls as appropriate in certain situations. Even at East Side, where girls feel free to "act masculine," it is assumed that girls will also display interest in "feminine" activities. In commenting on why BJ was coming to the club less frequently, Shelby, a former club member and current staff, says: "BJ's problem is that she never liked girly things. She would never get involved in any of the girls' stuff. She would never sit down and get her nails done or something." Improper display of femininity could also be used to put down girls. One afternoon, while discussing their dislike of Jeannie, another club member, Christine and Peaches shifted from discussing her actions to her physical appearance.

> They began to make comments about Jeannie's physical appearance, noting her short height and short hair. Christine said something about Jeannie commenting on Peaches' short hair. "But, man, her hair is much shorter!" They agreed that Jeannie had shorter (and worse) hair than either of them.

Thus, maintaining at least some feminine physical attributes is necessary. This is reflected in the amount of attention girls pay to hair and nails. Many change their hairstyles frequently. Young girls often wanted to play with my hair, literally braiding my own White femininity into their activity. Elaborate fake nails are popular. Such physical "playing" has been observed in other studies of African American girlhood. Wendy Luttrell suggests it gives girls an opportunity to try-on a particular type of femininity and glamour associated with respected "ladies."[42] In this way, the concern with physical appearance is again meshed with the girls' class status. Long nails are a sign that one does not do manual labor, suggesting a middle-to-upper-class femininity. I, too, often refer to femininity as something I and others put on and take off with our clothes. Cultural narratives tell us that skirts are feminine, suits are masculine. This is the language we have to discuss gendered characteristics. I do not mean to suggest that the use of such tropes is negative. My interest is in the ways in which teens use and transform this language in their daily activities and how such discourse influences our goals and identities.

The youth sometimes use East Side as a space in which to play with traditional feminine norms through their own activity. An example of such activity occurred one evening while BJ, John, and Jeannie, three Black teens, were chatting in the main hallway of the club. BJ and Jeannie are both dark skinned. John is light skinned. BJ is known as a tomboy who often plays on the boys' sports teams instead of the girls'.

> A Hispanic or biracial girl with long wavy black hair walked by them. BJ stood up and started walking in a hip-wiggling way behind her, singing, "I want to be a super model!" John and Jeannie laughed. BJ continued to sing and walk in an exaggerated way like a model. The girl stopped at the front desk and turned around, looking at them. She didn't say anything and eventually turned back around. [*This was an interesting interaction. It felt like BJ was responding to the girl's looks, which was thin, well dressed, made up, and with long hair. . . .*] I went back upstairs later and when I came back down, BJ took my hand and said, "Come on, walk with me, walk with me!" I took her hand and walked with her down the hallway. "I wanna be a super model!" she started singing. I played along with her and swung my hips and flipped my hair. John and Jeannie laughed, and BJ said, "Look at her! And she's wearing the Titanic necklace!" I shook my head and laughed. I walked to the front desk and, as I walked away, BJ said to Jeannie and John, "actually, she's the girl from *Save the Last Dance*." [*Save the Last Dance is a movie in which a White girl goes to a predominantly Black high school. She is a ballet dancer and winds up dating a Black boy from the high school and learning to dance hip-hop. I couldn't help wondering how much of that analogy was based on my being White in the predominantly Black club, since I do not look like [the actress in the movie]. It also interested me that the two girls I witnessed BJ making "models on the runway" were either White or light skinned.*]

BJ's mimicking of femininity appears tied into the race-gender system, which Nicole described earlier. The "cult of true womanhood" associates fair skin with femininity. BJ is dark skinned. She is also very athletic, a trait not commonly considered feminine. In interviews, BJ describes her athleticism as split from her feminine side. I never saw her personally mimic femininity in the exaggerated manner she had us mimic it here. She did, however, begin to display a more feminine physical appearance as she reached mid-adolescence.

Femininity, Sexuality and the Female Body

Girls recognize expectations for the female body and express anxiety over their own developing physiques. This revolves around fears of not being attractive, as well as being viewed as too sexual. A number of girls talk about struggles with weight. Te Te, a 14-year-old girl, mentions this numerous times during her interviews.

> I got bigger size wise. But I'm gonna lose it, watch. I'm gonna get skinny. My mom was like me but when she got to 16 she lost everything. . . . [In the future I am going to be skinny] 'cause I'm tired of being plump.

Overweight girls' bodies are the target of other youths' criticism at the club. Adults at East Side do not appear to intervene in these situations on any regular basis. As with girls' participation in the gym, it is not staff's actions that lead to a negative environment in this area. It is the lack of consistent proactive steps to curb harassment. Such youth behavior is not necessarily actively ignored, but it flies under the radar of many of the adults. Earlier we saw two boys telling Dynasty to go on a diet. This was not an isolated incident. Dynasty was, in fact, often the object of such harassment, and her younger brother reported that Dynasty quit the girls' sports team because she was teased about her weight by other girls. Despite this, Dynasty became friends with these girls over the years. This did not exempt her from teasing, however.

> While [Dynasty] was working, Jeannie and Nicole were chatting and laughing behind us. Jeannie began to say, "What Dynasty eats for lunch, two Big Macs, fries . . . Dynasty is big. It's a fat lunch," and laughing. I turned and looked at Jeannie. Dynasty didn't respond and continued to work on the web page. . . . Jeannie looked at me and then said, "We're just kidding, you know that Dynasty, right? We're not hurting your feelings, right?" Dynasty shook her head, still looking at the computer screen. "Nah," she said, shrugging. Jeannie continued a little but then moved her conversation on to other topics, continuing to laugh and giggle with Nicole.

Jeannie looked at me before asking Dynasty if they hurt her feelings. This suggests that my presence influenced the interaction. I was torn about

whether or not to intervene. Dynasty claimed not to be hurt. It is hard
to imagine an adolescent girl not being affected by such comments, especially by girls with whom she is friends. My own silence makes me com-
plicit in the harassment. It is also in line with the actions, or lack thereof,
of other adults.

Weight is not the only area of girls' bodies that is up for grabs, literally
and metaphorically. The following is an excerpt from one of the research
assistant's field notes from an afternoon in East Side's gym.

> The two girls . . . have slipped back into the room and are now mingling
> freely with the boys. The older one, who has a very developed figure,
> seems to take a lot of teasing, especially physical teasing like nonsexual
> grabbing and playful punching. She takes it in stride and returns much
> of it.

Through their relationships with each other, the youth are reacting and
giving meaning to gendered bodies. No one appears to contradict these
actions, thus reinforcing that mature girls' bodies are public property.

The silence surrounding the treatment of girls' bodies creates a climate
in which some girls are cautious of how they present their gendered selves.
Carla, a 14-year-old girl, talks about how she purposely makes people at
East Side think that she is younger than she is so that she will not get a
bad reputation. She is aware of her physical body and the way in which it
is perceived by others. One of the words that she uses to describe herself
is "thick." In talking about what that means to her, she says the following:
"Thick, well, everybody keeps tellin' me, even little girls and little boys and
big boys, everybody. Like I said I'm gifted. My momma's big, too. When I
look in the mirror, I see a sexy young woman."

Carla later discusses how she manages people's perceptions of her based
on her body. She demonstrates what Wendy Luttrell has termed "body-
smarts," an awareness of how her body is perceived by others and a realization that this perception is at odds with her own sense of self:[43] "Just
because, for instance, me, my shape, they think I'm fast. . . . [I don't think
of myself as beautiful at the club] 'cause some little girls they fast and do
anything, and I don't do that." The club serves as a protective space, keeping her from having to negotiate the public perceptions of her body that
she faces on the street. Yet it is also a space in which she does not feel

empowered to actively confront such issues. Instead, she uses East Side as a refuge in which to negotiate her gendered body through secrecy. Although East Side is often a safe space for self-construction that confronts gender stereotypes, in this case the club supports rather than challenges the status quo.

The girls both resist and reconstruct traditional femininity in ways linked to their social positioning. Although distancing themselves from certain stereotypes, they police the boundaries of femininity through their activity, especially surrounding physical appearance. The gendered nature of physicality and sexuality is reinforced by the media. Shows like *Elimidate,* which makes heterosexual dating an extreme sport, are frequently on the television in East Side's teen lounge. Such hyper displays of masculine and feminine heterosexual norms no doubt influence teens' views of appearance and sexuality. I am drawn into their construction of "appropriate," heterosexual, gender display. One evening a group of girls express concern that I am planning to wear jeans for a night out on the town. They urge me to go home and change into a skirt. The girls' linking of physicality with femininity is demonstrated by their relationships with each other as well as to the Other female teen.

Ho's and Hootchie Mamas: Other Girls

Women have served as objects of the male gaze and desire, rendering us as Others to the male self.[44] Yet this also makes us objects to ourselves and other women.[45] It is not uncommon for girls to define themselves by distinguishing themselves from other girls.[46] The East Side girls' Other is distinctly sexualized.

> [*Are there any teens you don't want to be like?*] I see the girls around here they having babies and whatever. —Carla, 14-year-old female

> [I don't want to be like] a runner. A ho'. —Kay, 15-year-old female

Their support of the cultural dichotomy of the good versus bad girl is not surprising. All girls' constructions of self are limited by dominant notions of femininity. As they reach adolescence, they are taught to take on the male point of view, part of which is men's image of the "good girl." Adolescent girls learn how to resist and react to boys' sexuality, rather than how to explore their own emerging feelings.[47] The image of the sexualized female Other is in line with the stereotype of the "urban girl." The East Side girls are familiar with this image.[48] They talk about learning to "respect themselves" as part of becoming women, often through participation in various girls' groups at the club. While this self-respect in part involves resisting male violence, it also includes managing one's reputation and protecting one's virtue. This is achieved by not "running around with" multiple guys. Thus, womanhood is tied to relations with men and sexual tension between men and women. This tension is epitomized by the "loose woman" who serves as Other to the "good woman."

Historically, through social discourse and stereotypes, Black women were positioned outside of "appropriate" femininity, as sexually permissive.[49] The East Side girls reconstruct the image of the "loose woman." They insert themselves into the "cult of true womanhood" by insisting on a sexualized female Other against whom they can construct themselves. In doing so, they sometimes jeopardize their relationships with other Black females, relationships that could serve as spaces for self-valuation and empowerment.[50]

Rumors and reputations are one way in which the female Other is constructed and maintained at East Side. The following incident occurred in the spring of my first year there.

> I asked Elizabeth [a young teen female member] how she felt as a girl at the club and how she felt girls were treated at the club. "Oh it's bad. There's a problem," she said. "They're all saying things to you and trying to touch on you and stuff." I asked her if she meant the boys, and she said yes. . . . She then said that the girls talk about the other girls, too, and some girls let the boys touch them. She said that she tells them to stop because she's not going to let those boys touch her. She said that some girls talk about her and call her a "B.H."[51] and say that she "sucks guys things. . . . But I don't cause I'm a virgin, and I'm not going to be fooling around with no project boys. I talked to my cousin about it, and she said that they're just jealous because I'm a virgin and they're not and look at a bunch of them already got babies."

Elizabeth reacts to other girls' attempts to place her in the "bad girl" box by constructing those girls as Others' to her self. Race and class complicates this Othering when she says she won't "be fooling around with no project boys." Notably, the club is *not* a safe space for Elizabeth. It is a combination of boys' behaviors, her relationships with other girls, and a lack of staff intervention that create a "bad" environment for her as a girl.

Like Carla, Elizabeth's body is physically developed for her age. The sexual maturation of girls' bodies is linked to rumors about their sexual activity. These rumors are perpetuated by girls in the club. The irony of this in a neighborhood with high teenage birth rates is great. Yet this activity is one way girls construct themselves. They mark the boundaries of "appropriate femininity" and define themselves in relation to girls who cross those lines.

Nearly all the girls describe strategies they use to manage their reputations. Many of the girls talk about preferring not to hang out with groups of girls because they "talk too much" or "spread your business around." Girls choose their friends and acquaintances carefully, with an eye toward protecting their reputations.

I pick the girls I want to hang with 'cause I don't really like hanging with girls 'cause all they do is sit around and talk about people. But the girls I hang with they do what I like to do. We can talk about anything without no problems. —Alyiah, 15-year-old female

Boys don't talk like girls do. If you tell your friend a secret she'll run off and tell people. Most of the boys won't do that. . . . I prefer to spend time by myself. That way my name won't be in a lot of drama. So I watch and know when to hang out with someone and when not to. —Peaches, 16-year-old female

At the same time, the girls are aware of the danger hanging out with boys poses to their reputations. Alyiah reflects this concern when she says, "I prefer to spend time with girls 'cause I don't care what nobody say, but if you spend a lot of time with boys they think you're doing something and they call you names. [*Who?*] People around the neighborhood." Kay mixes her concerns about girls and boys.

I don't really like [girls]. They talk too much. . . . [She says that she admires a lot of characteristics in boys.] Except for when they talk about certain people like they ho's or something or when they fight girls. They don't talk as much as females. They can take care of themselves. . . . I can't take care of myself. I'm not old enough. My boyfriend takes care of me.

Although Kay doesn't like it when boys talk about girls as "ho's," she admires boys' abilities to take care of themselves. Her goal is to not depend on anyone. She reports that now, however, her boyfriend takes care of her. She relies on his family for support, living with them on and off. Too young to move out on her own, Kay depends on her boyfriend to help her escape her own troubled family life. This reliance on her boyfriend puts her in a precarious place in the gender system. Kay's statement also demonstrates dual concerns with sexuality and independence. There is a desire for agentic traits associated with masculinity. Yet there is a simultaneous adherence to feminine norms of sexuality, much of which are based in notions of men's psychology and sexual desires.[52]

Negotiating one's gender and sexuality is part of identity construction for all women.[53] The East Side girls' activity around reputation management provides a glimpse into the ways in which they, too, are engaged in these negotiations within their local contexts and relationships. The girls have goals somewhat free of gender norms. Yet they balance those goals with a concern for feminine sexuality in order to protect themselves in the larger world. They use images of local teens and societal gender norms to inform their constructions of self and Other. Their narratives of the Other reflect their unique relationship to the gender system, determined by their local positioning within larger society. The boys, too, engage in Othering of boys from their neighborhood. Their activity is discussed in the next chapter, where John's narrative highlights the construction of masculinity.

Conclusion

Adolescents are simultaneously discovering expanded social worlds and biologically developing bodies. They are more aware of their own sexed and gendered bodies, as well as the ways in which their bodies are seen by others. Developmentally, puberty leads to a new awareness of the biology of sex. Socially, teens are more apt to be recognized and treated as male or female in relation to their sexuality. The combination of social and personal recognition of gender influences where and when gender is salient and in what ways teens apply gender to their own self-construction.

East Side sometimes helps youth confront and resist gendered stereotypes through the provision of cross-gender activities and strong role models. At other times East Side serves as a site wherein stereotypes are enacted and re-created. Thus, East Side becomes a microcosm of the larger social world and, at times, a negative climate for girls. The individual youth at East Side construct and maintain gendered identities through their activities. These activities are constricted by and enacted within both social structures and interpersonal relationships. The youths' relationships to the gender system are influenced by their race and class. In some ways this reflects findings from prior studies. Youth mimic the gendered divisions of the adult social world in their own lives.[54] But their relationship to the gender system is more complex than much prior research would predict. Males' bodies are marked in a way we typically associate with females. Females express a desire for agentic traits that are historically defined as masculine. Yet there is a simultaneous upholding of gender norms of sexuality and appearance. The East Side teens' negotiation of gender includes constructing masculine and feminine Others in relation to their neighborhood, other people, and society. Thus, gender is not a static, stand-alone category. Gender interacts with race and class, influencing personal experience and identity through complex processes enacted within our local contexts, activities, and relationships.

7

■   ■   ■   ■   ■   ■   ■   ■   ■

"Manly, Take Charge, the Head Man, the King"

John's Story

I walk down the street and people just moved out of my way. White
people just . . . lock their doors. People walk by you on the street . . .
All the kids who live in low-income developments are gangbangers,
that's what they say. . . . White people look at us, think we're ignorant.
I just want to show them we're not ignorant.   —John

John, is a light-skinned, 17-year-old Black male who has been
coming to East Side for 12 years. He is in the 11th grade and resides with
his mother, younger sister, and cousin in the housing project near the
club. John has two older siblings who no longer live with them. His aunt,
who lives nearby, works at the club periodically. His sister and cousin are
also club members. John's attendance at East Side fell off in my final year
there; by springtime he was coming only sporadically. This is not surprising. John had a difficult relationship with many of the staff.

John is "Black and Italian," with a fair complexion, freckles that dot the
bridge of his nose, and deep, almost black eyes. He is tall and of average
build, with a batch of curls shorn close to his head. John usually wears big

t-shirts, baggy jeans, a baseball hat or do-rag, and a bulky winter jacket, unzipped and sliding off the back of his shoulders. He rarely smiles, tending to look rather surly. Despite this, he at times breaks into a cheery grin that brightens his eyes. As my relationship with him evolved, I was pleasantly surprised by the congenial young man who revealed himself to me from behind his stony front.

John's story brings to the fore three issues that have been touched on in the preceding chapters. First, John's narrative highlights the role race, and the conflation of gender, race, and class, play in structuring teens' daily experiences. He describes racism's effect on his life more explicitly than other youth. He also discusses the ways in which other people's perceptions of him influence his own identity construction. John is extremely cognizant of the construction of himself and his Black peers as Other by Whites. He resents this image, saying that, "White people look at us, think we're ignorant. I just want to show them we're not ignorant."

Second, John demonstrates the ways in which teens engage in their own Othering. For him, this occurs most profoundly in the realm of masculinity. John defines himself as male in relation to females and homosexual men. He uses masculine heterosexuality as a means for asserting his own male identity. John's narrative of self is sprinkled with references to "getting sex" from girls and to dislike of "faggots." At East Side he is often seen policing gender norms and boundaries.

Third, I use John's story to demonstrate how we construct our identities within our interactions and relationships with other people.[1] John often confronts my positionality more explicitly than do other youth. John's case study is, therefore, a natural place for me to analyze narrative on two levels: (1) as presentation of self to me as an individual researcher, and (2) as representation of an identity in the larger world. In doing so, I remind us that identity is often a situational endeavor and researchers must remain reflexive about our role in the research process.

The Relationship between John and Me

Michelle Fine encourages researchers to "work the hyphen," to interrogate the space between researcher-participant.[2] It is within that space that knowledge is constructed. In our interactions with others, we create our selves. My relationship with John brings to light this space more explicitly than do my relationships with other youth. This is likely because John openly emphasizes the many dimensions that separate us. He plays these up, at times making me uncomfortable. As a result, I am cognizant of the activity in which we each engage in that space between us. Because of that heightened sensitivity, I use his narrative to explore the researcher-participant interaction as a site of meaning-making.

John enjoyed giving me a hard time. In my first few years at the club, he and his friends often poked fun at me. It was a test of my own comfort as a researcher to ask John to be in the study. I assumed that he would not want to participate, and was surprised that he agreed to do so. He was one of my first interviews, and I was nervous about it. My field notes reveal my unease.

> I had been a little nervous about interviewing John. . . . He was never particularly friendly to me and seemed to be more cold. . . . However, John seemed to be honest with me, especially when it came to race issues. He was the first youth so far to really openly discuss race as an issue and said that it is a daily issue in his life because White people always look at Black people. He also talked about how being a Black male has impacted him and how he is treated differently by Whites. At first he seemed almost defiant in his talking about these issues with me. But as the interview progressed and I discussed his feelings with him, he seemed to become less defiant and more simply matter of fact. He even broke into a smile once or twice, which I had never seen him do. John seems to have a lot of resentment of White people who make judgments about him and staff who think things about him that aren't true and/or try to act as if they know what the kids today go through. I wonder if my listening to him and not asserting that I understand his situation but letting him tell me about it . . . softened his attitude toward me. After the interview, when I saw him around the club later in the evening, his attitude toward me was noticeably different from his previous behavior toward me. He was friendly, joked with me a couple of times, and even patted me on the shoulder once to say hello.

My interactions with John were no doubt influenced by his desire to present a particular gendered and raced self to me. Our social positionings affected the interview situation and our interactions. John's concern with masculinity, and his hostility toward Whites, demand that we read his discourse about these subjects in the context of his interactions with me. My knowledge of John's feelings increased my anxiety during the interviews, which may have led me to either downplay or emphasize my own race and gender. Because of that anxiety, I may have questioned John less, allowing him to get away with playing with me at times.

John often used provocative language in our interviews. This was likely motivated in part by wanting to see my reaction. I was not immune to the power of words such as "faggot" and "pussy." I never objected to his use of them, perhaps fearing such objection would shut him down rather than open up dialogue. But John could imagine his words' effect on me. This makes for an interesting reading of self-construction. In the interview situation John may have felt a power differential between us. I am White. To many kids at East Side, that means I am also rich. These are groups toward which John is hostile. Using derogatory gendered language may have been one way in which John could claim power in our interactions. Because I am always present in my observations of John, my analysis of his gendered self-presentation is limited to cross-gender situations.

I dealt with such issues throughout the study and have written about them elsewhere.[3] In discussing them here I am not suggesting that John was the only participant with whom issues of positionality emerge. Yet because of our personalities and positionalities they are most evident here. As I move forward in my analysis, I consider John's desire to present a particular type of self to me. I also assume that such a desire holds it own information about the construction of gender, race, and class as components of identity. Because I work from symbolic interactionist and interpretive frameworks, I consider John's presentation of self in his daily interactions, including those with me, to be the stuff of which identities are made.

John's Sense of Self

John describes himself as, "tall, Black, I don't know. I'm John Robinson. [My mother's] son." When asked for the five words that best describe him, he provides only four: "smart, impatient, real, fun." John says that being real is his most important trait: "I be myself everywhere. I don't change my ways for nobody." John reports that his family would describe him as "caring but can be mean, helpful, and the same shit as everybody else." He doesn't know what the club staff would say about him except that they would say "some stuff that's not true. Well some of it's not . . . [they would] say stuff to make you think bad of me."

John's positioning of himself against others' perceptions of him is a constant theme in his narrative. He constructs himself in opposition to people's negative judgments. John appears obsessed with who he does not want to be. For example, John considers his freshman report card a significant event in his life. " 'Cause they thought I was bad, and I had good grades. I proved them wrong, and I was happy about that." John builds a story of self in which he struggles to resist the negative possible selves he sees Others putting forward for him.[4] Yet this stance does not always lead to positive outcomes. John has a tenuous connection to school, no obvious links to the labor market, and little emotional connection to East Side.

Many East Side youth discuss being misjudged by the outside world. John is the only youth in my study to feel that he is misjudged and disrespected at the club. He feels that staff do not appreciate the teens' experiences at all.

> [Some] staff grew up around here and they say they went through the same things, but they didn't. The police and all that. They didn't have to deal with that. . . . Rick didn't deal with the police cause he's White. Gettin' harassed by the police—all the kids here do. . . . Rick try to make [it about] gangs, hoodies, stop wearin' hoodies, that's what get you shot. No it don't. If you're Black, you get shot. Period.

John comes to the club now only, " 'cause where else you gonna be." This draws attention to the lack of resources available to youth in East Side's neighborhood.

John's insistence that staff members misjudge him is echoed by his mother. She notes that John used to do bad things, but some people have trouble accepting that he has changed. John, too, admits that he was bad when he was younger. Yet he also talks about how he used to give people money and "do so much stuff to make other people happy." He no longer will put other people first: "I don't give nobody nothing cause nobody give me nothing." But John also says that he is no longer bad: "I don't fight and all that crap anymore. 'Cause it didn't . . . get me nowhere." Although John has a tenuous relationship with the club, he acknowledges its part in reforming his behavior: "I got kicked out for fightin' all the time. And people looked for me to be bad. I like to prove people wrong." John does not see his good behavior as being rewarded. He continues to act in opposition to people's expectations, nonetheless, narrating a story of self triumphing against negativity.[5] Other youth experience East Side as a positive space that nurtures development through relationships with caring adults. In contrast, John's development appears motivated by the disrespect and lack of support he perceives at East Side. The club is a site in which he develops an identity in response to others' perceptions of him.

Despite his insistence that he has transformed from a "bad" kid, John still falls prey to negative behaviors. He constructs his own boundaries of right and wrong. John reports resisting media images of the urban Black teen. He thinks other kids are influenced by them, however: "They see them lookin' wearin' nice clothes and driving nice cars, and they want that. It's either rappin' or sellin' drugs, those ways, or playin' basketball." In his own self-construction, John re-creates many of the images he reports to resist. He seeks out the material trappings that he criticizes. Although he stays clear of drugs and gangs and considers athletic goals to be "kids' stuff," he enjoys shooting dice for money. John photographs guys shooting dice as something he wants to be in the future. He differentiates between dice hustlers and drug hustlers. He emulates the former but does not admire the latter. John takes a photograph featuring his bed with a pile of money on it to represent a place that is important to him. He explains this is " 'cause that's where the money comes in at. That's my life savings." The picture also represents "what I'm about, money." He constructs his own definitions of good and bad with which he draws boundaries between himself and others. He also uses these definitions to resist, at least discursively, the images that he sees others constructing of him.

John's overriding concern with who he is *not* may be preventing him from achieving a strong sense of who he *is*. From an Eriksonian perspective, adolescents sometimes overidentify with groups to fight off feelings of uncertainty about their own identities. This need for overidentification creates a polar need: that of shunning the out-group. Thus, John's intolerance of everything he claims that he is not may serve as a protective mechanism, a defense against uncertainty about his identity.[6] Although a balance of positive and negative selves supports achievement of one's goals,[7] John's obsession with the negative self may come at the expense of a more balanced identity.

"People Walk by You on the Street": On Being Black and Male

One of the first things John says to me in our interview is that White people perceive him negatively.

> Yeah [I sometimes act in a way that's not really me]. Job interview, round different races and stuff. Way I talk and stuff, way I dress, I pull my clothes up, turn my hat straight. . . . 'Cause White people look at us, think we're ignorant. I just want to show them we're not ignorant. [How does that make you feel?] Don't make me feel nothing.

I have to assume that if what John says is true, he is not acting "like himself" around me. Given that this is one of the first things John says to me, it is also a way of asserting himself and putting me on notice. I can interview him, but I can't be sure that I'm getting the "real him." But his self-presentation to me is part of his identity construction and positioning of himself both in and against White society. His narrative tells us something about the activity of identity construction within a social structure that is hostile to aspects of one's self.

John reports that he is treated differently all the time because he is Black.

> I walk down the street and people just moved out of my way. White people just . . . I had a little cousin say he wish he was White cause they get treated better. [So it's a daily experience for you?] Yea—they lock their doors. People walk by you on the street.

John thinks that Blacks, men, and people from his neighborhood all face a lot of prejudice. He says that he is always treated differently because of his gender, race, and class: "Outside all the boys get stopped by the cops." In describing this treatment, John says:

When I was in school I had a fight. I went to jail 'cause I live in [the projects near East Side]. "You live in [the projects] you're a King." That's
what the cops said. All the kids who live in low-income developments are
gangbangers, that's what they said.

John's report of his treatment at the hands of the police indicates an awareness of how he is constructed by others as an urban, Black male. There are
at least two ways to read this story. The first is that it is a truthful representation of an event. This is the way in which he experienced the incident.
If so, this story represents an event that reinforces John's ideas about the
outside world, particularly Whites and people in authority, stereotyping
him and his peers. A second possibility is that John's story is constructed
for a particular audience. John knows that I am likely to be distressed by a
story about police prejudice. It is possible that John chooses to construct
himself and his experiences in a way that he suspects I will find sympa-
thetic. In this reading, John purposely constructs himself as the urban,
Black, male Other to perpetuate a view of himself as struggling against
discrimination.

Regardless of his motivation, John constructs a narrative that emphasizes the prejudice he faces as an urban, Black male. Yet John thinks beyond the personal. He links the policeman's attitude with its effects on
his peers: "That's why some kids gangbang 'cause if I don't do it, I'll still
go to jail. So they get involved. [*And you are sort of the opposite?*] Yea
—I like to prove 'em wrong." John expresses disdain for gangbanging. Yet
he describes how his daily experiences could lead teens down another
path. He feels that gangs and violence have not affected who he is but
acknowledges that they influence other kids in the neighborhood who
"feed into it."

In contrast to his own self-description, club staff view John as the
"product of the streets" from which he distances himself. One staff member describes John as "very, very unfortunate." But he blames the environment as well as John for John's attitude.

He has no guidance, has no respect, receives no respect. Very poor in
character. Needy. And just very poor, poor soul. He's really unfortunate.
He's a product of this environment, of this society. He is what happens
when there is nothing positive in your environment. . . . He just doesn't

care anymore. . . . He doesn't understand that there are expectations and standards everywhere you go. There are authoritative standards everyone has to answer to. . . . He was never held to a standard of expectation in any environment . . . so how could he come to a structured environment [like East Side] . . . and be successful?

Over my years at the club, I watched John battle with club staff. I saw him grow from a teasing, if sometimes hostile, child to a surly and disengaged teen. Yet I also watched him interact positively with people at East Side. He may not have gotten along with staff, but he did not fight with other kids. Nor was he disrespectful to other adults. For example, earlier I related an incident when John bumped into an older woman who was entering the club. He immediately turned to her and apologized. Despite staff's construction of him as a disrespectful teen, this was not his universal identity. Rather, it appears locked into his relationship with adult authority within the club.

Rick, the club director, acknowledges that teens have to "front" on the streets. He accepts that many youth will display different behavior on the corner than in the club.[8] John seems unable to turn off this outer self when interacting with club staff. Given John's hostility toward Whites, it is possible that Rick's being White and Sean's being Hispanic intensifies his difficulties with East Side. Yet John also does not get along with Charles, an African American staff member, so the conflict seems to be as much about authority as it is about race.

John's raced and gendered body serves as a social marker that is ascribed with particular meaning, especially for authority figures. African American males are disproportionately represented in jails as well as in schools' disciplinary records.[9] Acts of resistance by Black males are read by authority figures within a context that emphasizes Black male criminality.[10] The high incarceration rate of Black males is one of the oppressive contexts within which John is constructing his identity.[11] Thus, John cannot escape this first impression of himself. This impression is determined by the meanings we have ascribed to the confluence of Blackness and maleness. John must acknowledge these first impressions and attempt to act in the face of them.[12] For many East Side members, the club serves as a place where they can escape these first impressions and cultivate positive identities. For John, however, East Side seems to perpetuate such experiences.

John's interviews are an example of how he manages such interactions. At the start he expresses hostility to Whites. Although his general anger at being mistreated does not abate, his hostility toward me appears to dissipate over the course of the first interview. I suspect that John expects to be objectified in the interview as he is on the streets. I believe that through listening to him and respecting him as a subject of his life, rather than as an object of my study, John and I move beyond first impression management. Yet given his position as an urban Black male in a hostile society, any "fronting" he is doing may be part of his "real self," a self that he has to present to the world.

"She's Not Black, I'm Black": Constructing a Black Self

John does not like "the way society treats Black people." He does not think there is anything he can do to change that. John operates outside of traditional pathways to financial success. This likely reflects his feelings of powerlessness in the face of discrimination. We may question how well he resists the structures of discrimination against which he rails. But John does not express any sense of internalization of others' negative views of him. In fact, he repeatedly mentions fighting those images. It has been suggested that racial minorities do not internalize negative stereotypes but develop coping strategies, in part determined by their own self-schemas. Coping can take the form of a "fight or flight" reaction to stigma, leading to either increased motivation or withdrawal from a particular domain.[13] The result of this process is similar to an "oppositional identity," a sense of self that rejects aspects associated with the majority culture.[14] Both suggest that an individual uses her agency to reject particular cultural norms as a reaction to social stigma.

Such theories are applicable but limited. If we do not consider social structure as influencing the development of identities, we place too much of the burden on youth.[15] By setting up a dichotomous identity structure located in individual identification with cultural groups, we remove the possibility of collaboration between members of "opposed" cultural groups. Yet these groups may be situated in similar ways along other axes of social power. For example, rather than seeing global capitalist structures as the culture against which to define oneself, Black youth are set up to define themselves against Whites.[16] Although the image of "the Man" as the

White capitalist machine does capture part of the larger social structure, it subsumes all Whites. This image does not separate out those Whites who may share similar social positions with Blacks in terms of access to market resources. Whites, in turn, are trained to fear losing their jobs not because of activity at the top end of the global capitalist system but because of the influx of racial and ethnic minorities into the local labor market.[17] This discourse is being drawn on yet again in current debates on immigration. "Oppositional" identities are produced that serve the needs of capitalist culture, creating new markets for rebellion that support the status quo.

As evidence of this, John himself polices racial barriers within the club. John and Moonie, a 12-year-old Hispanic girl, share social positioning as residents of a low-income housing project. But John makes sure that Moonie understands that her own positioning is different from his. One evening in the Teen Lounge, John tells Moonie to stop "talking Black." He turns to a staff person for reinforcement, saying, "She's trying to talk Black. And she's not Black. I'm Black. Black and Italian." Moonie retorts, loudly announcing that John is "Black and White!" John again refutes her, and Moonie slugs him in the arm. Their interaction reflects a policing of "appropriate" behavior based on race/ethnicity and rejection of shared culture based on class and geographic positioning. John refers to Moonie as "trying" to talk Black, inferring that her dialect does not come naturally for her. Moonie attempts to discredit John's construction of her by challenging his own racial "purity." John expresses resentment against others' treatment of him based on race. Yet he reconstructs the "natural" racial boundary between himself and Moonie. This attribution of behavior or speech to one or another race or ethnicity was not uncommon at East Side.

John is biracial, a fact he rarely acknowledges. When he does acknowledge it, he uses the word "Italian" and rejects the word "White." He lives with his mother, who is Black, and never mentions his father, with whom he has only tenuous contact. John defines himself as Black and identifies closely with issues of racial prejudice. This is not surprising. John is treated by the outside world as an African American male, specifically as a Black male from the projects. As noted, individuals from multiple racial backgrounds are often forced to choose one race or ethnicity with which to identify. This choice is influenced by social factors, including knowledge of physical appearance and others' perceptions.[18]

John's choice to identify himself solely as Black may be informed by his social experiences outside his neighborhood. This is suggested by his discussion of discrimination. His racial identification may also be influenced by his social positioning as a resident of an urban public housing project, in which the majority of residents are African American. John's light skin tone may heighten his desire to identify himself as Black and increase the importance of being seen as *not* White. As noted earlier, skin color is still important in Black communities. One study using data from the National Survey of Black Americans suggested that light skin is perceived as feminine within the African American community.[19] John is extremely focused on masculinity. John's dual concerns with race and gender may be related to ensuring his identity as a Black man despite his fair skin.

John's self-schema not only emphasizes a singular, Black racial identity but also rejects larger White society. In erasing that part of himself that is White, he disconnects himself from social structures perceived as being part of White society. For him, this apparently includes school and the legal labor force. Daphna Oyserman and colleagues' work with low-income, urban, minority adolescents suggests that incorporating into one's identity one's minority status as well as one's membership in the dominant society (i.e., one is Black *and* American) may help racial and ethnic minorities overcome obstacles of discrimination.[20] John appears to reject this duality.

John's construction of himself as a Black male rests heavily on his knowledge of himself as Other and on his rejection of White culture's power to define him. He claims his identity through refuting Others' perceptions of him and Whiteness as a part of himself. When it comes to gender, however, John relies on the very process of Othering that he resents when it comes to race and class.

"You Think You're a Man": East Side as a Developmental Context

Men's identities are bound up by notions of power and prestige that juxtapose men to both women and subordinate masculinities.[21] Masculine independence relies on the existence of the feminine Other.[22] Sexuality, race, ethnicity, and economic status are all differentially located on the axis of power within the structure of hegemonic masculinities.[23] The East Side youth are growing up in a neighborhood in which violence is prevalent, especially public violence involving young males. These racial and economic contexts of development influence their constructions of gender.[24]

Talking the Talk

John's discourse of masculinity constantly references sexuality. Defining the boundaries of gender around sexuality may be important for John because he is not athletic. Focusing on masculine sexuality may be a means to assert a gendered identity for boys who do not identify with activities considered "masculine" by their peers. Signithia Fordham, in her study of an urban high school, found that academically high-achieving Black males were preoccupied with what it meant to be male, with a particular focus on sexuality.[25] Many boys at East Side play basketball and express sports-related aspirations. John calls such goals "kid stuff," saying that, although he is a boy, he does not like to play basketball. He is quick to define masculinity as not dependent on athletic prowess. Masculine, he says, is "manly, take charge, the head man, the king." John names the characteristics he admires in boys as "being smart, not being in a gang." John's definition of masculinity discursively constructs manhood to include him as male, despite his lack of participation in the "masculine" world of sports. Not all males at East Side name athletic skills as part of the definition of masculinity, but some mention physical strength or report admiring the athletic prowess of other males.

Boys and girls at East Side engage in Othering in their constructions of gender. Youth use phrases such as "not like a girl" to define masculine and "not real masculine" to describe feminine. Their definitions of gender rest on a shared image of the opposite gender. Many youth have difficulty describing masculinity or femininity without referring back to gender itself. Feminine is "acting like a girl"; masculine is "manly." Sometimes youth use an example of what it means if someone of the opposite sex displays a trait. Masculine is defined as "tomboy," and feminine is described as "gay." Thus, gender norms are tied up with an image of the Other that helps define the expectations for the self.

Like other youth, John defines femininity in relation to men rather than women. He describes feminine as "sensitive, gay." Asked if he is feminine, he says, "Hell, no." Asked if there are any adults that he does not want to be like, John replies, "Yea, faggots. I don't like faggots." When I ask him why not, he replies, " 'Cause they're faggots! Like men!" John uses Other men, gay men, to define the opposite of masculine. In doing so, he draws a boundary against which he defines himself as male. John also says that he does not want to be like Rick, who he calls a pussy, or his sister, who he says has "an ugly ass attitude." John's construction of self against Other rests on the feminine. This Othering occurs though sexuality, the feminization of men, White men in particular, and girls with bad attitudes. Research with both African American and working-class White male adolescents has demonstrated a similar construction of manhood via the emasculation of females and Other males.[26] In rap music, the enemy is often feminized.[27] This construction of the male self makes visible the relational nature of gender. Masculinity is dependent on femininity to define that which it is not.[28] The power of the male self rests on the subjugation of the feminine, whether in the form of the biological female body or other, subjugated masculinities. Females and Other males are set up to receive all that is "expelled" from hegemonic masculinities.[29]

It is possible that John is playing with me (being purposively provocative) or presenting a hypermasculine self to a White female. It is difficult to sort out in his narrative what is "truth" from what is representation. John's demeanor suggests both "doing" and "representing."[30] He is acting and reacting in the moment (doing) while strategically using verbal symbols to name himself (representing). Yet the provocation for John's comments is less important than the comments themselves. Within the interview John is putting forth a specific idea of masculinity. He is protecting its bounds and ensuring that he remains distinctly inside the lines of what he sees as masculine activity. By choosing feminine-gendered language to insult Rick, John further asserts his own masculine agency against a feminized Other, perhaps both Rick and me. The emasculation of other males is a common tool by which men coproduce their own identities while subjugating others.[31]

The teens at East Side police interactions that violate heterosexual norms. The following incident occurred one evening while some teens were hanging out with a staff member.

The [6-year-old] boys at the side of the room were at times jumping up from their chairs and running and jumping on each other. Shelby [a female staff member] kept telling them to calm down. There was some talk about how one of the boys had kissed another one on the lips. "You're gonna get a whupping when I tell that," Shelby said, shaking her head. "You kissed him on the lips? You gay?" [a teen girl] asked. "Don't be saying that to my [kids]!" Shelby snapped at [the girl. . . . The conversation turned to other topics. . . . John came into the room and sat down]. . . . There was something else said about the boy who had kissed the other boy on the lips. John whipped his head around. "You gay?!" he said. "Stop that. Shelby doesn't want you saying that to the [youngest kids]," Janet [a former member] said.

John is involved in this policing. But he is not alone. Youth and staff work together to monitor the boundaries of "acceptable" gender behavior, making East Side a site that often supports, rather than contests, the traditional gender system. Instead of challenging the construction of homosexuality as negative, the staff member reinforces it, suggesting that mentioning homosexuality is not appropriate in front of the children. She does not seem to object to the negative portrayal of boys kissing; in fact, she suggests it leads to punishment.

In constructing himself during interviews, John is very conscious of heterosexual gender norms and activity. He narrates an identity that abides by those norms and sets himself up as different from and in opposition to the gendered Other. John's descriptions of females are linked to gendered sexuality. The characteristics that he admires in girls are being smart and "not being a ho." Whereas he says that he admires intelligence in both boys and girls, sexual restraint is named only in relation to girls. For boys, you may recall, John says that "not being in a gang" is important. John's construction of gender includes a division of violence and sexuality, with Other boys involved in gangs and Other girls sleeping around.

John's narrative of gendered identity often conflicts with the photographs he takes as part of this research project. John says that being smart and "not being a ho'," the characteristics he admires in girls, also describe him. But in his interview, he claims that most of his friends are girls and talks about these relationships as being based on sex: "Why would I want to sit down with another dude when I can be with a girl? . . .They got what I want . . . sex." Yet he photographs a group of male friends as people who are important to him. The only photograph he takes of a girl is of his steady girlfriend. John says that she does not deserve to have her picture taken but later retracts this statement saying, "she's there for me."

Given the discrepancy in his narrative, one minute saying he is not a ho' and the next saying he wants sex from girls, it is likely that John is presenting an image to me. John's photographs tell a different story of John's daily life than the narrative of self he constructs for me during the interview. His photos show primarily groups of male friends and dice hustlers, with a few shots of his family, his home, and his girlfriend. This suggests that at least part of his narrative is constructed for the benefit of me as the interviewer.

Not surprisingly, John expresses great resentment toward one staff member who he feels questioned his masculinity.

> [Sean] always say turn your hat straight. If I wanna have my hat turned ... He say not in my club. Last I checked this ain't his club. He just have a thing about me. He called me a girl and stuff. You're a girl. You think you're a man. All the staff got opinions of me but don't know nothing about me. . . . I don't care what they think.

John and Sean had a contentious relationship. Each complained of a lack of respect from the other. I do not know whether this incident occurred as John describes it. Certainly he and Sean do battle over club rules and John often wears a hat, in open defiance of those rules. Whether or not Sean used the phrase "You're a girl. You think you're a man," I do not know. But John's report of his reaction to Sean's attempt to discipline him is telling. He construes it as a threat to his masculinity. One could imagine that, as a 17-year-old, the incident could have been constructed around age: "You're a child. You think you're an adult." Or, "You're a boy. You think you're a man." Rather, John reports being feminized. He protects himself from this feminization by declaring, "I don't care what they think," asserting that they "know nothing" about him.

Male heterosexuality has bounds within which the East Side boys construct their image of positive masculinity. These norms are constructed in relation to the local context and supported by the culture at East Side. Gangbangers are a common Other taken from the streets of the neighborhood. Nearly all the youth talk about not wanting to be like gangbangers and drug dealers. Some teens photograph males from the neighborhood who represent these categories. For the boys, the males stand as a constant reminder of who they could become. This is reinforced by club staff and programming. The masculinity present on the streets around East Side provides the boys with an image against which they construct their own gendered selves. Thus, the social construction of gender occurs within, as well as between, groups.[32]

As noted earlier, the teen boys talk about not wanting to father a lot of children with different women. Although high teen birth rates in the inner city have led some to discuss hypermasculinity in terms of both violence and sexuality, the East Side boys tend to reject such displays of masculine sexuality.[33] The following exchange occurred during one of the focus groups that I conducted.

> *Male 1*: Yeah. Majority of 19-, 20-year-olds, around here, they ain't got no GED, no high school diploma, nothing.
> *Male 2*: They got kids.
> *Male 3*: Kids, all that level.
> *Male 1*: And they proud of it, too.
> *Female 1*: I hear —— got three kids.
> *Male 1*: And not takin' care of none of them. [Laughter and inaudible comment.]
> *Female 2*: [mimicking voice] Hey, you, watch my kids for me while I go out? I met this fine girl!

The boys use local young men as personifications of masculinity. They describe their own masculinity in opposition to them, highlighting family responsibility and caretaking. Staff reinforce this through discussions emphasizing the importance of responsible fathering and the difficulties facing Black men from their neighborhood.

African American men have had a different relationship to the gender system than their White counterparts. Whereas Black women were removed by race from the "cult of true womanhood," Black men were often blocked by racism from achieving masculine status through economic success. Much has been written about the role of economic structure and historical shifts in the labor market in relation to African American males' social positioning.[34] This has led to theories suggesting that academic disengagement in African American males is based in a desire to construct masculine identities that oppose White social structure.[35] Such an approach strays close to blaming the victim. It also ignores similar processes among White youth. In the 1980s and early 1990s, when deindustrialization was changing the landscape of industrial cities across the United States, academic disengagement and resistance was noted in studies of White working-class males.[36] By focusing on the racial aspects of such resistance, we allow the larger economic system off the hook. White working-class male school resistance is rooted in labor relations and historical conflicts between laborers and managers.[37] It also reflects a decrease in the availability of decent jobs for working-class males and perpetuates the construction of racial Others who serve as scapegoats.[38] Black males have historically had fewer opportunities for non-menial labor and, thus, may have disengaged earlier from the education and labor systems as sources of masculine pride than White working-class males.[39] By positioning African American male resistance as antithetical to White social structure we make it more difficult for Black and White working-class people to collaborate for social change.

The assumption is often made that any paid labor supports a masculine identity. But certain types of labor, especially positions viewed as demeaning or subservient, may be considered antithetical to manhood. No job may be preferable and more "manly" than a demeaning one.[40] In a *New York Times* Op-Ed, sociologist Orlando Patterson chided social scientists for being unable to let go of our adherence to the belief that structural and economic factors are to blame for the disconnection of many Black males from "mainstream" culture. He points out that economic researchers have found that new, low-paying jobs are taken by immigrants, not unemployed Black youths, even in the presence of living wages. To him, this points to the need to consider culture as an underlying factor.[41] But culture is developed within social structure, as well as in response to it. Even when jobs are available, the meaning of those jobs to individuals and groups must be considered. A job that is seen as subservient may threaten one's identity, especially for members of groups who feel devalued by society.

It is no coincidence that the social welfare system in the United States has been set up with two distinct tiers. One is considered acceptable to draw on because it is based on an assumed period of independence (unemployment insurance and social security). The other is considered demeaning because it represents dependence (Temporary Aid for Needy

Families, food stamps). The fact that the latter tier has been feminized through media and political depictions of "welfare queens" serves to bolster the gendered nature of autonomy and dependence.[42] Black women's traditional advantage over Black males in the labor market is historically rooted in their participation in the domestic help and service industries. Such jobs are low in both respect and pay.[43] If men were to take such jobs, they might risk breaking the dichotomy between themselves and the female Others against whom their definition of masculinity rests.

Walking the Walk

John's presentation of himself within a sexualized masculine framework is not limited to the interview situation. Many observations of John around East Side involve discussions about or references to sexuality. One afternoon John was involved in a conversation about how one of the research assistants looks like a teacher from the local school. John turned the conversation into one about first the teacher's sexuality and then his own sexual prowess.

> [John] said, "You know Miss ——? She's a teacher by day and a —— [he paused and rocked his hips and his pelvic region gyrated back and forth] by night." "What?!" I asked. "You know, a dancer," [John] answered, exaggerating the word "dancer." I shook my head and laughed. I asked him his name. . . . "I'm John—student by day and lover by night!" He smoothly swayed his hips from side to side as he said this.

This interaction seems to both denigrate the teacher and build up John. Yet John later defends the research assistant against another youth's sexual harassment, yelling at the offending boy, "You best getcho nasty ass up those stairs!" John acts defensively toward another boy's attempt to sexualize and demean an adult female. While seemingly contradictory, these interactions work together to present a specific masculine trope to the female researcher. John demonstrates sexual prowess as well as male gallantry. He displays himself as both a lover and a protector of females, two traditionally male roles in cultural discourse.

On another afternoon, John uses exaggerated sexuality to involve himself in a conversation. I am talking with some girls about the recent departure of a popular female staff person. John enters and begins to listen to our talk.

> "The parents . . . did a petition and sent it to [regional headquarters] to get rid of Cheryl," [Janet said]. "Why?" I asked. " 'Cause she was talking to us about sex. And the parents complained about that. But we're grown, ya know? What we do in that young women's group is our business. That was our space to talk about what we wanted to. And I tell you, if it weren't for Cheryl, half these little girls would be runnin' around fuckin'. I'll put that right out there 'cause that's the truth. She's the reason these girls aren't gettin' down." [Two other girls] both began nodding vigorously in agreement and making comments like "uh huh" and "that's the truth!" . . . "What about Charles?" I asked. "He's gone too, right?" "Yeah, he gone," Janet said. "Charles taught us how to fuck," John said, jumping onto one of the tables and dropping himself down through the hole in the center of it. "Yeah, without Charles none of us be getting the girls," he said laughing and snaking his way along the floor. Janet rolled her eyes at him. [*I assumed that John was joking and just reacting to Janet saying that Cheryl kept the girls from having sex. His demeanor suggested that this was all in jest. However, it is an interesting gender moment—the girls suggesting that the female staff's role is to keep them from having sex and the boy saying the male staff's role was to get them girls. Given what we have heard about [the boys' discussion] group, I doubt this was really what went on.*]

John does not get along well with Charles. All the boys in Charles's discussion group say that they learned about puberty and STD's and that boys should not irresponsibly father babies or sleep with lots of girls. Some mention watching videos about domestic violence, teaching them that men should not "be beating on women." Such male discussion groups can be positive sites for the construction of nonviolent masculinities.[44] Even John later acknowledged Charles's attempts to dissuade boys from sexual activity. John's acting out during this incident, therefore, appears to be an effort to demonstrate his own masculinity in relation to the girls.

I have positioned John's posturing around issues of gender and sexuality as an indication that the two are linked within his own conception of masculinity. But it is also possible that John is simply trying on a particular type of masculinity. His exaggerated discourse of sex is not necessarily atypical for adolescent boys. The possibility that this is simply a form of playing with masculinity is given some weight by John's discussions of people that he admires. John expresses admiration for nonsexual qualities in both males and females. He names his mother as the person who has the most influence on him because "she was always there," raising him and doing her best even though he gave her a lot of problems. He also looks up to a male cousin, who he says is a good guy who "just do right. He's doin' right by other people. Honest, a good guy." John's use of this discourse as a form of self-presentation demonstrates engagement with media images of the sexual male, whether or not he enacts such an identity outside of the club.

Conclusion

John's identity construction relies on an image of himself as a young, Black male living in an urban housing project. He is angry about being objectified as an Other by society, especially by people in authority. He expresses resistance to the stereotypes he confronts. But John also reconstructs those images through his behavior. He has trouble living within authority structures and clashes with the club directors and staff whom he feels disrespect him. John enjoys making money through gambling, despite his rejection of kids in his neighborhood who see gangs, drugs, or sports as a means to the same ends. He also sets himself up as diametrically opposed to Whites, policing the boundaries of "authentic" Black identity. In doing so, John decreases the possibility of collaboration with low-income Whites and Hispanics, people who may share his difficulties in accessing social power. Access to power is clearly an issue for John, and he battles for individual agency on many fronts.

John's narrative demonstrates the ways in which individual agency and activity interact with structure to construct raced and gendered identities on a local level. It also reveals that adolescents rely on the image of the Other as they negotiate their own sense of self. But beyond that, John highlights his own perception of self as Other and the complex ways in which gender, race, and class braid together to position him and his male peers in the social system.[45] John poignantly demonstrates the tension between self-presentation and self-construction. He presents a strongly sexualized persona to me and other female researchers. Yet his behaviors and relationships outside of these interactions suggest a less central role for gendered sexuality in his own identity. His expectations and future goals for himself are also positioned less in relation to gender than to the confluence of gender, race, and class. The importance of this tripartite system must be considered when thinking about how gender informs and constrains individual lives. The ways in which local contexts, such as youth programs, both contest and reinforce these systems is highlighted by John's simultaneously contentious and continuous relationship with East Side and its staff.

8

■   ■   ■   ■   ■   ■   ■   ■   ■

"If I Never Came Here I'd Be Irresponsible, Like a Little Kid"

After-School Programs as Sites of Development and Identity Construction

In recent years, there has been considerable interest in the potential of after-school programs for providing safe and supportive places for youth to learn and grow. Particular attention has been paid to the role of such organizations in the lives of youth living in high-poverty neighborhoods. The most visible manifestation of this interest was endorsed by a real life kids' action hero, the Terminator himself. Before becoming governor of California, Arnold Schwarzenegger stewarded California Proposition 49 to victory, promising permanent funding for after-school programs statewide. After-school programs were also part of the initial No Child Left Behind Act of 2001, which provided financial support for 21st Century Community Learning Centers. Subsequent federal budgets have decreased funding for that portion of the initiative.[1]

If we are to press forward with financial support for the efforts of youth organizations, we must have a deeper understanding of what makes these sites successful and how developmental processes occur within them. As I argue throughout this book, such an effort requires an understanding of the developmental needs of adolescents in context. Environments that do not fit adolescents' developmental needs can be harmful.[2] Furthermore, we must take a positive stance toward youth, considering not only how we can prevent problems but also how we can promote development.[3] This goes beyond prevention and intervention. It requires attending to the development and support of the inherent competencies in all youth.[4]

Researchers and practitioners are increasingly taking a developmental approach to studying youth organizations. Although early work on after-school programs focused on behavioral outcomes, skill enhancement, and risk prevention, recent work highlights the broader developmental potential of such settings. Two recent reviews suggest that programs do not need to focus solely on academics to achieve positive effects in academic areas.[5] These findings support the idea of positive youth development as a holistic concept. This is encouraging. Too often we separate the process of human development from the practice of social policy and programming. For those of us concerned with youth development, this fissure is particularly troubling. Creating successful programs for youth requires fusing development and practice. We must consider the policies we expect to affect young lives in light of the developmental needs of the youth whom we hope to reach.

The increasing focus on after-school programs as sites for positive youth development stems from a desire to help improve the life chances of youth growing up in high-poverty neighborhoods. It also reflects an anxiety about youth crime and high-risk behaviors. Much like the media blitz around teen pregnancy in the 1980s, today's focus on the "3–6 PM risk" is partially driven by genuine concern for the well-being of youth. Yet it is also fueled by recognition of the social costs of juvenile delinquency.[6] Mentoring and after-school programs, which offer both supervision and support to youth deemed "at-risk," are increasingly being touted as a panacea. But much remains unknown about the potential of such programs.

It is my contention that after-school programs have promise beyond risk prevention and behavior promotion. Such sites can serve as positive developmental settings that assist youth in negotiating the broader task of adolescence: identity development. Yet to adequately meet the developmental needs of minority, economically disadvantaged adolescents, we must understand how they construct identities and the ways in which they use local contexts and relationships to negotiate this task. The voices and experiences of the East Side youth provide insight into the ways in which such settings, and the people in them, serve as sites for positive development and self-construction. These youth are actively engaged in constructing identities within the rubrics of gender, race, and class. Too often the contexts that are available to them do not provide optimal support for this task. Adolescents recognize this. After describing the violence he and his peers continually negotiate in his neighborhood, Bob pauses and looks at me: "I'm gonna have problems when I grow up," he concludes. This is not how a 14-year-old should view his chances for the future. It is incumbent upon us, as a society, to pay attention to these teens' experiences and respond to their developmental needs. After-school programs can serve as safe spaces wherein youth can come together and negotiate identities in relation to each other and the larger world. But to create such spaces, we must first hear youths' voices.

Inside the Black Box: Youth Organizations as Developmental Settings

In 2002 the National Research Council released a report indicating that youth organizations provide important and positive support for youth. Other researchers were deeming after-school programs as especially important for children growing up in high-poverty and high-crime neighborhoods.[7] Yet researchers could do little to answer the question of why or how certain organizations succeeded. Youth organizations, the NRC report concluded, function like a "black box"; youth enter, and some emerge with positive outcomes, but we cannot yet say how we get from here to there (Figure 8-1).[8]

Since that time, researchers and practitioners have attempted to identify key components of successful programs. A number of factors have been linked to positive outcomes and have been suggested as indicators of program quality. Features such as a safe and healthy environment; varied, challenging, age-appropriate, and consistently implemented activities and programs; opportunities for skill-building; and adequately trained personnel have been found to be important. A number of psychosocial and emotional aspects have also been identified. These include psychological safety, positive social norms, youth engagement, and, perhaps the most common factor, positive staff-youth relationships.[9] All of these, of

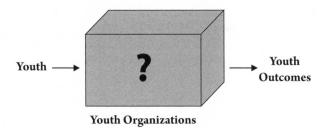

Fig. 8-1. The Black Box

course, are predicated on youth attendance. Attendance cannot be taken for granted. Participation in after-school programs decreases as youth enter adolescence, so getting teens in the door can be a challenge.[10] It is all the more important, therefore, for practitioners to pay attention to the aspects of after-school programs that teens themselves find supportive. This entails consideration of specific activities and programming, as well as the broader socioenvironmental characteristics of these settings.

One of the challenges of identifying supportive factors is that there have been few methodologically rigorous studies of after-school sites. Evaluations of programs are plagued by weak research designs and overblown expectations for program effects. Staff and youth attrition also complicate study designs.[11] One of the few national evaluations of an after-school program, the 21st Century Community Learning Centers Evaluation, failed to find large impacts on youth. Researchers had difficulty interpreting its results because of variation in program implementation, activities, and attendance across sites. These factors were hard to isolate and investigate due to the design of the evaluation, which did not include long-term observations of sites. Statistical controls in the middle-school portion of the study and problematic measures of after-school care also hindered its findings.[12]

Many after-school program evaluations focused solely on problem prevention or intervention, emphasizing structured prevention and assistance programs and specific, individual youth outcomes.[13] A recent meta-evaluation of after-school programs indicated overall positive results for both academic and psychosocial outcomes. This gives some hope to the research and programming communities, especially since academic outcomes were found even in programs focused on social skills. The key seemed to be using evidence-based approaches to skill building.[14] This meta-analysis has been criticized, however, for including formal intervention and prevention programs that are not traditional after-school programs. Yet its results are supported by a second review, which also found positive results, especially for those youth most at risk.[15]

Although structured programs have been pointed to as an important facet of successful after-school programs, we now know that unstructured programming and socioenvironmental aspects of the spaces also promote positive outcomes.[16] Research designs focused on capturing youth outcomes alone cannot capture such environmental factors. Despite a growing body of literature suggesting the need for ecological-developmental studies, there is still a dearth of empirical work that takes such an approach.[17] We have more information about factors that indicate quality programs, but we still do not know in what ways these factors drive outcomes.[18] This makes clear the need for more intensive work on youth organizations. A deeper understanding of the processes that are at work in such sites, and how these processes are linked to adolescents' developmental needs, will help researchers and practitioners develop better evaluation tools and effective programs.

The East Side teens' narratives suggest that this organization, at least, is supporting the development of identities that are in rich connection to other people. The club serves as a distinct setting for youths' self-construction, especially with regard to relational traits. Most youth feel that East Side encourages and appreciates many aspects of their personalities, especially relational characteristics. It is striking that the majority of the youth I interviewed said they would not be "who they are today" without East Side. These teens do not say simply that their grades would be lower or that they would be engaged in behaviors typically considered risky. They say that they would not be themselves. East Side, in their minds, has helped to shape their identities. Their statements point to the potential for youth organizations to take a more expansive view of youth development, to work toward supporting the construction and negotiation of positive identities that will be with youth throughout their lives.

In the remainder of this chapter, I review the three broad themes addressed in earlier chapters: the self in interpersonal relationships, the raced and classed self, and the influence and construction of gender. I collapse the latter two themes into one discussion of the social Other, highlighting the interactive influence of these categories on youths' lives and experiences.[19] I consider these themes in relation to what we can learn from East Side about creating positive developmental settings for teens growing up at the juncture of marginalized social categories. The thread that ties these themes together within East Side is the developmental needs of the teens themselves. Adolescents need spaces in which they can (1) integrate various social roles, both chosen and ascribed; (2) receive a sense of individual validation, as well as belonging to a community of which they are contributing members; and (3) be provided with a balance of individual autonomy and adult support. Whereas the activities at East Side provide opportunities for meeting these needs, it is the relationships within the club's walls that serve as particularly powerful contexts of identity construction for these youth. These relationships help the teens build relational selves but also serve as sites for the negotiation of social identities including gender, race, and class.

Respect, Responsibility, and Role Models: Adolescents' Connections to Others in After-School Sites

As infants, we come to distinguish "me" from "you." As we grow, we continually negotiate being an individual within a community, learning to balance the needs of self and other. Yet despite research on adolescent peer groups, family relationships, and social organizations, there has been little revision of the traditional framing of the primary task of adolescence as one of individuation of identity. Despite concern over civic apathy in young adults, there has been little work exploring the development of a relational identity during adolescence.[20]

Following from researchers such as Ruthellen Josselson and Niobe Way,[21] my research pushes the field of identity development to consider how boys and girls grow up and construct identities in relation to other individuals and the culture at-large. The voices of the East Side teens suggest processes of negotiation of personal relationships and larger social structures. These negotiations influence youth identity and shape how adolescents envision their roles in the adult world. The story of East Side as a local context of self-construction provides insight into the developmental potential of youth organizations to assist youth with the complex task of identity construction. Such sites seem especially promising for nurturing relational selves.

My findings suggest that we have been too quick to dismiss the importance of the connected self for adolescents. The East Side youth nearly all describe themselves using a balance of independent and interdependent characteristics. Both boys and girls list qualities such as respect, responsibility, kindness, truthfulness, and caring as important self-characteristics. Because I used open-ended questions, rather than quantitative measures of interdependent versus independent self-constructs, I was able to access youths' spontaneous descriptions of self. The importance of teens' relationships with others emerges consistently from their narratives. A key element of that relational identity is the primacy of respect and responsibility in youths' self-constructions. This contradicts our cultural myth of adolescence, yet it sustains traits that have been historically central to African American communities.

My fieldwork confirms the primacy of respect and responsibility and provides insight into the processes and contexts that nurture these pro-social, connected qualities. Through activities and relationships at East Side, youth develop and are given respect and responsibility. They view these characteristics as integral to their identities. At the same time, they proclaim individual traits, displaying a balance of individual and connected qualities that mirror their participation in the club. The teens describe themselves as individuals with unique talents who are contributing members of a community. They also report being viewed this way by club staff. The bidirectional respect that characterizes most youths' experiences at the club allows for engagement in the setting and the potential for other, positive processes to take effect. These include tri-level role modeling and the development of narratives of self-transformation.

"Kids Look Up to Me": Tri-Level Role Modeling

One of the unique aspects of many after-school programs, including East Side, is the wide age range of their participants. Once they leave elementary school, youth are often in nonfamilial settings where the maximum age difference is four years. This limits their access to young adult role models as well as their opportunities for seeing themselves as role models for others. Despite the increased focus on mentoring, researchers have given little consideration to the developmental benefits of teenagers mentoring younger kids. Seeing oneself as a role model to others gives one an important sense of belonging in the community and connectedness to others. It also offers a chance for individuals to serve as experts, showing them the positive aspects of themselves that they have to offer. These two processes are particularly important for adolescents as they try to balance relatedness and autonomy.

After-school programs have the added benefit of embedding these youth-youth relationships within adult-youth relationships. Thus, the teens have adult mentors, many of whom are not much older than them. These adults often come from similar backgrounds as the youth. Such natural mentors have been found to reduce the negative effects of stress and promote urban youths' abilities to seek social support.[22] The teens also find support for the development of their sense of themselves as role models and mentors. Here again, they are able to play out narratives of relatedness and autonomy. They serve as adult-like figures for the kids and rely on their own relationships with adult staff for support as needed.

Given the salience to the East Side youth of their ties with both adults and kids, after-school programs should attempt to cultivate tri-level relationships. Adult staff are important to this process. Giving staff time to nurture their relationships with youth has been cited as an important factor for organizations to consider in their planning.[23] East Side youths' close ties to Charles and Cheryl, in particular, were apparent throughout this study. These staff's relationships with youth represent in many ways the club at its best. Yet Charles's and Cheryl's overrepresentation in the youths' narratives also points to one of the challenges faced by after-school programs. The prevalence of high turnover rates in youth programs means that there are not always adults such as Rick, Cheryl, and Charles who have long-standing relationships with the teens. Retaining staff is a challenge that, when met, provides important developmental support.

I argue that a well-trained and effective adult staff is necessary but not sufficient. After-school programs must also provide contexts in which youth can use their relationships with staff as models for their own developing selves. Through working with younger kids, youth come to see themselves as experts and as contributing members of the community. They also begin to see a place for themselves in the adult world. Such relationships help nurture the responsibility that teens report as important to their identities. Serving as a role model or mentor entails a sense of responsibility to the mentee. The changing nature of youths' roles at the club provides increasing levels of responsibility to youth as they age. They move from participant, to scaffolded coach or mentor, to worker. The responsibilities inherent in these roles are to the club as well as to other people. Thus, it is a sense of responsibility that reflects an interconnected sense of identity.

It is with some awe that Lorenzo says, "I never thought kids would look up to someone like me." Lorenzo is a kid who has a tough life. There are a number of obstacles for him to overcome to succeed by traditional standards. Although the tri-level role modeling he experiences at East Side is not a panacea—Lorenzo struggles with school and occasionally drops out—it gives him a valued position in the East Side community. East Side embeds him in supportive relationships that become part of his sense of self. This also seems to be the case for a number of East Side youth. Thus, nurturing adult-youth relationships and providing opportunities for relationships that span age boundaries are ways in which after-school settings can provide developmentally appropriate and supportive settings for teens.

Respect as a Component of Relationships

The respectful nature of the adult-youth relationships within East Side is important to consider, especially because many programs serve youth from socially marginalized populations. Youth-led evaluations of programs for inner-city teens have identified respect and trust as key components of successful interactions and organizations.[24] The youth at East Side specifically emphasize the importance of bidirectional respect, a concept that is linked to the sociohistorical positioning of African Americans in the United States. That youth are wary of according respect to people whom they don't feel respect them indicates the situated nature of identities. Settings that serve youth should consider teens' experiences of self in broader society. They must ensure that the relationships that youth experience within the program setting counteract, and help youth to negotiate, possible negative interactions they may have in other contexts. Being respectful is important to the East Side youth. The existence of bidirectional respect in their relationships with adults is particularly important as it fosters respectfulness.

Interdependent Selves: Moving beyond Gender Differences

The East Side youth demonstrate that the development of connected selves is not a result of gender alone. Rather, it is a more complex interweaving of social positions. Because the bulk of initial identity research was conducted with White males, the priming of individualism over connection during adolescence may be a false dichotomy. The East Side males assert that relationships are important to their sense of self. This supports other research on working-class and ethnic and racial minority boys.[25] Connection and individuation are not oppositional in the East Side youths' lives or identities. Given the importance of connections to others throughout human life, it is vital that we support adolescents in developing both relational and independent selves.

Boys' abilities to nurture selves that are in positive relationship to others within East Side has important implications for social policy aimed at adolescents. Despite traditional notions about the distinct needs of boys and girls, both genders receive important benefits from the relationships that they develop at the club. Boys and girls describe themselves as being connected to other people. Many attribute these relational qualities to their participation at East Side. It is clear that we must pay attention to these relational aspects of selfhood if we are to create programs and environments that address adolescents' developmental needs. Settings that serve adolescents should take into account their relational climates. Some educators are calling attention to the importance of coordinating social, emotional, and academic learning, stressing the importance of fostering respectful and supportive relationships in schools.[26] Through practices such as tri-level role modeling and embedding academic and recreational activities within relationships with caring adults, East Side appears to be doing this successfully.

"I Used to Be Bad, I'm No Longer Bad": Narratives of Self-Transformation

One mechanism by which East Side becomes an important site of development and identity negotiation is youths' use of the club as a setting for narrating stories of self-transformation. Many of the older adolescents narrate a sense of self that experiences a positive change, from "hard-headed" or "bad" kid to "good" or "responsible" teen. Youth often link this transformation to their experiences at the club. Youth state that their relationships and participation in activities at East Side lead them to change negative aspects of themselves. Youths' parents, too, note that East Side positively socializes kids, bringing them out of their shells and teaching them to get along with others. Thus, East Side becomes a literal site of self-construction, as youth build turning points in their life stories around the club. This again points to the broad potential of after-school programs as contexts for youth development.

Offering a site in which youth can "grow up" and continue to participate over the years provides opportunities for youth to engage in developmental tasks. From a community psychology framework, the potential of after-school programs to serve as "empowering communities" seems apparent.[27] Although much work on community narratives has focused on adults, I suggest it is imperative that we apply this lens to adolescence as a developmental period. Because adolescents are both individuating and finding a social niche, they must have environments in which they can "play with" and "try on" different selves and discourses. This allows them to resist and reconstruct the narratives they confront in the wider society. The activities of the teens at East Side demonstrate just such consideration and reconstruction of, as well as resistance and accommodation to, social discourses. Such reconstruction and resistance is accomplished through their participation in a community that allows them to challenge and reshape those narratives that don't fit.

Many of the processes at work at East Side are conceptually linked to features of empowering organizations. These include a strength-based belief system, an accessible and multifunctional opportunity role structure, a support system that provides a sense of community, and a committed leadership. Youth at East Side report experiencing many of these factors at the club. They also link their participation to positive growth in areas aligned with the club's system of values. Teens' growth is supported by both adult and peer role models. Peer role models have been considered an important part of empowering communities.[28] Further research is necessary to provide the outcome data needed to determine whether East Side is truly functioning as an empowering community. My study provides a basis for further study of comprehensive after-school programs as sites of empowerment for at-risk youth through the process of self-construction.

East Side's long-term role in the lives of its members and its deep ties to the community enhance its potential as a site of youth empowerment. Because of Rick's long-standing relationship with the club and its community, he knows many of the kids' parents and teachers, as well as other local adults and kids. East Side hosts community events, including housing authority meetings, census drives, and emergency support services. As one example, during a summer power outage, the club provided space for local families to eat meals donated by charitable organizations. The parents I spoke to are happy to have East Side in the neighborhood. Some parents had attended the club as kids and reminisced about their own days there. It gives them peace of mind to have a safe space for their kids in the after-school hours. The low membership fee, which is waived if a family cannot pay it, makes East Side a good choice for affordable, safe child care in walking distance of their homes. One of the East Side teen girls emphasizes this when she tells me that she comes to the club in the afternoons so that her mom "doesn't have to worry."

After-school programs can be positioned to foster positive developmental processes through providing sustained relationships, displaying respect for the whole teen, and offering opportunities for youth to engender and develop prosocial traits as a natural part of their interactions in the site. Such factors have been previously identified as part of the 5 C's of positive youth development (PYD)—competence, confidence, character, connection, and caring—discussed in chapter 1. The findings from this research provide evidence that the process of PYD does occur through relations between people and their contexts.[29]

The potential of youth organizations to serve as sites for the development of a connected self is important and has both theoretical and practical implications. Yet key questions remain unanswered. In particular, in this study I did not directly observe or address youths' lives outside of the club. Although photographs and interviews touch on youths' outside lives, I have no evidence to demonstrate whether the prosocial qualities that youth report at East Side are carried over into other areas of their lives. This raises the question of to what extent these connected selves are context-specific. Certainly, their development is contextual. The youth talk about their relationships in the club as nurturing relatedness. More research is needed to examine whether these prosocial characteristics that youth describe as important parts of their identities transfer to other situations and are sustained over time. Furthermore, although there are important implications of these findings for the development of moral and civic identities, the empirical link is yet to be made.

Who Am I to You: Adolescents and the Social Other

For youth growing up at the intersection of marginalized social categories, the task of identity construction poses additional challenges to those confronted by their majority peers. For such teens, identity development and integration require negotiating other people's views of them. Those views may not accurately represent who they are. This demands an ability to balance understanding of such negative views with strategies for resistance to them. Empirical work has largely neglected the ways in which individuals make meaning in their lives through engaging with social structures in local contexts. Symbolic interactionism showed initial promise as it suggested the possibility of understanding the intersections of individual identity, interpersonal interactions, and society. Yet social identities have largely remained essentialized, and social structures have generally been omitted as explanatory and addressable variables in empirical work.[30] Research that tackles these issues with teens is especially valuable; helping adolescents contest negative or constricting social structures should empower them to confront social barriers to their own advancement. To help youth negotiate the construction of a self that deals with social categories and stereotypes without being subsumed by them, one must acknowledge that no social category stands alone. As such, no category has universal meaning.

My findings are in line with Jocelyn Hollander and Judith Howard's suggestion that social positions are interactive and simultaneous and "should be studied not merely as individual-level variables but as systems of social hierarchy."[31] In a special issue of the *American Journal of Community Psychology*, Meg Bond emphasized this point. She noted that studies on the lives of women of color do more than add to our knowledge base. Rather, she points out, such studies can alter our understandings and point to new sources of differences. This view locates difference in the dynamic intersections of gender, race, and class rather than in one category alone.[32] Such an approach is precisely what the narratives of youth in my study suggest. The meaning and influence of gender, race, and class on their lives must be considered in context.

Along with concurring with the call for more studies of both between-group overlap and within-group difference, I also suggest that we reconceptualize the way in which we consider the relationship between the individual and society in the study of difference. The results of my research indicate the active ways in which meaning-making occurs within local sites and relationships and in dialogue with larger cultural discourse and structure. If we conceptualize identity as a dynamic relationship between the individual and society, we can move away from blaming the individual for not meeting "normative" standards. This is not meant to deemphasize individual agency. Rather, it privileges the understanding of human agency within context, calling for an examination of the processes by which macro and micro contexts are integrated, assimilated, and resisted during individual self-construction. This requires empirically linking Uri Bronfenbrenner's ecological levels of development through probing the processes by which the outer layers become infused in the inner. East Side serves as a site for youth to grapple with the constraints and tensions resulting from the intersectionalities of their gender, race, and class positionings. These negotiations occur through their relationships and interactions with other people. Staff are able, in some areas at least, to work with the teens to provide them with tools for negotiating their social identities. Yet at times youths' activities at East Side reproduce, rather than challenge, the status quo. Exploring these processes as they occur within East Side allows us to consider the potential for after-school programs to serve as sites in which youth can negotiate the various categories of their identities. By doing so, they can engage with and resist social discourse in the process of constructing their own sense of self in the world.

East Side youth are particularly aware of their positioning as "project kids." Their narratives braid gender, race, and class. Yet youth also move fluidly between these categories in describing their daily experiences. Youth express frustration at being typecast without their consent. They resist images of the "project kid" through both action and discourse. Yet they, too, reconstruct the "project kid" in their own activities, defining themselves against this image. East Side teens use the club as a site for this separation. The club distances them from the kids on the streets of their neighborhood. It also provides a location for the development of positive identities as they move into the adult world. East Side does this by seeing and respecting the whole teen, moving beyond the first impressions that youth have to negotiate in other environments. Furthermore, the club is a site in which youth experience a sense of belonging to a community of others who are "like them." They can try on and nurture possible future selves free from stereotypes of "project kids" and resist stereotypic gender norms and identities.

"It's a Relief to Get Back to Myself": A Place That Recognizes and Respects the Whole Teen

Within the walls of East Side, most youth do not feel stigmatized or stereotyped. The vast majority of teens feel that race "isn't an issue" at East Side because everyone is "like them." Yet racism and classism are both discussed openly. Staff acknowledge the challenges faced by the youth as a result of their race and class positioning. Cheryl states that certain local stores will not hire "her girls." Sean and Charles talk explicitly about adults from outside the projects stereotyping local teens. These staff make the kids aware of such issues as they emphasize that youths' own behaviors and self-presentations can reinforce or challenge such stereotypes. Most important, they do so from a base of respect for these teens.

By recognizing the whole youth, seeing beyond social categories such as race and class, East Side allows teens to cultivate positive identities free from the stereotypes they face in other environments. Many youth feel that teachers and other authority figures make judgments about them based on first impressions. Yet most youth I spoke with feel that club staff hold no such negative views of them or their peers. This seems intricately tied to the notion of respect, particularly bidirectional respect. The idea that one is seen as a whole, respected person, outside of the rubrics of race and class stereotypes, is particularly important for youth whose daily interactions are filled with negotiations of other people's unfounded assumptions about them.

In addition to seeing beyond race and class stereotypes, the staff at East Side also value and support youths' strengths in various domains that may not be appreciated in other contexts of their lives. Lorenzo's skill in working with younger kids is not apparent at his high school, where his identity as a student is one that leaves him feeling less than competent. At East Side, although he is encouraged to work harder at being a good student, staff also recognize and prize his other skills. Youths' comments about getting "back to themselves" or all the parts of them "coming together" when they step inside East Side's doors speak to the power of such a place.

Not all youth experience this positive integration of self at East Side. John, for one, does not. He reports a lack of respect from staff and feels that they stereotype him just as people outside the club do. John's perceptions are at least partially accurate. Staff do consider John an "unfortunate kid." John acknowledges that "some of" what staff say about him is true. Yet John continues to come to the club, at least periodically, despite his conflicts with staff. Perhaps John is simply proof that no site can successfully reach all youth. There will always be some who simply do not connect. Yet East Side's very presence in his neighborhood has some value for him, even if he does not report the positive experiences of many of his peers. This underscores the importance of after-school programs in neighborhoods where there are few safe spaces for youth to socialize, let alone to take part in structured programs and activities. Whatever else John does, he shuns gangs and drug dealing. East Side provides him with a space where he is not in danger of being pressured to engage in such activities and is safe from the violence he may be vulnerable to on the streets.

This type of safe space can also provide an identity in and of itself. Although John does not make such an attachment, being an East Side member can be an identity that carries with it certain expectations and traits. As noted earlier, older teens at East Side are expected to serve as role models for the younger kids. This provides youth with identities as responsible community members. Other researchers have suggested that youth organizations in neighborhoods with high levels of gang activity can serve as a "holding ground," buying youth time to explore different options.[33] East Side does appear to act as such a site for many youth. Teens talk about themselves in opposition to local kids who do not come to the club, many of whom the East Side youth see as going down "the wrong road." The presence of East Side in this neighborhood allows youth an alternative to seeking identities and safety on the streets. For youth who remain involved in the club through adolescence, such an identity may become internalized, providing them with a narrative of self that grows with them as they age. This identity revolves around their participation in East Side and involves a communal narrative constructed in conjunction with their peers and the adult staff.

The internalized sense of self that is connected to this local context suggests another strength of after-school programs. Community psychologists have suggested that empowerment requires giving people the tools to construct their own community narratives as a means to resist negative, dominant, cultural narratives.[34] Having a youth-centered space in which they can create their own boundaries of self and Other in opposition to social hierarchies may be particularly important for adolescents.[35] This is especially relevant for youth who are circumscribed by social categories that have been given negative meaning by society. Such teens may need additional support to gain the resources necessary for controlling their lives and achieving their goals.[36] Having spaces within which one can escape dominant cultural narratives may be a key to developing an identity that can understand, negotiate, and also resist dominant cultural narratives. Yet transforming a space into a location for empowerment requires active engagement and guidance from adults in the setting. Youth narratives must be both affirmed and challenged in order for them to truly critically engage in discussion of social identity issues.[37] Thus, having the space is a start, but it is not enough. It takes effort for such a space to live up to its potential as a site of resistance and identity coconstruction.

Building an Adult Self

East Side also provides important practical supports for developing identities that will help youth succeed as they move into the adult world. The club allows for the construction of a community narrative and for the development of specific job skills and identities. Lorenzo and Nicole are particularly salient examples of this. Lorenzo is not very connected to school. East Side demonstrates to him that his skills in coaching and working with kids can be transferred to future jobs. Club staff encourage him to build on this by pursuing summer jobs at East Side and other clubs. Nicole is a successful student with strong career and academic goals. East Side provides her with internship and job opportunities that are not available elsewhere in her neighborhood. By working at the club, she cultivates a sense of herself as an adult employee who contributes to the East Side community and to her family. She also gets important experience that she will be able to cite when she applies for jobs in the future. She and Lorenzo both develop practical job skills at East Side, skills that are important for each of them in different ways.

Schools have traditionally had difficulty linking students to careers. Youth organizations may be able to play a key role in helping teens think about their future position in society. For youth who do not have access to the types of internships afforded by higher-income social networks, after-school programs can serve as sites where youth can gain specific skills and begin to experiment with possible career identities. Staff's role in helping youth think about their career goals and in providing practical support for applying to college are concrete examples of how after-school programs can help youth actively work toward positive future selves.[38]

It is the social climate at East Side, over and above any specific events or activities, that contributes to a supportive developmental environment for the youth. The attitudes of the staff are not only reflected in specific actions, such as assisting with job applications or scholarship searches, but are part of their overall treatment of the youth. In Bob's statement that Rick obviously "deeply cares about" the kids with whom he works, he pays tribute to the importance of this underlying trait. Bob embeds this in a discussion of how East Side is an important resource for low-income teens through its provision of computers and educational assistance. The accumulation of small, everyday activities and interactions has more of an influence than simply taking youth to a job or college fair once a year. When such activities are infused in the everyday events of the club, it lets teens know that these issues are important to the staff. It also provides them with support for their developing adult selves. As Bob points out, it is both the concrete tasks *and* the emotional climate that are important supportive features for the youth at East Side.

"Girls Are Just So Different from Boys": Resisting and Reconstructing Gender Norms

Boys and girls at East Side are aware that they are perceived as Other. They construct their own Others against whom they define their gendered selves. These Others are maintained through their activity and discourse. Within East Side, youth are in some ways able to resist stereotypic gender norms. Participation in cross-gender activities is not uncommon. Girls play sports. Some girls even play traditionally masculine sports, such as football or hockey. Many girls talk about having both masculine and feminine parts of themselves, both of which are displayed at East Side. They report wanting to be feminine sometimes, but none of them wants to be feminine all the time. Nearly all seem comfortable with being masculine, as they define it, now and then.

East Side boys are not so open to having a feminine side. However, both the construction of a connected sense of self and the role of the older boys in working with the kids may be seen as promoting characteristics that are traditionally thought of as feminine. The lack of gender difference in the sense of an interconnected self is notable and suggests that after-school programs can be places where independence and interdependence can be nurtured in both boys and girls. Programs such as Charles's male discussion group serve as safe spaces in which to nurture such identities. This may be particularly important for racial minority boys, whose physical presence can lead to differential treatment and threats of violence in other settings.

Many of the boys at East Side report being treated differently "all the time" because they are male. In a primarily African American community in which police harass boys more than girls, it is gender that gives meaning to this experience: it is gender that separates the boys from their female African American peers for this treatment. Gender is inscribed on the body differently for Black men than for White men. The Black male body has a particular meaning to White society that puts young Black males in a different position to structures of authority. This relationship between the Black male body and society is further influenced by the neighborhood context, which affects local processes and shifts the boys' social positioning.[39] It has been suggested that the positioning of minority men within the structure of hegemonic masculinities can lead to identities that emphasize violence and sexual prowess as ways to gain safety and respect.[40] Boys at East Side credit staff, and Charles's discussion group in particular, with helping them see that it is "tough enough being a Black man in America." This encourages them to resist the stereotypical images of masculinity they see in the media and on the streets.

The club also serves as a site of reconstruction of gender norms. Youth police those norms within the peer group. East Side is not free from gender stereotypes or their negative implications. Girls in particular are caught up in cultural discourses that require them to negotiate identities around sexuality and their physical bodies. Although they talk about their frustrations with rumors and reputations, they also re-create them through their activity and discourse. Girls spread rumors about other girls. They use the club as a barrier between themselves and the girls on the street who are "having babies and whatever." Even inside East Side, where other aspects of gender norms are challenged, the bad-girl/good-girl dichotomy remains.

If youth are to battle such strong cultural narratives, the adults in programs must actively work with them to do so. Whereas East Side staff talk explicitly about race and class issues, attention is not always given to deconstructing gender norms within the club. More explicit attention must be paid to such issues if youth programs are to serve as sites of true resistance to gender norms. It is important for settings that serve adolescents to recognize and support areas of resistance, as well as to monitor and understand areas of reconstruction.

Even in the arenas where East Side does help youth resist gender norms, greater effort is needed. The presence of Cheryl seemed to be the driving force that kept girls' sports alive. Once she left, despite Charles's support of the endeavor, the girls' sports program struggled to regain its initial momentum. Charles felt the tension of trying to support girls' sports activity while not being able to serve as an effective advocate and role model. Although he began coaching the girls' teams after Cheryl's departure, Charles noted that the girls often had to be pushed to really practice and play hard. He expressed a desire for another African American female staff person to take Cheryl's place. Cheryl, too, experienced periodic frustration with the girls' lax attitude toward practice. The simple presence of a female role model in sports is not enough. Active leadership is key in helping girls navigate the gender structure. It must be the culture and climate of settings, over and above programs or activities, that encourage active engagement in resisting gendered social norms and identities.

Conclusion

East Side as a context supports youth by meeting specific developmental needs: the integration of roles, individual validation, a sense of belonging, and a balance of autonomy and support (Figure 8-2).

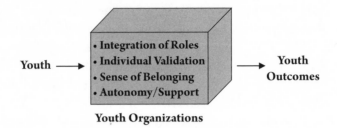

Fig. 8-2. Filling in the Black Box

These tasks are both broader and more specific than what is typically conceptualized in the goal statements of programs and organizations. On the one hand, these needs go beyond the objectives of focused initiatives, such as tutoring or violence-prevention programs. Yet they are narrower than the vague notion of "positive youth development" set forth in the mission statements of many youth-serving organizations. Components associated with successful after-school programs, particularly adult-youth relationships and skill-building, have been linked to programs that promote the more specific 5 C's of PYD.[41] The developmental needs that are often being met through the social processes and relationships within East Side map onto those 5 C's. Support and belonging are captured in connection and caring. Validation, autonomy, and integration of roles, when fostered positively, may produce competence, character, and confidence.

According to Erikson, the key task of adolescence, within which all these processes are enveloped, is the development of an integrated identity. Without resolving our identities during adolescence, he contends, we cannot move into healthy adulthood.[42] I dispute his positioning of intimacy as a need that comes after identity integration, which suggests that individuation occurs outside the bounds of our relationships with others. I do believe that a consolidated identity is an important endpoint of adolescence. I propose that this task occurs within and through our relationships with others. And in doing so, I position relationships as a mechanism for creating settings that promote identity construction, as well as overall positive development.

When well run, the environments of youth organizations meet these adolescent needs. They offer a broader-based approach to youth development, opportunities for inter-age interactions, and wide arrays of relationships and activities. The unique developmental opportunities available in after-school programs should be endorsed and promoted by researchers and practitioners alike. The experiences of the East Side youth, and their descriptions of how their identities have been influenced by their time at East Side, support work that has begun to identify possible benefits of unstructured youth programming to adolescents.[43] Yet this literature has been constrained by a lack of longitudinal research directly linking the intersection of context, process, and positive youth development.[44] To create more effective spaces, researchers have to continue to take on the challenge, directly studying the spaces of after-school programs in terms of the specific developmental tasks that are occurring within them over time.

Scholars must also strive to answer the call for more and better investigations of the outcomes associated with youth organizations. This is not to suggest that I endorse measuring organizational success with stringent measures of outcomes. Rather, I propose that researchers work to develop more effective means of measuring the ecological contexts of organizations in order to assess how well various programs are meeting important developmental needs. Additional work on long-term and specific behavioral outcomes is also needed, yet I would caution against expecting too much. After-school programs are but one environment in youths' lives. They cannot completely counteract the influence of all the other contexts in which adolescent development occurs. They may, therefore, have limited measurable effects in the short run. It has been argued that, because the influence of a year of schooling on academic outcomes is relatively small compared with what we might expect, we cannot presume that after-school programs could make large strides in far fewer hours.[45] Yet the narratives of East Side youth in my study indicate that many teens have internalized their participation in the community of the club, transforming the experience into a part of their identities. The long-term effects of their participation, therefore, may emerge over the years, as relationships and strengths that they develop through the program help them navigate various life challenges.

It is not my intention to romanticize the potential of youth organizations as positive settings for youth. East Side is not universally successful at engaging the teens within its walls, and there are youth who never set foot there in the first place. It takes a well-run organization staffed with competent and committed staff to create a positive space. However positive that space is, it exists as one system within the greater ecology of its members' lives. Some youth at East Side do get pregnant, drink alcohol, or get involved with illicit activities. But in a society in which many other environments provide less than optimal support, East Side supports youth through these incidents and helps bring out their innate competencies at times when they need them most. After-school programs should perhaps be thought of as one of many possible supportive environments. Sara Pedersen, Edward Seidman, and their colleagues have delineated the concept of contextual competence, which considers the resources available to youth in different settings. Their work demonstrates that high levels of engagement in multiple developmental contexts leads to adaptive psychosocial outcomes. They suggest that "more effective interventions likely facilitate youth engagement in multiple prosocial domains, allowing the youth to develop a reserve of diverse skills and to form positive relationships with a greater number of young people and caring adults."[46]

Well-run organizations can serve as sites that add to youths' contextual competence. Effective youth programs cannot fully transcend the challenges posed by their members' outside environments. Yet they can provide settings for prosocial engagement and positive relationships with both peers and adults. For youth who have support elsewhere in their lives, such organizations serve as an additional resource. But many communities in which such programs are situated have few resources for youth. A comprehensive after-school program can provide significant benefits by offering multiple activities, peer relationships, and caring adults under one roof. The voices of the East Side youth suggest that, when East Side is working well, it does just that, allowing for the development of diverse competencies, prosocial skills, and supportive relationships.

It is a social responsibility to continue to work to link theory and practice, to create spaces that nurture youth in constructing positive, holistic identities. Such identities can in turn cultivate a prosocial society that is concerned with its relationships as well as its resources. To build a truly positive society, we must turn away from focusing on individuation as the primary task of adolescence and look toward helping youth negotiate the contested terrain of self and other, group and me. We can take our lead from the three R's of the East Side youth: respect, responsibility, and role models. Future research should look for differences in the prevalence, salience, and meaning of these concepts for adolescents in various contexts and environments. Examining the relational processes of role modeling and self-transformation, which this research suggests are mechanisms through which development occurs, may help us understand how we can implement programs and policies that assist youth in creating prosocial selves.

In this work I demonstrate the importance of contextualizing identity development, embedding the process in its ecology. As such, I call into question universalized models of identity development that don't take into account the processes at work in specific places at specific times. Furthermore, I provide hope for enhancing the identity development process for teens. Identity is relational and contextual. Larger social structures are mediated through the local environment and interpersonal relationships. This means that researchers and policymakers can create environments that provide optimal support to youth.

At East Side, as at a multitude of similar sites across the country, teens like BJ, Lorenzo, Nicole, and John are constructing identities and developing selves. These teenagers live in neighborhoods in which they face multiple challenges to their health and development. As they engage in these settings and with the people in them, they help us see the transformative potential of the interaction of individuals with supportive environments and relationships. BJ confronts us with society's view of her neighborhood, forcing us to look for the beauty beyond the buildings. It may be a revelation to some people that there are birds in the projects. It is researchers' task, and society's responsibility, to see those birds and respond, to tap the full developmental potential of after-school settings and the youth they serve.

After each site visit, I typed up extensive field notes. These notes included a running record of what occurred during the visit, as well as analytical and reflexive notes that recorded my subjective feelings, reactions, and beginning analytic thoughts. I also wrote field notes for all the focus groups and interviews that I conducted. At times, I struggled with the ethics of fieldwork. I developed close relationships with many staff and youth over the years. There were instances when people shared things with me that were deeply personal, and which I was uncomfortable documenting in my field notes. Coming from a feminist perspective on researcher-participant relationships, I could not erase my humanity from my interactions.[2] Thus, my fieldwork was often a negotiation between my desire to paint an accurate, full picture of East Side youths' experiences and my need to respect the privacy and humanity of the people who were sharing their lives with me. I hope that in writing this text, I have respected the teens and staff's dignity and accurately represented their worlds without coopting them.

Five research assistants, four undergraduates and one graduate student, also did fieldwork at East Side from 1999 to 2002. In the first two years, two undergraduates per academic year visited East Side for four hours a week. In the third year, a graduate student visited East Side four hours a week. These site visits sometimes occurred on the same day that I was observing, but often we attended the club on different days. These researchers also took on the role of participant-observers. I used their field notes as well as my own during data analysis.

Data Collection and Analysis

I approached data collection and analysis with specific topics and coding schemes in mind. In reviewing my data I used a variation on the constant comparison method to look for patterns within the themes that I was exploring.[3] This technique involves circling between data collection, analysis, and theory. Data are continually compared to each other, common themes and patterns are uncovered, and future data collection and analysis are conducted with emerging patterns in mind.

Sample

To recruit the seventeen-person interview sample, I first approached youth who had either expressed interest in being part of the project or who I thought would be interesting participants. I also attended a staff meeting at which I explained my project and asked staff to recommend youth for the study. I made clear that I wanted youth who were involved in the club but who varied on other characteristics, such as academic success and involvement, family background, and risky behaviors. During the following weeks I got recommendations from staff. I then approached those youth, introduced myself, and explained the study. In total, five of the seventeen participants were recommended by staff. There were also a number of youth whom I had already recruited who staff said they would have recommended. Twenty-four youth were initially approached about taking part in the study. Seventeen said yes, signed the youth assent forms, and brought back signed parental consent forms. Three youth said yes but never remembered to bring back their consent forms. Three youth declined to be involved in the study, and one was going to be moving and no longer coming to the club.

I did not randomly select youth for this study because I was interested in how the Boys and Girls Club is used as a setting for identity work. Therefore, it was important to have youth who came to the club regularly or who had been coming to the club for a long time. I did not use a control group, as I wanted to uncover common themes among those youth who used the club as a supportive environment. Even within these criteria, my sample may be biased. Although I used staff recommendations in an attempt to recruit youth who were under my radar, I had an easier time recruiting youth with whom I had already established some relationship. This may bias the sample toward more outgoing or friendly youth. However, it may also enhance my findings because I may have elicited more nuanced information due to our established relationships. Staff did tell me that I had some "difficult" members as part of the study.

Observations

As noted, I was a participant-observer at East Side for four years. My field notes, along with those of the five other researchers, comprise the environmental context for the study. I use the field notes to paint a picture of the setting of the club. Because I am interested in the contextual nature of identity, it is important that I have a rich pool of data about the setting on which I am most focused. The field notes also triangulate and illuminate information gathered during the interviews. I went back through the field notes and found examples of the type of activities or situations mentioned by youth in interviews. This gives background to youths' interviews and compares youths' and researchers' views of the club.

The observational data also allows for in-depth case studies. Most of the older youth had attended the club for years. Many of them appear across the four years of field notes. I was able to go back and look at how the youth participated in the club over time. Thus, the field notes help to provide both additional specificity and generality, giving a context to the time-located interviews and photographs.

Focus Groups

In the winter of my third year at East Side I conducted two focus groups, one with youth 12–14 and one with youth 15 and older. The groups ranged from five to seven youth. Some of the youth in the focus groups became part of the interview sample. The data from the focus groups was used to help construct the interview protocol. Each focus group lasted 60 to 90 minutes, was facilitated by myself and a research assistant, and examined youths' experiences of the club as a site for self-construction.

Interviews

In my fourth year at East Side I conducted two semistructured interviews with the seventeen sample youth. The first interview (appendix B) began with open-ended questions about how youth see themselves and what aspects of themselves they most value. Further questions explored youths' feelings about gender and conception of self in relation to other people, their community, and society. The second interview (appendix C) began with discussion of the photographs that the youth took during the time between the two interviews. The second part of the interview expanded on the themes in the first interview. Each interview lasted 45 to 60 minutes, although a few lasted over an hour. Participants were given a gift certificate as compensation for their time after each interview. Interviews were generally conducted in private rooms with only the participant and myself present. A few times an interview could not be completed in one sitting due to time conflicts. In those cases the interview was completed as soon as possible, usually within a couple of days. All seventeen youth completed the first interview. Thirteen of the seventeen youth completed the second interview and a fourteenth completed part of the second interview. Two of those youth had not completed the photography project. With those youth I either skipped the photograph questions or asked them hypothetically.

The open-ended questions in both interviews were developed based on the topics in which I was interested exploring with the youth. I used data from the focus groups and pilot interviews (conducted the prior year), to determine which topics and questions resonated with youth. Based on that information I revised the interviews and developed additional questions to address areas that seemed to merit attention. Many of the questions included probes to elicit additional information. I also followed any interesting leads that emerged. Such "tell me more" techniques emphasize the importance of the interviewee saying how they see things over the interviewer sticking to a protocol.[4]

I drew from Jacqueline Eccles's work on racial socialization in my inclusion of questions about youths' perception and experiences of prejudice.[5] Results from her Racial Socialization Questionnaire suggest that it is not only objective and daily experience of racism but also youths' perception of racism that influences ethnic identity. Thus, I asked about both personal instances of discrimination based on gender, race, and class and perceptions of societal discrimination.

I also drew on the narrative analysis of life stories, as developed by Dan McAdams in the Life Story Interview.[6] The first interview included a question designed to capture a peak experience in a person's life. I use this to explore what types of events youth see as being significant and why. In particular, I was interested in the types of events youth would mention, especially whether they would highlight individual talents, caretaking or relationships with other people, or group involvements.

Photo Projects

To gain knowledge about or understand a particular question the researcher must start from the subject's viewpoint.[7] Photographs give youth the opportunity to literally provide their own view on the topics of inquiry. Photographs can serve as a tool for eliciting more detailed information and as an entry into environments to which I do not otherwise have access. They may be read as a text describing how the adolescent makes meaning of his or her world. Yet they also provide context: images of what the youth sees in daily life.[8] Furthermore, they give youth a more creative and autonomous means for describing themselves.

After youth completed the first interview, they were provided with a disposable camera. I also gave them a sheet of paper that introduced the photography project and explained its goals. I provided youth with instructions on how to use half of the film, asking for pictures of such things as an adult to whom they're close, favorite things in the club, and something that represents what they want to be in the future (appendix D). The rest of the film youth were to use for pictures of anything that they felt would tell me more about who they are. Once youth had finished their film, I collected the cameras and had the film developed. Youth were given a set of the prints and a photo album to take home. Eleven of the seventeen participants completed the project. During the second interview I laid the photographs out on a table and asked the youth to show me which photograph went with each of the assigned pictures, to describe the picture's subject, why she took it, and its meaning. I then had the youth pick out and talk about the five pictures that were most important to him or her. We then discussed any additional photographs. I recognize that what youth told me about the photos and what they took pictures of may have been influenced by my own position as a White, female, adult researcher.[9] I hope that, because the youth took the photos after they had already spoken with me, they were more comfortable with letting me into other parts of their lives. Based on content of the photographs, many of which included pictures of the inside of their homes and bedrooms, I suspect that most of the youth were open with me during the process.

Visual sociologists and anthropologists have argued for the benefits of using photographs in social science research. Photographs allow a segment of reality to be frozen and thus used throughout the research process. Furthermore, photos present the subjective view of the photographer, providing a window into what aspects of an environment he or she picks out as important.[10] Some branches of psychology have looked to photographs as an "instrument of self-recognition," a means of self-exploration.[11] Photographs used within the tradition of visual sociology are meant to make explicit statements about cultural patterns and social structure. Yet the danger of decontextualizing photographs and the importance of remembering that photographs take their meaning from context has also been emphasized.[12] Content analysis of photographs, although linking individual photos to larger theories and eliciting patterns of meaning, may also misrepresent the reality of the image or make false assumptions about the image's representivity or purposefulness.[13]

The practice of photo-elicitation attempts to get around this issue. This technique privileges the research participant's meaning-making of the photographs. It can serve as a useful adjunct to conventional interviews because it allows the photograph to be a basis of discussion rather than relying on interview questions that reflect the interviewer's frame and which the participant may or may not relate to or understand.[14] I expanded the photo-elicitation technique to allow participants not only to describe what photos meant to them but also to actually create the photos we used for the exercise, privileging their view of reality on two fronts.

I understood that what youth photographed would be determined by choice and by limitations on their movements and where they are allowed to take pictures (for safety or institutional reasons). To elicit knowledge of such limitations, I asked youth both about what they did photograph and what they did not. Limitations may themselves also highlight the difference between the adolescents' view of the world and ours.[15] For example, some youth were not able to take pictures of their favorite places because they did not have transportation to get there. Other youth said they did not take a photograph of "something they did not want to be" because "a crackhead wouldn't let me take a picture of him." Some youth took pictures of "crackheads" and gang members without apparent concern for their own safety.

Interactions with Staff and Parents

The staff and parents at East Side were incredibly supportive of and welcoming to me. They provided information about the club as an organization, as well as insights about individual youth. Over the years I had numerous informal conversations with staff and club leaders and with some parents. I also conducted semistructured interviews with some staff, the club director, and the assistant director and attended a parents' meeting at which I asked questions about the role of the club in their children's lives.

After I began to analyze the youths' interview data, I developed questions based on emerging patterns. I then conducted interviews with the staff people who appeared to know individual youth best. Which staff person I chose was based either on youth report of closeness to a particular staff or on my observations of high levels of interaction between a youth and staff person. The interviews with staff, the club director, and the program director focused on the role of the club in individual youths' lives. I also asked about their perceptions of general themes that were emerging across youth, such as the importance of respect and East Side as a site for the development of respect.

Data Analysis

The analytic process for this project was iterative. Qualitative research is a constant interplay of theory, data collection, analysis, and ideas.[16] Throughout the analysis I was drawn back and forth between themes, levels, and forms of data. I examined my notes for emerging themes and used these to inform future observations and interviews.[17] Interview topics were developed from the focus group data and the identity literature. After finishing the first set of interviews, I revised the second interview to ask about certain themes that emerged in youths' responses. As I conducted both sets of interviews, I paid close attention to emerging topics, on which I then probed during subsequent interviews. In addition, I began to focus my field notes more closely on areas that were surfacing as salient in the interview data. Overall, I approached analysis as a combination of revealing and exploding: uncovering themes that existed within the data on the general topic of identity construction and splitting open those issues to examine their meanings within the local context and the larger social realm.

After completion of data collection, I read the transcripts from both sets of interviews for content and themes, exploring continuities and differences in thematic content both within and between youth. I analyzed

the interviews for codes that came from the identity-development literature, as well as codes that came from the youth themselves.[18] I developed
specific coding guidelines and used a second, blind rater to check the reliability of my coding of youths' self-descriptions into individuated and connected words.[19] I reread all four years of field notes from all researchers
(six including myself), compiling a summary table that included notation
of places where major themes from the interview data could be seen in
interactions and events within the field notes. I noted where and when interviewees appeared in the field notes, but I also searched for instances related to the themes in the interviews that did not involve the interviewees.
This helped to ensure that the themes identified in the interview were not
unique to just the youth who participated in the study. To identify patterns within as well as across youth, I wrote narrative summaries of each
of the seventeen participants, compiling all the data from their interviews
and photo projects and any additional focus groups or pilot interviews
with which they were involved.

Throughout these processes, I compared data from across sources (field
notes, interviews, and photos) to search for patterns.[20] In doing so, I considered where and when sources contradicted as well as confirmed each
other. When sources provided triangulation of my findings, I went on to
explore differences across youth. When sources conflicted, I probed the
source of that conflict, examining whether my initial assertion had been
wrong or whether there was another factor that explained the difference.
For example, with John, there was tremendous difference between what he
said in his interview with me, the photos he took, and the records of his
behavior in field notes. Such complexity pushed me toward deeper analysis, requiring constant attention to the way that data were collected as well
as what the data "revealed." Given my focus on how identity is constructed
within relations with others, such consideration of data collection as a site
of knowledge and identity is well aligned with my underlying framework.

From this combination of reading and thinking I drew up outlines of
the major findings that emerged and delved back into the data to explicate
them in writing. As I came to the major themes on which I would focus, I
ensured that these themes were well represented across sources and youth.
Throughout the analytic and writing processes I also ran back and forth to
the library, diving into new pools of literature whenever a novel theme ma-
terialized and pushing my analysis in response to both theory and the data.

■   ■   ■   ■   ■   ■   ■   ■   ■

Appendix B

The Contextual Identity Interview:
Protocol for Interview 1

ID _____

M / F Age: _____ Race/ethnicity (as defined by youth): _____
Grade in school: _____ Age first at club: _____ No. of siblings: _____
Lives with: _____ Live in club neighborhood? Y / N
Pseudonym chosen by youth: _____

I want to start by asking you some questions about who you are and how you see yourself.

1. Tell me about yourself. Describe yourself to me.
2. Do you change at all depending on where you are? For example, are you different at the club than at school or at school than at home? How do you feel about that?
3. Do you *feel* differently at the club than you do at school? At home? School versus home?
4. Do you ever act in a way that you feel is not really who you are? In other words, do you ever change your behavior/dress/speech in

a situation in a way that makes you feel like you are not being yourself?

Follow-up probes:
If yes, what aspects do you change?
If no, do you observe other kids who seem to be different in different situations?
How does that make you feel?
Why are you not like these kids?

5. Are there aspects of yourself that are always the same, even if other things are different?
6. Give me the five words that you think describe you the best.

Follow-up probes:
Tell me a little bit about what these mean to you.
Which of these are the most important to you?
Are there any of these that would be different if I asked you only about how you were at the club? Only at school? Only at home?
Are any of these things that you think are encouraged or appreciated at the Boys and Girls Club?
Do you expect that you will also be these things in the future?

7. Give me five words that describe who you were in the past, when you were younger.

Follow-up probes:
Are any of these things different from who you are today?
Have any of these changed over time?
Why do you think that is?
Do you think that any of these changes are because of your participation in the Boys and Girls club?

8. Give me five words that describe who or what you think you may be in the future.

Follow-up probes:
How did you come to decide on these things?
Is there any particular person who has influenced you to want to be these things?

Is there any particular activity or group that you have been involved
with that has helped influence you to want to be these things?
Has the Boys and Girls Club or any staff here influenced this at all?

9. What are your goals for the future?
10. What are the five things you like best about yourself.

   Follow-up probes:
   Are any of these things that you feel are encouraged or appreciated at
   the Boys and Girls Club?
   Do you have role models that you look up to for any of these things?
   Do you think that you will be/want to be these things in the future?

11. Has anyone ever thought something about you or judged you in
   a way that you think was wrong? Do you ever feel that someone
   doesn't understand who you are and thinks things about you that you
   don't feel are true?

   Follow-up probes:
   Why do you think they made that judgment?
   If you could say something to that person, what would you tell them
   about yourself to change their minds about you?
   Does this ever happen at the Boys and Girls Club? How often? At
   school? How often?

12. You defined your ethnicity as _____. Can you
   think of an experience you have had that helped you understand
   what it means to be a _____ male or female or made you
   think about yourself as _____ ?
13. Describe an event from your life that stands out in your memory as
   being especially important or significant.
14. Can you identify the single person, group of persons, or organiza-
   tion/institution that has or have had the greatest influence on who
   you are? Please describe this person, group, or organization and the
   way in which they have had an impact on you.
15. Have you ever done something that you really didn't want to do to
   make someone else happy or to avoid conflict with other people?
   What did you do? Can you think of an example of a time that you put
   the wants or views of another person or group of people before yours?

Follow-up probes:
If no, can you think of a situation in which you would put another person's wants or desire before your own or do something you really didn't want to do?

Now I want to ask you some questions about the Boys and Girls Club and your participation in it.

16. What do you think are the most important things about the Boys and Girls Club?
17. Some kids have told me that one thing that is important to them about the club is that the people here are like them and that other kids at the club and the staff understand what they go through because they have had similar experiences. Other kids don't feel that way. What about you? If that is true for you, what does that mean to you? How are people here like you, and what types of experiences may be similar? If not, how are they different?
18. Some kids have told me that they felt more like themselves at the club than at school. Other kids don't feel that way. What about you? Why? What about at the club or at home? Is there somewhere else that you feel most like yourself? What does feeling like yourself mean to you?
19. Are there activities at the club that have influenced who you are? What about at school?
20. Have your relationships with staff at the club influenced who you are at all? How?

Follow-up probes:
Has staff helped you think about your goals for the future?

21. Does staff help you feel like you can be yourself in different situations? For example, some kids have told me that they have learned that they can be more street with their friends but not in school and that they have learned where and when they can act a certain way and when that might cause them trouble. Do you feel that is true for you? How has the club influenced you at all in that way? Do you still feel like you are yourself in these different situations, or do you feel like you are putting on an act?

22. Are there any ways in which the club has made you think about being a male/female? (Ask about specific activities at the club if not brought up.)
23. It seems to me that guys tend to use the gym more at the club and play more sports here, while girls often sit on the bleachers and talk. Do you think that this is true? Do girls and boys do the same activities at the club, or do they do different activities? What activities do they do? For those activities that are different, why do you think that is so?
24. Has there ever been an activity that you wanted to try that you felt that you could not do because you are a girl/boy? Why did you think that you could not do it? Did anything change your mind? Could something change your mind? Are there any activities at the club that you would not have done if you hadn't gotten to try it here?
25. How old were you when you first starting coming to the Boys and Girls Club? Have you changed at all since then? How?

    Follow-up probes:
    Has your participation in the club changed at all over this time? How? Why?
    Do you think that you would you be the same person you are today if you didn't come to the club?

Now I want to ask you some questions about some more broad topics.

26. How much do you think that people from your racial/ethnic group face prejudice?
    Not at all   A little   Some   A lot
27. How much do you think that people of your gender face prejudice?
    Not at all   A little   Some   A lot
28. How much do you think that people from your neighborhood face prejudice?
    Not at all   A little   Some   A lot
29. Have you ever had an experience when you felt you were treated differently because of your race or ethnicity? Can you tell me about that? How often does this happen?

Follow-up probe:

If no, do you think any of your friends or relatives have had an experience when they were treated differently because of race or ethnicity? Can you tell me about it?

30. Have you ever had an experience when you felt you were treated differently because you're a boy/girl? Can you tell me about that? How often does this happen?

Follow-up probe:

If no, do you think of any of your friends or relatives have had an experience when they were treated differently because of their gender? Can you tell me about it?

31. Have you ever had an experience when you felt you were treated differently because of the neighborhood you live in? How often does this happen?

Follow-up probe:

If no, do you think of any of your friends or relatives have had an experience when they were treated differently because of the neighborhood they live in? Can you tell me about it?

32. Tell me about somebody you admire (this can be someone you know or someone you don't know). Why do you admire them? What things about them do you admire?
33. The person you just told me about was a male/female. Can you think of a female/male that you admire? What do you admire about him/her?
34. What things or characteristics do you admire in girls? Are any of those things that you think that you are? Would you want to be any of them?
35. What things or characteristics do you admire in boys? Are any of those things that you think that you are? Would you want to be any of them?
36. Are there things about our society that you don't like? What are they? What do you think that you could do to change them?

■ ■ ■ ■ ■ ■ ■ ■ ■

Appendix C

The Contextual Identity Interview:
Protocol for Interview 2

ID _____

Let's begin by talking about the pictures that you took. Choose the five pictures here that are the most important to you and that you think tell the most about who you are.

1. Tell me about each of these pictures. What are they of? Why did you take this picture? How does it tell about who you are?

   (More in-depth probing of answers, why they framed the picture as they did, what was excluded, what were they doing when they took the picture.)

2. Tell me about some of the other pictures. Why did you take them? What do they mean to you? How do they describe who you are?

   (More in-depth probing of answers, why they framed the picture as they did, what was excluded, what were they doing when they took the picture.)

3. Are there things or places or people that you wanted to photograph but couldn't or didn't? What are they? Why did you want to? Why didn't you?

Now I want to ask you a few more general questions about yourself.

4. Can you think of some adults who you look at as people who you would like to be like? Why do you want to be like those people?
5. What about other kids or teenagers? Are there kids or teens that you would like to be like? Why?
6. Are there adults who you see as examples of things that you do not want to be? Why?
7. Are there kids or teenagers that you see as examples of things that you do not want to be? Why?
8. What is your definition of success?
9. What is your definition of a successful man?
10. What is your definition of a successful woman?
11. Where is your favorite place to be? Why?
12. Who are your favorite people to be with? Why?
13. What is your favorite thing to do? Why?
14. What are some things that make you feel good?
15. What are some things that make you feel bad?
16. Gangs and violence seem to be pretty prevalent around here. Have they affected who you are in any way?
17. Are there any things that make you feel good or bad about yourself in the media, like in TV shows, music, movies, or magazines? Does the media influence who you are or who you want to be in any way? What about other kids?
18. What does it mean to be feminine? Are you feminine? Do you want to be feminine?
19. What does it mean to be masculine? Are you masculine? Do you want to be masculine?
20. Are most of your friends boys or girls? Why?
21. Do you prefer to spend time with boys or girls? Why?

Follow-up probes:
Is this true no matter where you are (club, neighborhood, school, etc)? Why/Why not?

22. If I asked your friends at the club to describe you, what do you think they would say? What about your friends at school? What about your family? What about club staff?

   Follow-up probes:
   What types of things would people say that are the same?
   What types of things would they say that are different?
   Probe similarities and differences that emerge—why?
   Are you ever that with _____?

23. Do you have different groups of friends who you hang out with? What makes the groups different? In what ways do you feel that you are similar to each group of friends? In what ways do you think that you are different from each group of friends? How do you feel about this?

24. Is there any group that you consider yourself part of? This could be either a group that you are a member of because you participate in it, like a sports team or the Boys and Girls Club or a church group, or a larger group that you are a member of based on your ethnicity, gender, etc. (e.g., I consider myself as part of a larger category of women and Jews). How are you similar and different from other people in this group?

   Follow-up probes:
   When you achieve something, do you ever feel as if you are making other members of the group proud or being a good representative of the group?
   When other people from the group achieve something, do you ever feel proud as a member of the group?
   Do you ever do things specifically for the good of the group?

25. Now think about your best friend. How are you similar and different from your best friend?

   Follow-up probes:
   When you achieve something, do you ever feel as if you are making your best friend proud?
   When your best friend achieves something, do you ever feel proud?
   Do you ever do things specifically for the good of your best friend?

■   ■   ■   ■   ■   ■   ■   ■   ■

Appendix D

Photography Project

Express Yourself!

Show me who you are in pictures

I am giving you this camera to take photographs to help you tell me more about yourself. I would like you to take this camera out with you for a few days and take pictures with it. There are a few things that I want you take pictures of, but the rest is up to you. Please take:

- **5 pictures inside the Boys and Girls Club.** These could be kids or staff who you like, your favorite places in the club, and/or activities that you enjoy or that are important to you.
- **1 picture of an adult who you are close to.**
- **1 picture of a friend who you are close to.**
- **1 picture of something that represents what you would like to be in the future.**
- **1 picture of something that represents what you do not want to be in the future.**
- **1 picture of a place that is important to you (outside the Boys and Girls Club).**

- **1 picture of something you enjoy doing.**
- **1 picture of a group of people who are important to you.**
- **1 picture of somewhere you like to spend time alone.**

You can take pictures of more than one of each of these things if you want. Please use the rest of the pictures to show anything else that is important (people, places, activities, objects, anything that you think helps tell the story of you and your life). Try to take photographs in **all different places, over a number of days**. Please *don't use up all your photos in one place, at one time, or on one thing* just because you are having fun. I want to see all of the different things that are important to you! Think of this as a picture story that shows who you are.

Some quick questions to get you started thinking about your photographs:

- Who are the important people in your life?
- What are your favorite activities?
- What are your favorite places to be with friends? With family? By yourself?
- What are your talents and skills?

I will come back on _____ to pick up your finished roll of film and take it to be developed. After that we will talk about your photographs and you can tell me what they mean to you and how they help explain who you are. I will give you a scrapbook in which you can put your photos to bring home with you. Thanks for your help! Have fun taking pictures!

Appendix E

Coding Guidelines for Individuated versus Connected Self-Descriptors

Each youth responded to the question "Give me the five words that you think describe you the best." Each of the words that the youth provided are to be coded as either "Individual" or "Connected." Individual words describe a trait that is an individual characteristic, independent of the youth's connections with other people. Connected words refer to the youth's relationships with others. The words are coded in the context of the youth's descriptions of what the words mean to them. Therefore, there are some words that may be coded in different ways for different youth, depending on how the youth describes the meaning of that word. Each word that a youth gives gets its own code, independent of the other codes for that youth.

Individuated

Individual self-descriptors are those words that describe a particular trait of the individual independent of the individual's interpersonal relationships with other people. Such characteristics do not require the presence (physical or emotional) of other people for existence.

A trait that refers to the youth in relation to a rank ordering of people is still individual if the characteristic itself does not specifically have to do with those relationships. For example, a youth saying that she is smart and talking about that in terms of saying she is the "smartest in my class" is an individual trait. Although she provides the reference point of her class, the actual characteristic "smart" does not rely on those other people for its meaning or existence.

Thus, individuated words may contain an element of social comparison and yet retain their individuated core nature. This may occur in a situation such as the above, when a trait is rank ordered. It may also occur in a situation in which an individual trait leads to participation in a group activity, such as being athletic or a good actor. In such cases, the individual may consider themselves talented in this trait *in comparison with other people*—for example, on their team or in their acting troupe. Whereas part of the trait as enacted may rely on the presence of other people (i.e., a basketball player playing on a team, an actor as part of the cast of a play) the trait itself reflects *individual* talent, which at its core is independent of other people. Thus, Michael Jordan is an individually talented basketball player who can display that talent either in the context of team playing or as a solo demonstration.

Similarly, youth mentioning that people say that they are a particular thing does not necessarily make it a connected word. The word may still be individual if it refers to an individual talent or skill or trait even if that talent/skill/trait is recognized or appreciated by other people or takes place in a group setting (i.e., a sports team or a dance troupe). Thus, an individual trait can stand on its own and does not require interpersonal relations for its existence.

Examples of Individuated Words:

Intelligent. I think I am intelligent because I do well in school and all my teachers say I am very smart. It is important to be intelligent to succeed.

Athletic. I am very talented at sports.

Silly. I like fooling around and being silly. I'm just a silly person.

Connected

Connected self-descriptors are those words that describe a particular trait of the individual that exists in relation to other people. These may be interpersonal relationships or group relationships (i.e., "caring" refers to a personal relationship, whereas "activist" refers to a connection with a larger group of people). Such characteristics may refer directly to relationships (i.e., family man) or may refer to ways of interacting with other people (i.e., respectful). Connected words give a sense of the youth linked to and in interpersonal relationship with others. A connected word is not meaningful outside of the context of relationships with other people.

Social comparison, although theoretically related to connectedness, is not synonymous with it. Connectedness, as used herein, refers to how one sees oneself *in relation with,* rather than *in contrast to,* others. While social comparison implies a notion of oneself within a social group, it still refers to a sense of oneself as an individual within and distinguished from the group. Social comparison is closer to the construction of self in relation to the "Other." Connected traits, however, relate to the actual relationship between an individual and others. The difference between describing oneself as "athletic" versus as "a good sportsman" highlights this difference. Being an athlete may include having good sportsmanship toward others, but it may not. Rather, being a good athlete more specifically refers to having the skills associated with being good at a number of sports. It may be that one is a good athlete in reference to other people who are not. But even without the mental or physical presence of those others, the individual is still a good athlete because he or she can enact that athleticism without other people present (in solo practice, for example). Being a good sportsman, in contrast, specifically refers to how one interacts with other athletes.

The cut off for individual versus connected is that a connected trait *requires* a relationship to another person in order to exist and have meaning. Again, some words may be defined as connected based not on the word itself but on the description of its meaning as provided by the youth.

Examples of Connected Words:

Responsible. I am responsible, and people can count on me to do what is required.

Generous. I always share things with people, and I like to help people however I can. I always give my friends presents and share candy and stuff.

Silly. I like to make people laugh. My friends say that they like to be around me because I am so silly and it makes them happy to be with me when I am silly.

Notes

Notes to Chapter 1

1. Niobe Way has been a major exception to this rule. Her studies of urban boys' friendships, cited throughout this book, have begun to turn attention to the important role of relationships in the lives of boys. Her volume of work on boys lives, coedited with Judy Chu, features research that focuses on the contextual and relational nature of boys' development (Way & Chu, 2004b).

2. The names of all organizations, locations, and individuals in this work, with the exception of my own, have been changed to protect the identities of the participants. With one exception, the youth chose their own pseudonyms (one girl could not come up with a name so I chose one for her). I also changed the pseudonyms of two youth who had selected names of other East Side club members.

3. Bronfenbrenner, 1979.

4. Weis & Fine, 2000.

5. Strauch, 2003.

6. In the mid-20th century, Erik Erikson (1959, 1968) developed stages of identity development based on Freud's psychosexual stages. Adolescence was defined as the time period in which issues of identity come to the fore, with the main developmental task of adolescence being the consolidation of identity.

7. Erikson, 1959; Harter, 1990, 1999; Harter, Bresnick, Bouchey, & Whitesell, 1997.

8. Markus & Nurius, 1986; Oyserman & Marius, 1990a, 1990b.

9. Cooley, 1902; Erikson, 1959; James, 1890; Marcia, 1980; Mead, 1934.

10. Anderson & Snow, 2001; Blumer, 1969; Bottero & Irwin, 2003; Denzin,

2001; Hollander & Howard, 2000; B. B. Lal, 1995; Snow, 2001; Stryker, 1980, 1987.

11. Tajfel, 2001; Tajfel & Turner, 1986; Tarrant et al., 2001.

12. L. Bloom, 1996; Bruner, 1990; Gergen, 1991; Weigert & Gecas, 2005.

13. Cote, 2006.

14. W. E. Cross, 1991; W. E. Cross Jr. & Fhagen-Smith, 1996; Phinney, 1989; Phinney & Rosenthal, 1992; Phinney & Tarver, 1988.

15. For example: D. DuBois, Burk-Braxton, Swenson, Tevendale, & Hardesty, 2002; French, Seidman, Allen, & Aber, 2000; Oyserman & Harrison, 1998; Scott, 2003; C. A. Wong, Eccles, & Sameroff, 2003; Yoder, 2000.

16. Nasir & Saxe, 2003.

17. For example: J. Bloom, 2007; Gosa & Alexander, 2007; Noguera, 2003; O'Connor, 1999.

18. For example: Lee, 2004; Lopez & Lechuga, 2007; Oboler, 2002; Spencer, Fegley, Harpalani, & Seaton, 2004; Stevenson, 2004; Ward, 2007.

19. Schwartz, 2005, p. 296.

20. For examples and discussion of the image of the urban teen in social science research, see Leadbeater, 2007; Taylor, Smith, & Taylor, 2007; Way, 2007.

21. Fine & Weis, 1998.

22. Adams & Marshall, 1996, p. 437.

23. L. Bloom, 1996; Stewart, 1994.

24. W. E. B. DuBois, 1903.

25. Bruner, 1990; Gergen, 1991.

26. The "looking glass self" is a term created by Charles H. Cooley to describe the ways in which we incorporate others' views of us into our own self-concepts (Cooley, 1902). I should note here that I use quotation marks within this volume in three specific ways: (1) to indicate the language of the participants, (2) to signify that I am using a specific term coined by another scholar, and (3) to signify that I am using a linguistic term in line with its popular meaning, although I may be uncomfortable with that meaning. For example, I may put "at-risk" in quotes because, while it is a linguistic shorthand that is recognizable to readers, it has connotations of individual level traits which do not reflect the fact that it is environmental contexts that often place youth at risk.

27. Lerner, 2002; Rogoff, 2003.

28. Lerner, 2002.

29. The recent emphasis on the interaction between humans and their contexts in the developmental literature harks back to evolutionism and symbolic interactionism, which view human behavior as a process involving the interactions of humans and our social and natural environments (Reynolds, 2003b).

30. Calculated based on 2004 data from the Annual Demographic Survey, March Supplement on youth ages 12–18 living below 100% of the poverty line (http://pubdb3.census.gov/macro/032005/pov/new34_100_01.htm).

31. Bishaw, 2005.

32. Gosa & Alexander, 2007; Roderick, 2003; Taylor et al., 2007; Western, 2006.

33. Coll et al., 1996; Greene, Way, & Pahl, 2006; S. Quintana, 2004; Rosenbloom & Way, 2004; C. A. Wong et al., 2003.

34. J. Bloom, 2007.

35. Bottero & Irwin, 2003; Callero, 2003; Schwalbe et al., 2000.

36. Galletta & Cross, 2007; Ogbu, 1988.

37. Fine & Weis, 1998; Heath & McLaughlin, 1993a; Leadbeater & Way, 1996; McLaughlin, 1993; Spencer, Dupree, & Hartmann, 1997; Spencer & Markstrom-Adams, 1990; Way, 1998; Weis & Fine, 2000.

38. Gilligan, 1982; J. B. Miller, 1976, 1990.

39. S. E. Cross & Madson, 1997; Gabriel & Gardner, 1999; Gardner, Gabriel, & Lee, 1999; Larson & Wilson, 2004; Markus & Kitayama, 1994; Singelis, 1994; Triandis, 1989.

40. Chu, 2004; Way, 2004; Way & Chu, 2004a.

41. Ghosh, Mickelson, & Anyon, 2007.

42. Throughout the book I use "others" with a lowercase "o" to indicate specific people with whom we have interpersonal relationships. I use "Other" with a capital "O" to denote the social images we create to help define our own sense of self in opposition to that which we are not.

43. I define and explain this concept in full in chapter 4.

44. L. Bloom, 1998; Brunskell, 1998; R. Campbell & Wasco, 2000; Cosgrove & McHugh, 2000; Fine, 1992; Harding, 1987; Mies, 1983; Olesen, 1994; D. Smith, 1999; Stack, 1996; Stewart, 1994.

45. Fay, 1975; Lazar, 1998.

46. Helfenbein, 2006.

47. The Generalized Other is Mead's conception of the way in which we carry with us the viewpoints of other people. As children learn to see things, including themselves, from other people's perspectives they eventually internalize this process and come to be able to see themselves from the points of view of groups of others. This internalized concept is the Generalized Other (G. H. Mead, 1934). See also Bronfenbrenner, 1979.

48. Beall, 1993; P. Berger & Luckmann, 1966; Brunious, 1998.

49. Oyserman & Markus, 1998.

50. Augoustinos, 1998.

51. Butler, 1990; Lorber, 1994; Okin, 1998; C. West & Zimmerman, 1981.

52. Erikson, 1968, p. 42.

53. Cote, 2006.

54. Chu, 2004; Stevenson, 2004; Tolman, Spencer, Harmon, Rosen-Reynoso, & Striepe, 2004; Walker, 2004.

55. Fine & Weis, 1998.

56. Branch, 1999; Clark, 1992; J. Eccles et al., 1993; Flannery, Huff, & Manos, 1998; Li et al., 2002; Spergel, 1992; Vigil, 1988, 2003; Wood et al., 1997.

57. Burton, Allison, & Obeidallah, 1995; Burton, Obeidallah, & Allison, 1996;

Harter, 1990; Harter et al., 1997; Heath & McLaughlin, 1993a, 1993b; McLaughlin, 1993; Pastor, McCormick, & Fine, 1996; Ward, 1996.

58. Bumbarger & Greenberg, 2002; Catalano, Berglund, Ryan, Lonczak, & Hawkins, 2002.

59. Hamilton, Hamilton, & Pittman, 2004; Lerner, Almerigi, Theokas, & Lerner, 2005; Lerner, Lerner et al., 2005; Lerner, Phelps, Alberts, Forman, & Christiansen, 2007.

60. P. Berger & Luckmann, 1966; Brunious, 1998; Filmer, Jenks, Seale, & Walsh, 1998; Sabo, Miller, Farrell, Barnes, & Melnick, 1998; D. Smith, 1987, 1999.

61. Coffey & Atkinson, 1996.

62. Kuchment, 2004.

63. Chu, 2004; Way, 1998, 2004; Way & Chu, 2004a.

64. W. E. Cross & Strauss, 1998; J. Eccles, 2001; Oyserman, 1999; Oyserman, Gant, & Ager, 1995; Oyserman, Kemmelmeier, Fryberg, Brosh, & Hart-Johnson, 2003; Phinney, 1989; Phinney & Tarver, 1988.

65. For example: Ghosh et al., 2007; Gosa & Alexander, 2007; Noguera, 2004; O'Connor, 2003.

66. Nasir & Saxe, 2003.

67. Helfenbein, 2006.

68. Beall, 1993.

69. Lee, 2004; Luttrell, 2003; Noguera, 2003; Spencer et al., 2004; Stevenson, 2004; Ward, 2007.

70. John's story provides an excellent opportunity for considering interview data on two levels, that of what is said and that of how it is said. John's presentation of self in his interviews, as well as in his club activities as captured in field notes, provides a text for analysis of the construction of gender as much as, if not more than, his own verbal narrative of the subject.

71. Hirsch, 2005.

72. For reviews, see Durlak & Weissberg, 2007; Lauer et al., 2006.

73. Boys and Girls Clubs of America website (http://www.bgca.org/whoweare/mission.asp).

74. Deuces and Kings, short for Latin Kings, are two local gangs.

75. This is discussed in detail in chapter 3.

76. When I describe a youth's race or ethnicity in the text, I use the word(s) he or she chose to describe himself or herself. Thus, I go back and forth between Black and African American, depending on the youth.

77. Miles & Huberman, 1994.

78. Institutional ethnography is one such practice, arising from the sociological tradition. Institutional ethnography uses individual experience as an entry point into the social relations of institutions and societies, which are lost in research that is abstracted from daily life (M. L. Campbell, 1998; DeVault, 1995; Grahame, 1998; D. Smith, 1987, 1999). Generalizability comes not from assuming universal experience but from the linking of micro experience to the macro relations that organize

social settings (DeVault, 1995). Although I did not conduct a formal institutional ethnography, I used the ideas driving this methodology to consider the links between the micro world of the club and macro society in the lives of the youth. In terms of identity theory, symbolic interactionism and personal expressiveness theory both influenced my work. The former posits that people act based on the meaning that we give to things, that such meanings arise from social interactions between people, and that meanings are modified and used through a process of interpretation on the part of the individual (Blumer, 1969). The latter posits that activities provide a forum for self-expression, self-discovery, and self-actualization in every day life (Waterman, 1990, 1993).

79. M. L. Campbell, 1998; Noblit & Hare, 1988; Olesen, 1994, 2005.
80. Cook & Fonow, 1990; Mies, 1983; D. Wolf, 1996.
81. R. Campbell & Wasco, 2000; DeVault, 1995; Katz, 1996; Ladner, 1971.
82. Deutsch, 2004.
83. Dill, 1987; Fine, 1992; Harding, 1987; Marcus, 1986.
84. L. Bloom, 1998; J. Lal, 1996; Williams, 1996; D. Wolf, 1996.
85. Coll et al., 1996.

Notes to Chapter 2

Parts of this chapter were previously published in Deutsch (2005), which uses the framework of moral identity development to examine the Boys and Girls Club as a site for the construction of prosocial selves.

1. G. S. Hall, 1905.
2. Lesko, 2001.
3. Erikson, 1959, 1968.
4. Adams & Marshall, 1996; Erikson, 1959, 1968; Harter, 1999; Kroger, 1989; Lavoie, 1994.
5. Harter, 1990; Harter, Bresnick, Bouchey, & Whitesell, 1997; Howarth, 2002; Markus & Nurius, 1986.
6. Burton, Obeidallah, & Allison, 1996; Howarth, 2002.
7. Steinberg, 1990.
8. Larson & Wilson, 2004.
9. Burton, Allison, & Obeidallah, 1995; Catalano, Berglund, Ryan, Lonczak, & Hawkins, 2002; Dimitriadis, 2001; Halpern, Barker, & Mollard, 2000; Harter, 1999; Heath & McLaughlin, 1993a, 1993b; McLaughlin, 1993; McLaughlin, Irby, & Langman, 1994; National Research Council & Institute of Medicine, 2002.
10. Adams & Marshall, 1996; Lykes, 1985.
11. Donne, 1624.
12. Lerner, Brentano, Dowling, & Anderson, 2002; Newman & Newman, 2001.
13. Cooley, 1902; James, 1890; G. H. Mead, 1934.
14. Erikson, 1959, 1968.
15. Spencer & Markstrom-Adams, 1990.

16. Gergen, 1991; Rattansi & Phoenix, 2005. For a discussion of youth identity within the fluid boundaries of modern-day Europe, see Rattansi and Phoenix.

17. Larson & Wilson, 2004.

18. Adams & Marshall, 1996; Erikson, 1959, 1968; Flum & Lavi-Yudelevitch, 2002; Harter, 1999; James, 1890; Kroger, 1989; Lavoie, 1994; Lesko, 2001; Lykes, 1985; Steinberg, 1990.

19. A sample set of self-descriptions was given to a second coder for a reliability check. Kappas for both individuated and connected words were .88 to .89.

20. All words were coded within the context of the individual participant's descriptions of what the words mean to him or her. See appendix E for coding guidelines.

21. S. E. Cross & Madson, 1997; Gilligan, 1982; Lykes, 1985; Madson & Trafimow, 2001; Marcia, 1980; J. B. Miller, 1976, 1990.

22. Gilligan, 1982.

23. Tice & Baumeister, 2001.

24. Singelis, 1994.

25. S. E. Cross & Madson, 1997; Tice & Baumeister, 2001.

26. di Leonardo, 1999.

27. Adamson, Hartman, & Lyxell, 1999; Hirsch, Mickus, & Boerger, 2002; Hirsch et al., 2000; Pagano, 2001; Roffman, 2001.

28. Ferguson, 2000; Gregory, Nygreen, & Moran, 2006.

29. Brown, Way, & Duff, 1999; D. DuBois & Hirsch, 1990; Loder & Hirsch, 2003; Way, 1996, 1998.

30. Larson & Wilson, 2004.

31. D. DuBois & Hirsch, 1990.

32. Flum & Lavi-Yudelevitch, 2002.

33. Debats, 1999.

34. Deutsch, 2005; Larson, Wilson, Brown, Furstenberg, & Verma, 2002; Nasir & Kirshner, 2003; Reimer, 2003.

35. Catalano et al., 2002; Goldsmith, Arbreton, & Bradshaw, 2004.

36. Aron & McLaughlin-Volpe, 2001; Sedikides & Brewer, 2001; Tice & Baumeister, 2001.

37. Ryan & Deci, 2000; Ryan, Deci, & Grolnick, 1995.

38. Chu, 2004; Way, 2004.

39. Way, 1998, 2004; Way & Chen, 2000.

40. Josselson, 1989, 1992, 1994.

41. Barker, 1998; Howarth, 2002; Spencer, 2003; Tajfel, 2001; Tarrant et al., 2001.

42. Newman & Newman, 2001; Stevens, 1997.

43. Damon, Menon, & Bronk, 2003; Hart, Atkins, & Ford, 1998; Nasir & Kirshner, 2003; Reimer, 2003; Sherrod, Flanagan, & Youniss, 2002; Youniss, McLellan, & Yates, 1997; Youniss & Yates, 1999.

44. Damon, 1998, p. 623.

45. Chu, 2004; Cunningham & Meunier, 2004; Reichert, Stoudt, & Kuriloff, 2006; Tolman, Spencer, Harmon, Rosen-Reynoso, & Striepe, 2004.

46. Lawrence-Lightfoot, 2000.

47. DeFrancisco & Chatham-Carpenter, 2000.

48. Britt, 1999; Strausberg, 2003; Worrill, 2001.

49. Dimitriadis, 2001; Hemmings, 2002; Stevens, 1997.

50. Bourgois, 1995; Bowman, 1995; Burton et al., 1995; Hemmings, 2002; Seaton, 2004.

51. Britt, 1999; DeFrancisco & Chatham-Carpenter, 2000; Lawrence-Lightfoot, 2000.

52. When text is italicized within brackets in an excerpt from field notes, it indicates analytical notes written by the researcher at the time the field notes were written. When text is italicized within brackets within a quote from a youth, it represents a question posed by the researcher during the interview. Nonitalicized text in brackets indicates that I modified the original quote to clarify its meaning.

53. Damon, 1998.

54. Ansah, 1998; Chideya, 1998.

55. Reichert et al., 2006.

56. Aspy, Roebuck, & Black, 1972.

57. Bryk & Schneider, 2002; Gregory et al., 2006.

58. Lopez & Lechuga, 2007. The issue of the distinctiveness of East Side as a setting for mutual respect, especially in contrast to school, is discussed in more detail in later chapters.

59. Catalano et al., 2002.

60. Britt, 1999; "A call for self-respect," 1999.

61. Aspy et al., 1972; Britt, 1999; Lawrence-Lightfoot, 2000.

62. Lawrence-Lightfoot, 2000.

63. Blau & Stearns, 2002.

64. Strausberg, 2003.

65. DeFrancisco & Chatham-Carpenter, 2000; Flum & Lavi-Yudelevitch, 2002.

66. Larson & Wilson, 2004.

67. Catalano et al., 2002; Goldsmith et al., 2004; Greenberg et al., 2003.

68. Britt, 1999; Stevens, 1997.

69. For many youth, East Side served as a site for self "transformation." A number of youth talked about being "bad" before coming to the club and developing positive and prosocial traits, becoming "good," through their experiences at East Side. This is discussed in depth in the case study of Lorenzo (chapter 5). I have also written about this elsewhere, in considering the link between youth development organizations, the nurturance of prosocial selves, and moral development (Deutsch, 2005).

70. McAdams & Bowman, 2001; McAdams, Diamond, de St. Aubin, & Mansfield, 1997; Rappaport, 1995, 2000.

71. Recent research on positive youth development programs suggests that

fostering prosocial norms and providing opportunities and recognition for prosocial behavior are features of positive youth development programs (Catalano et al., 2002; Goldsmith et al., 2004).

72. Folbre, 2001.

Notes to Chapter 3

This chapter is a modified version of a previously published work. The citation of the original is N. L. Deutsch (2007), "From island to archipelago: Narratives of relatedness in an urban youth organization," in R. Josselson, A. Lieblich, and D. P. McAdams (Eds.), The meaning of others: Narrative studies of relationships (pp. 75–91), Washington, D.C.: American Psychological Association. Copyright 2007 by the American Psychological Association. Reprinted with permission. That chapter considers Lorenzo's story through the framework of Josselson's theory of relatedness.

1. Fordham, 1996; Myers, 1998; Steele, 1997; Steele & Aronson, 1995.

2. Gosa & Alexander, 2007; Noguera, 2003; Roderick, 2003; Spencer, Fegley, Harpalani, & Seaton, 2004.

3. Fashola, 2003; Noguera, 2003.

4. Bryk & Schneider, 2002.

5. For explorations of the interconnections between societal images of African American males, trust and support between teachers and Black male students, the discipline gap, and academic achievement, see Fashola, 2003; Ferguson, 2000; Gregory, Nygreen, & Moran, 2006; Noguera, 2003.

6. Roderick, 2003; Spencer et al., 2004.

7. Gee, 1996.

8. W. E. Cross & Strauss, 1998; Doss & Gross, 1994; Koch, Gross, & Kolts, 2001.

9. Dimitriadis, 2001; Halpern, Barker, & Mollard, 2000; McLaughlin, Irby, & Langman, 1994.

10. Catalano, Berglund, Ryan, Lonczak, & Hawkins, 2002; Goldsmith, Arbreton, & Bradshaw, 2004.

11. Greenberg et al., 2003.

12. Hirsch, 2005.

13. Hirsch, 2005.

14. Fine & Weis, 1998; O'Connor, 1999.

15. Western, 2006.

16. Roderick, 2003.

17. Camino & Zeldin, 2002; Larson, Wilson, Brown, Furstenberg, & Verma, 2002; Maccoby, 1998.

18. McAdams & Bowman, 2001; McAdams, Diamond, de St. Aubin, & Mansfield, 1997.

19. Baumeister & Newman, 1994; McAdams & Bowman, 2001.

20. Grotevant & Cooper, 1998; Steinberg, 1990.
21. Josselson, 1994.
22. Chu, 2004; Way, 1998, 2004.

Notes to Chapter 4

1. Tatum (1997) has discussed this with relation to African American adolescent identity. Yet the idea has roots in the early self-theories of symbolic interactionism (Blumer, 1969; Cooley, 1902; James, 1890; G. H. Mead, 1934; Reynolds, 2003a).

2. This idea has been widely discussed in fields including anthropology, cultural studies, and African American and gender studies. Early and well-known explorations include Simone de Beauvoir's (1952) characterization of woman as "other" to man's "self," Edward Said's (1978) explication of how colonizing nations constructed themselves in opposition to the Eastern "Other," and W. E. B. DuBois's (1940) assertion that the White European world rests on the idea of a racial other. See also Kenny, 2000.

3. Fanon, 1967; Said, 1978; Smedley, 1998; Stoler, 1997.

4. Ann Arnett Ferguson's book *Bad Boys* (2000) has been instrumental in illustrating how media images of Black males have worked themselves into the national psyche in a way that influences our individual interactions with Black males in local settings.

5. Haymes, 1995; hooks, 1990.

6. I consider axes of power to be the categories that allow access to power within any given society. In contemporary America these include race, socioeconomic class, gender, and sexuality. Within this chapter I am particularly focused on race and social class.

7. Rosenthal, 2001; Tajfel, 2001; Tajfel & Turner, 1986.

8. Celious & Oyserman, 2001; Diamond & Hartsock, 1998; Pringle & Watson, 1998; Sapiro, 1998.

9. Tajfel, 2001; Tajfel & Turner, 1986.

10. Cameron, 2004; De Vries, 2003; McCoy & Major, 2003; Tarrant et al., 2001; Verkuyten, 2005.

11. Frable, 1997.

12. Negy, Shreve, Jensen, & Uddin, 2003.

13. W. E. Cross, 1991, 2004; Phinney, 1989; Phinney & Tarver, 1988; Rotheram-Borus & Wyche, 1994; Spencer, 2003; Spencer & Markstrom-Adams, 1990.

14. Tatum, 1997.

15. Coll et al., 1996; S. M. Quintana & Segura-Herrera, 2003; Rosenbloom & Way, 2004; Steele, 1997; C. A. Wong, Eccles, & Sameroff, 2003.

16. D. DuBois, Burk-Braxton, Swenson, Tevendale, & Hardesty, 2002; French, Seidman, Allen, & Aber, 2000; Oyserman & Harrison, 1998; Scott, 2003; C. A. Wong et al., 2003; Yoder, 2000.

17. Phillips & Pittman, 2003.

18. Shorter-Gooden & Washington, 1996; Waters, 1996.

19. Gosa & Alexander, 2007.

20. J. Bloom, 2007; Cole & Omari, 2003; O'Connor, 1999, 2003.

21. Bottero & Irwin, 2003.

22. Fordham & Ogbu, 1986; Ogbu, 1988.

23. C. A. Wong et al., 2003.

24. Herman, 2004.

25. Coll et al., 1996.

26. Luttrell, 2003; Villenas, 2001.

27. C. A. Wong et al., 2003.

28. I thank Wendy Luttrell for providing me with the notion of the social marking of boys' bodies. Her comments on a paper investigating the construction of gender helped point me to the idea of boys' bodies as being read by others in similar ways to how girls' bodies are discussed as being culturally enscripted.

29. Howarth, 2002.

30. P. Berger & Luckmann, 1966; S. Hall, 1989.

31. Bronfenbrenner, 1979; Spencer & Markstrom-Adams, 1990.

32. Hemmings, 2000; Spencer & Markstrom-Adams, 1990.

33. S. Hall, 1989.

34. Gee & Crawford, 1998; Heilman, 1998.

35. Eidelman & Biernat, 2003; Howarth, 2002.

36. "Gangbanger" is a term common in the city where East Side is located. It is used by teens to describe an active gang member.

37. Halpern, Barker, and Mollard, 2000.

38. Signithia Fordham (1996), for example, found that high-achieving African American males rated gender as more important than race in their own self-definitions. This differed from their low-achieving male peers and from both high-achieving and low-achieving females.

39. S. Hall, 1989. This idea gained support and began to garner national attention in late 2007 when the Pew Research Center released a report which found that 37% of Blacks felt that African Americans were no longer a single race (Pew, 2007).

40. Haymes, 1995.

41. Olsen, 1996; Tolman, 1996; Way, 1998.

42. Haymes, 1995.

43. Fordham (1996), for example, found this phenomenon among some high-achieving Black students who distanced themselves from their low-income Black peers and even blamed low-income Blacks for their conditions.

44. Deutsch & Hirsch, 2002; Fine, Weis, Centrie, & Roberts, 2000.

45. W. E. Cross & Strauss, 1998; hooks, 1990; Tatum, 1997.

46. J. Hall, 2001; Heath & McLaughlin, 1993b; Helfenbein, 2006.

47. Rappaport, 1995, 2000.

48. Adamson, Hartman, & Lyxell, 1999; Fine, 1994.
49. Howarth, 2002; J. Wong, 2002.
50. Brunious, 1998.
51. Rotheram-Borus & Wyche, 1994.
52. Fine, 1993; Musick, 1993; Phillips & Pittman, 2003; Stevens, 1995.
53. Chavous et al., 2003; D. DuBois et al., 2002; C. A. Wong et al., 2003.
54. Coll et al., 1996; Rosenbloom & Way, 2004; C. A. Wong et al., 2003.
55. This is consistent with other work which has found boys report more discrimination than girls overall (Greene, Way, & Paul, 2006).
56. Ratings of generalized prejudice based on race and neighborhood are correlated $(r = .52, p < 0.03)$. Reporting an instance of racial discrimination is correlated with reporting an experience of neighborhood-based discrimination $(r = .53, p < 0.03)$. Yet neither of these correlation coefficients is large enough to suggest equation of the two types of prejudice or discriminaton.
57. W. E. Cross, 1991; W. E. Cross & Strauss, 1998; French, Seidman, Allen, & Aber, 2006; Phinney, 1989; Phinney, Cantu, & Kurtz, 1997; Phinney & Chavira, 1992; Phinney & Rosenthal, 1992; E. P. Smith, Walker, Fields, Brookins, & Seay, 1999; Umana-Taylor, Diversi, & Fine, 2002.
58. O'Connor, 2003.
59. W. E. Cross & Strauss, 1998; Steele, 1997; Steele & Aronson, 1995.
60. M. Mead & Baldwin, 1971, pp. 224–225.
61. Oyserman & Markus, 1990a, 1990b.
62. Cornel West, 1993.
63. Flum & Lavi-Yudelevitch, 2002.
64. West, 1993.
65. Waters, 1996; Way, 1998.

Notes to Chapter 5

1. Because words were coded within the context of youths' uses of them, "outgoing" in this case was coded as "individuated."
2. During adolescence, teenagers begin to notice discrepancies in their behavior across different contexts. Part of the task of adolescence is to come to terms with these discrepancies and to become comfortable with the idea that we may display different sides of ourselves in different environments without being hypocritical or dishonest (Berk, 2000).
3. Adamson, Hartman, & Lyxell, 1999.
4. Adamson et al., 1999.
5. Rosenbaum, 2001a, 2001b.
6. Although she refers to her grandparents as Indian, I assume she means Native American, as many youth at East Side talked about having Indian heritage but are far more likely to have American Indian than East Indian ancestors.
7. It has been argued, however, that such boxes on administrative and census

documents are not meant for self-expression but for providing accurate information to address issues of racial and ethnic discrimination. For a discussion of this issue, see Denton (1997).

8. Denton, 1997; R. E. Hall, 2001; Poston, 1990.

9. When I conducted my pilot interviews I asked participating youth to give me their opinions on the questions that I asked. I specifically asked them to tell me if they thought a question was not good or didn't make sense or if there was anything I should have asked about that I did not. I revised the interviews based on youths' comments, although I did not always remove questions if I felt that they were important to my study.

10. Dill, 1987; Fine, 1992.

11. Hill, 2002; Kinnon, 2000.

12. R. E. Hall, 2003.

13. Robinson & Ward, 1995.

14. Collins, 1991; Hill, 2002.

15. Luttrell, 2003.

16. Cockburn & Clarke, 2002.

17. L. Bloom, 1996, 1998.

18. Collins, 1991; Way, 1998.

19. Cockburn & Clarke, 2002.

20. Bem, 1974.

21. Abrams, 2003; Fine, 1993; Proweller, 1998; Tolman, 1994.

Notes to Chapter 6

1. Connell, 1995.

2. Beall, 1993.

3. Connell, 1987.

4. Although theorists and researchers working with minority and low-income populations, both youth and adults, have begun to examine the "braiding" of gender, race, and class (Collins, 1991; DeFrancisco & Chatham-Carpenter, 2000; Ferguson, 2000; Fine, 1992; Frosh, Phoenix, & Pattman, 2000; Goodey, 1998; J. Hall, 2001; Luttrell, 2003; Stevens, 1997; Waters, 1996), more empirical work is needed to truly understand their interactive influences on individual lives.

5. Butler, 1990; C. West & Zimmerman, 1981.

6. Connell, 1987.

7. Connell, 1987.

8. Thorne, 1990, 1993.

9. Aydt & Corsaro, 2003; Bem, 1983; Caldera, Huston, & O'Brien, 1989; Fagot & Hagan, 1991; Maccoby, 1998; N. Marshall, 2003; Ruble & Martin, 1998; Thorne, 1990, 1993.

10. Lorber, 1994; Okin, 1998, p. 116.

11. The most obvious gendered stratification of the social world is structural,

the division of society into the realms of public and private and the gendered division of the labor force. Through these divisions, the state not only reflects gender inequalities but also creates and institutionalizes them (Dressel, 1988; Pringle & Watson, 1998; Quadagno & Fobes, 1995).

12. Deutsch & Hirsch, 2005.

13. Ridgeway & Smith-Lovin, 1999; Wingrove, 1999.

14. A. Rich, 1980.

15. Chodorow, 1989.

16. Having a "good record" means having a good reputation, having led a positive and successful life to date.

17. Echabe & Castro, 1999, p. 299.

18. African American women's independence has been reinscribed by the state as dependence through the image of the welfare queen. As the labor market and social forces have removed some pathways to financial independence, society has constructed a new portrait of female dependence. This form of dependence puts women in relation to the state rather than to individual men. Yet it ignores the ways in which we are all dependent on the state for survival, making dependence once again a gendered (and raced and classed) trait. For a theoretical and historical discussion of this trend, see Fraser and Gordon's (1994) extensive tracing of the history of dependence as a trait and its relation to the state and gender systems.

19. Echabe & Castro, 1999; Ridgeway & Smith-Lovin, 1999.

20. It should be kept in mind that the order of questioning did not depend on the participant's gender but on the gender of the person they named first.

21. Psychoanalytic theories of gender identity indicate that girls identify with their mothers as role models for their own gender identity, whereas boys must separate from their mothers to ensure their identity as men (Chodorow, 1989). Boys may be able to separate out the admirable traits their mothers exemplify. Given their age, the girls may be trying to individuate from their mothers. Thus, they may be more inclined to separate themselves from their mothers as role models when there are aspects of their mothers' lives that they do not want to emulate.

22. Way, 1998.

23. Collins, 1991; DeFrancisco & Chatham-Carpenter, 2000; hooks, 1981; Stevens, 1997.

24. Collins, 1991.

25. Fraser & Gordon, 1994; Riley & Kiger, 1999.

26. Connell, 1995; Fraser & Gordon, 1994. The unique position of African American women within this system is discussed further later in this chapter.

27. Fraser & Gordon, 1994.

28. Moynihan, 1965.

29. Collins, 1991.

30. See hooks, 1981. A 2005 New York Times article alluded to the change in women's roles without a corresponding change in men's roles in work and family life as a possible force behind the increasing rate of young, educated, White women

who are choosing full-time motherhood over full-time work (Story, 2005). The unbalanced shift in roles has placed burdens on both men and women to find alternative gendered identities without a road map for how to enact such identities in their daily lives. For African American women this is a historically longer-standing struggle.

31. hooks, 1981; Kelly, 2001.

32. Dawkins, 1999; Fine & Weis, 1998; Goodey, 1998; J. Hall, 2001.

33. Chu, 2004; Stevenson, 2004.

34. B. Wilson, White, & Fisher, 2001.

35. Abrams, 2003; L. Bloom, 1998.

36. Collins, 1991; R. E. Hall, 2003; Hill, 2002.

37. Connell, 1995.

38. Violence was actually suggested as a means to "help" African American men "regain" their masculinity in the 1960s. At that time, Senator Patrick Moynihan recommended military service as a way for "Negro youth" to be socialized into "a world run by strong men of unquestioned authority" (Moynihan, quoted in hooks, 1981, p. 105).

39. Stoltenberg, 1994, p. 42.

40. hooks, 1981.

41. Engel, 1994; B. Wilson et al., 2001.

42. Luttrell, 2003.

43. Luttrell, 2003.

44. "Ho's" and "hootchie mamas" are slang words referring to whores and sluts (girls who sleep around with a lot of boys). Other authors have also noted the prevalence of these characters in urban neighborhoods (Collins, 1991; Ebron, 1989).

45. J. Berger, 1972; De Beauvoir, 1952; Wollstonecraft, 1792.

46. Brown, Way, & Duff, 1999.

47. Fine, 1993; Gilligan, 1993; Proweller, 1998; Tolman, 1994, 1996.

48. Olsen, 1996; Tolman, 1996.

49. Collins, 1991; J. Hall, 2001; Harden, 1997; Hill, 2002; Schein, 1997; Stoler, 1997.

50. Collins, 1991; J. Hall, 2001; Tolman, 1994, 1996.

51. This probably stands for "bitch-ho."

52. Gilligan, 1993.

53. L. Bloom, 1998.

54. Heilman, 1998.

Notes to Chapter 7

1. Here, again, I draw on the idea of self and identity as profoundly social and created in our interactions with others and the meanings that we give to the language and actions within those exchanges (Blumer, 1969; G. H. Mead, 1934).

2. Fine, 1994.

3. Deutsch, 2004.
4. Oyserman & Markus, 1990a, 1990b.
5. McAdams & Bowman, 2001; McAdams, Diamond, de St. Aubin, & Mansfield, 1997.
6. Erikson, 1959.
7. Oyserman & Markus, 1990a, 1990b.
8. Others have also noted this phenomenon, sometimes called the need for a "cool pose," among urban males (for example, Cunningham & Meunier, 2004; Reichert, Stoudt, & Kuriloff, 2006).
9. Gregory, Nygreen, & Moran, 2006.
10. Ferguson, 2000.
11. Western, 2006.
12. Winston, 2004.
13. Oyserman, Kemmelmeier, Fryberg, Brosh, & Hart-Johnson, 2003.
14. This has been discussed particularly with regard to academic achievement as "acting White" (Fordham, 1996; Fordham & Ogbu, 1986; Ogbu, 1988; Tatum, 1997).
15. For example, see work challenging Ogbu's oppositional identity construct as not giving due consideration to the historical structure of school policies (Galletta & Cross, 2007).
16. For discussion of how this "closing ranks" to White America has reinforced Black male power, and thereby supported patriarchy as a "response" to racism, see West, 1993.
17. For discussion of how White, male, working-class youth construct their own identities in opposition to the Black Other, see Weis, 1990.
18. R. E. Hall, 2001; Poston, 1990.
19. Hill, 2002.
20. Oyserman et al., 2003.
21. Connell, 1995.
22. Butler, 1990.
23. Kaufman, 1994; Lehne, 1998; Limon, 1994; Nonn, 1998.
24. Researchers working with White and racial minority boys in urban centers of the United States and Europe have found that fear of violence may result in a felt need for the presentation of a particular type of exaggerated masculinity (Goodey, 1998; Seaton, 2004).
25. Fordham, 1996.
26. J. Hall, 2001.
27. Ebron, 1989.
28. Connell, 1995; Fine, 1992.
29. Connell, 1995.
30. Moje, 2004.
31. Connell, 1995; Goodey, 1998; J. Hall, 2001.
32. For discussion of this issue with regard to race, see Clay 2003.

33. Cunningham, 1999; May, 2001; Seaton, 2004; Spencer, 2001.

34. Barker, 1998; Bowman, 1995; Connell, 1995; W. J. Wilson, 1987.

35. Fordham, 1996; Fordham & Ogbu, 1986; Ogbu, 1988.

36. J. Hall, 2001; Weis, 1990, 1993.

37. Connell, 1993; Weis, 1990, 1993.

38. Fine & Weis, 1998; J. Hall, 2001; Weis, 1990, 1993.

39. hooks, 1981.

40. Bourgois, 1995; hooks, 1981; Weis, 1993.

41. Patterson, 2006.

42. Fraser & Gordon, 1994.

43. hooks, 1981.

44. Barker, 1998.

45. Fine, 1992.

Notes to Chapter 8

1. The Afterschool Alliance, a nonprofit awareness and advocacy organization, tracks federal policy decisions affecting afterschool programming (http://www.after schoolalliance.org/policy_news.cfm). Additional information on No Child Left Behind and its funding of the 21st Century Community Learning Centers is available on the U.S. Department of Education website (http://www.ed.gov/programs/21stcclc/index.html).

2. J. Eccles et al., 1993.

3. Bumbarger & Greenberg, 2002; Catalano, Berglund, Ryan, Lonczak, & Hawkins, 2002.

4. Recently there has been a call for an integrative model that links prevention and treatment research in psychology, with positive development and health promotion seen as the one of the goals of intervention (Weisz, Sandler, Durlak, & Anton, 2005).

5. Durlak & Weissberg, 2007; Lauer et al., 2006.

6. The 3–6 PM hours are when youth are most likely to be unsupervised and juvenile crime peaks.

7. Carnegie Council on Adolescent Development, 1992; Deutsch & Hirsch, 2002; Halpern, Barker, & Mollard, 2000; Hirsch, 2005; Hirsch et al., 2000; Lauer et al., 2006; McLaughlin, 2000; McLaughlin, Irby, & Langman, 1994; National Research Council & Institute of Medicine, 2002; Riggs & Greenberg, 2004; Roth, Brooks-Gunn, Murray, & Foster, 1998.

8. National Research Council & Institute of Medicine, 2002.

9. Catalano et al., 2002; Chung & Hillsman, 2005; J. S. Eccles & Gootman, 2002; Goldsmith, Arbreton, & Bradshaw, 2004; Hirsch, 2005; Luttrell, 2005; Mahoney, Eccles, & Larson, 2004; B. M. Miller, 2005.

10. Cotterell, 1996; Goldsmith et al., 2004.

11. Catalano et al., 2002; Kane, 2004; Riggs & Greenberg, 2004.

12. James-Burdumy, Dynarski, Moore, Deke, & Mansfield, 2005; Kane, 2004.

13. Bumbarger & Greenberg, 2002; Catalano et al., 2002; Riggs & Greenberg, 2004.

14. Durlak & Weissberg, 2007.

15. Lauer et al., 2006.

16. Anderson-Butcher, Newsome, & Ferrari, 2003; Catalano et al., 2002; Deutsch & Hirsch, 2002; Roffman, Pagano, & Hirsch, 2001.

17. Riggs & Greenberg, 2004.

18. Anderson-Butcher et al., 2003; Bradford, 1991; Bumbarger & Greenberg, 2002; Carnegie Council on Adolescent Development, 1992; Catalano et al., 2002; Dynarski et al., 2003; Halpern et al., 2000; Larson, 1993; National Research Council & Institute of Medicine, 2002; Roth et al., 1998.

19. My findings help make concrete the theoretical writings on the processes and interactions of identity that occur at the crux of social categories. Yet, whereas I address gender and race explicitly and class implicitly through neighborhood location, I do not touch on sexuality. This is an omission of which I am aware, and I recognize the shortcomings this lends to my work, especially in the area of gender construction. Further research is obviously needed in this area.

20. The major exceptions to this rule include research on female identity (which has focused on interpersonal relationships) and research on racial and ethnic identities (which has explored individuals' relationships to society).

21. Josselson, 1994; Way, 2004.

22. Rhodes, Davis, Prescott, & Spencer, 2007.

23. Hirsch, 2005.

24. London, Zimmerman, & Erbstein, 2003.

25. Way, 2004.

26. Bryk & Schneider, 2002; Greenberg et al., 2003.

27. Maton & Salem, 1995; Rappaport, 1995, 2000.

28. Maton & Salem, 1995.

29. Lerner, Almerigi, Theokas, & Lerner, 2005.

30. Hollander & Howard, 2000; B. B. Lal, 1995; Snow, 2001; Stryker, 1980, 1987.

31. Hollander & Howard, 2000, p. 348.

32. Bond, 1997.

33. Halpern et al., 2000.

34. Rappaport, 1995.

35. Helfenbein, 2006.

36. Maton & Salem, 1995.

37. Gruenewald, 2003; Rubinstein-Avila, 2006.

38. The club holds college fairs, takes kids on college tours, and helps youth access information about scholarships and applications.

39. Spencer, Dupree, & Hartmann, 1997.

40. Goodey, 1998; Seaton, 2004; Stevenson, 2004.

41. Lerner, Lerner, et al., 2005.

42. Erikson, 1959, 1968.

43. Anderson-Butcher et al., 2003; Halpern et al., 2000; Hansen, Larson, & Dworkin, 2003; Hirsch, 2005; Kahne et al., 2001; Larson, 1993.

44. For discussion, see Lerner, Almerigi, et al., 2005.

45. Kane, 2004.

46. Pedersen et al., 2005, p. 81.

Notes to Appendix A

1. For more information on my position at East Side and how my role as insider-outsider influenced my research, see Deutsch (2004).

2. Olesen, 2005; D. L. Wolf, 1996.

3. Coffey & Atkinson, 1996; Glaser & Strauss, 1967; Walsh, 1998.

4. Seale, 1998.

5. J. Eccles, 2001.

6. McAdams, 1993, 2001.

7. Lazar, 1998.

8. Orellana, 1999.

9. Orellana, 1999.

10. Secondulfo, 1997.

11. Henny, 1986, p. 21.

12. Becker, 1995; Secondulfo, 1997.

13. Orellana, 1999; Secondulfo, 1997.

14. Harper, 1986.

15. Orellana (1999) notes that children in her study were limited by the degree of spatial autonomy they had. She also points out that youths' photographs capture the world as they literally see it, reflecting not only different social positions from adults but also different physical positions.

16. Coffey & Atkinson, 1996; Walsh, 1998.

17. C. Marshall & Rossman, 1999.

18. Erickson, 1986; Huberman, 1994.

19. I developed a specific coding protocol for individual versus connected self-descriptors to code the youths' answers to the question "give me the five words that describe you the best." This coding protocol and examples are provided in appendix E.

20. Erikson, 1986; Glaser & Strauss, 1967; A. Strauss & Corbin, 1994; A. L. Strauss, 1998.

References

Abrams, L. S. (2003). Contextual variations in young women's gender identity negotiations. *Psychology of Women Quarterly, 27,* 64–74.

Adams, G. R., & Marshall, S. K. (1996). A developmental social psychology of identity: Understanding the person-in-context. *Journal of Adolescence, 19,* 429–442.

Adamson, L., Hartman, S., & Lyxell, B. (1999). Adolescent identity—a qualitative approach: Self-concept, existential questions, and adult contacts. *Scandinavian Journal of Psychology, 40,* 21–31.

Anderson, L., & Snow, D. A. (2001). Inequality and the self: Exploring connections from an interactionist perspective. *Symbolic Interaction, 24*(4), 395–406.

Anderson-Butcher, D., Newsome, W. S., & Ferrari, T. M. (2003). Participation in Boys and Girls Clubs and relationships to youth outcomes. *Journal of Community Psychology, 31*(1), 39–55.

Ansah, K. (1998, March 21). Telling the real story about race relations. *Pittsburgh Courier,* p. A7.

Aron, A., & McLaughlin-Volpe, T. (2001). Including others in the self: Extension to own and partner's group memberships. In C. Sedikides & M. Brewer (Eds.), *Individual self, relational self, collective self* (pp. 89–108). Philadelphia: Psychology Press.

Aspy, D. N., Roebuck, F. N., & Black, B. (1972). The relationship of teacher-offered conditions of respect to behaviors described by Flanders' interaction analysis. *Journal of Negro Education, 41*(4), 370–376.

Augoustinos, M. (1998). Social representations and ideology: Towards the study of ideological representations. In E. U. Flick (Ed.), *The psychology of the social* (pp. 156–169). New York: Cambridge University Press.

Aydt, H., & Corsaro, W. A. (2003). Differences in children's construction of gender across culture. *American Behavioral Scientist, 46*(10), 1306–1325.

Barker, G. (1998). Non-violent males in violent settings: An exploratory qualitative study of prosocial low-income adolescent males in two Chicago (USA) neighborhoods. *Childhood, 5*(4), 437–460.

Baumeister, R. F., & Newman, L. S. (1994). How stories make sense of personal experiences: Motives that shape autobiographical narratives. *Personality and Social Psychology Bulletin, 20*(6), 676–690.

Beall, A. E. (1993). A social constructionist view of gender. In A. E. Beall & R. J. Sternberg (Eds.), *The psychology of gender* (pp. 127–147). New York: Guilford Press.

Becker, H. (1995). Visual sociology, documentary photography, and photojournalism: It's (almost) all a matter of context. *Visual Sociology, 10,* 5–14.

Bem, S. L. (1974). The measurement of psychological androgyny. *Journal of Consulting and Clinical Psychology, 42,* 155–162.

Bem, S. L. (1983). Gender schema theory and its implications for child development: Raising gender aschematic children in a gender-schematic society. *Signs, 8,* 598–616.

Berger, J. (1972). *Ways of seeing.* London: Penguin Books.

Berger, P., & Luckmann, T. (1966). *The social construction of reality.* Garden City, N.Y.: Doubleday.

Berk, L. E. (2000). *Child development.* Boston: Allyn & Bacon.

Bishaw, A. (2005). *Areas with concentrated poverty: 1999.* Washington, D.C.: U.S. Census Bureau.

Blau, J. R., & Stearns, E. (2002). Adolescent integrity: Race and ethnic differences. *Critical Sociology, 28*(1–2), 145–167.

Bloom, J. (2007). (Mis)reading social class in the journey towards college: Youth development in urban america. *Teachers College Record, 109*(2), 343–368.

Bloom, L. (1996). Stories of one's own: Subjectivity in narrative representation. *Qualitative Inquiry, 2*(2), 176–197.

Bloom, L. (1998). *Under the sign of hope: Feminist methodology and narrative interpretation.* Albany: State University of New York Press.

Blumer, H. (1969). *Symbolic interactionism: Perspective and method.* Englewood Cliffs, N.J.: Prentice Hall.

Bond, M. A. (1997). The multitextured lives of women of color. *American Journal of Community Psychology, 25*(5), 733–743.

Bottero, W., & Irwin, S. (2003). Locating difference: Class, "race" and gender, and the shaping of social inequalities. *Sociological Review, 51*(4), 463–483.

Bourgois, P. I. (1995). *In search of respect: Selling crack in El barrio.* New York: Cambridge University Press.

Bowman, P. J. (1995). Family structure and the marginalization of black men:

Commentary. In M. B. Tucker & C. Mitchell-Keman (Eds.), *The decline in marriage among African Americans: Causes, consequences, and policy implications* (pp. 309–321). New York: Russell Sage Foundation.

Bradford, S. (1991). *OJJDP and Boys and Girls Clubs of America: Public housing and high risk youth.* Washington, D.C.: Office of Juvenile Justice and Delinquency Prevention, U.S. Department of Justice.

Branch, C. W. (1999). Pathologizing normality or normalizing pathology? In C. W. Branch (Ed.), *Adolescent gangs: Old issues, new approaches* (pp. 197–211). Philadelphia: Brunner/Mazel.

Britt, D. (1999). Teaching our sons to respect women. *Essence, November,* 166–215.

Bronfenbrenner, U. (1979). *The ecology of human development.* Cambridge: Harvard University Press.

Brown, L. M., Way, N., & Duff, J. L. (1999). The others in my I: Adolescent girls' friendships and peer relations. In N. G. Johnson, M. C. Roberts, & J. Worell (Eds.), *Beyond appearance: A new look at adolescent girls* (pp. 205–226). Washington, D.C.: American Psychological Association.

Bruner, J. (1990). *Acts of meaning.* Cambridge: Harvard University Press.

Brunious, L. (1998). *How black disadvantaged adolescents socially contruct reality: Listen, do you hear what I hear?* NY: Garland.

Brunskell, H. (1998). Feminist methodology. In C. Seale (Ed.), *Researching society and culture* (pp. 37–47). London: Sage.

Bryk, A. S., & Schneider, B. (2002). *Trust in schools: A core resource for improvement.* New York: Russell Sage Foundation.

Bumbarger, B., & Greenberg, M. T. (2002). Next steps in advancing research on positive youth development. *Prevention and Treatment, 5,* n.p.

Burton, L. M., Allison, K. W., & Obeidallah, D. (1995). Social context and adolescence: Perspectives on development among inner-city African-American teens. In L. J. Crockett & A. C. Crouter (Eds.), *Pathways through adolescence: Individual development in relation to social contexts* (pp. 119–138). Mahwah, N.J.: Lawrence Erlbaum Associates.

Burton, L. M., Obeidallah, D., & Allison, K. W. (1996). Ethnographic insights on social context and adolescent development among inner-city African-American teens. In R. Jessor, A. Colby, & R. A. Shweder (Eds.), *Ethnography and human development* (pp. 395–418). Chicago: University of Chicago Press.

Butler, J. (1990). *Gender trouble: Feminism and the subversion of identity.* New York: Routledge.

Caldera, Y. M., Huston, A. C., & O'Brien, M. (1989). Social interactions and play patterns of parents and toddlers with feminine, masculine, and neutral toys. *Child Development, 60,* 70–76.

Callero, P. L. (2003). The sociology of the self. *Annual Review of Sociology, 29,* 115–133.

A call for self-respect (1999, March 20). *Pittsburg Courier,* p. A6.

Cameron, J. E. (2004). A three-factor model of social identity. *Self and Identity,* 3(3), 239–262.

Camino, L., & Zeldin, S. (2002). From periphery to center: Pathways for youth civic engagement in the day-to-day life of communities. *Applied Developmental Science,* 6(4), 213–220.

Campbell, M. L. (1998). Institutional ethnography and experience as data. *Qualitative Sociology,* 21(1), 55–73.

Campbell, R., & Wasco, S. M. (2000). Feminist approaches to social science: Epistemological and methodological tenets. *American Journal of Community Psychology,* 28(6), 773–791.

Carnegie Council on Adolescent Development (1992). *A matter of time: Risk and opportunity in the out-of-school hours.* New York: Carnegie Corporation of New York.

Catalano, R. F., Berglund, M. L., Ryan, J. A., Lonczak, H. S., & Hawkins, J. D. (2002). Positive youth development in the United States: Research findings on evaluations of positive youth development programs. *Prevention and Treatment,* 5, n.p.

Celious, A., & Oyserman, D. (2001). Race from the inside: An emerging heterogeneous race model. *Journal of Social Issues,* 57(1), 149–165.

Chavous, T. M., Bernat, D. H., Schmeelk-Cone, K., Caldwell, C. H., Kohn-Wood, L., & Zimmerman, M. A. (2003). Racial identity and academic attainment among African American adolescents. *Child Development,* 74(4), 1076–1090.

Chideya, F. (1998). Money. Power. Respect? *Emerge,* 10(1), 34.

Chodorow, N. (1989). *Feminism and psychoanalytic theory.* New Haven, Conn.: Yale University Press.

Chu, J. Y. (2004). A relational perspective on adolescent boys' identity development. In N. Way & J. Y. Chu (Eds.), *Adolescent boys: Exploring diverse cultures of boyhood* (pp. 78–104). New York: New York University Press.

Chung, A., & Hillsman, E. (2005). Evaluating after-school programs. *School Administrator,* 62(5), 18–21.

Clark, C. M. (1992). Deviant adolescent subcultures: Assessment strategies and clinical interventions. *Adolescence,* 27, 283–293.

Clay, A. (2003). Keepin' it real: Black youth, hip-hop culture, and black identity. *American Behavioral Scientist,* 46(10), 1346–1358.

Cockburn, C., & Clarke, G. (2002). "Everybody's looking at you!" Girls negotiating the "femininity deficit" they incur in physical education. *Women's Studies International Forum,* 25(6), 651–665.

Coffey, A., & Atkinson, P. (1996). *Making sense of qualitative data.* Thousand Oaks, Calif.: Sage Publications.

Cole, E. R., & Omari, S. R. (2003). Race, class and the dilemmas of upward mobility for African Americans. *Journal of Social Issues,* 59(4), 785–802.

Coll, C. G., Lamberty, G., R., J., McAdoo, H. P., Crnic, K., Wasik, B. H., et al.

(1996). An integrative model for the study of developmental competencies in minority children. *Child Development, 67*(5), 1891–1914.

Collins, P. H. (1991). *Black feminist thought: Knowledge, consciousness and the politics of empowerment.* New York: Routledge.

Connell, R. W. (1987). *Gender and power.* Stanford: Stanford University Press.

Connell, R. W. (1993). Disruptions: Improper masculinities and schooling. In L. Weis & M. Fine (Eds.), *Beyond silenced voices: Class, race and gender in United States schools* (pp. 191–208). Albany: SUNY Press.

Connell, R. W. (1995). *Masculinities.* Berkeley: University of California Press.

Cook, J. A., & Fonow, M. M. (1990). Knowledge and women's interests: Issues of epistemology and methodology in feminist sociological research. In J. M. Nielsen (Ed.), *Feminist research methods: Exemplary readings in the social sciences* (pp. 69–93). San Francisco: Westview.

Cooley, C. H. (1902). *Human nature and the social order.* New York: Schocken.

Cosgrove, L., & McHugh, M. C. (2000). Speaking for ourselves: Feminist methods and commmunity psychology. *American Journal of Community Psychology, 28*(6), 815–838.

Côté, J. (2006). Identity studies: How close are we to developing a social science of identity?—An appraisal of the field. *Identity: An International Journal of Theory and Research, 6*(1), 3–25.

Cotterell, J. L. (1996). *Social networks and social influences in adolescence.* New York: Routledge.

Cross, S. E., & Madson, L. (1997). Models of the self: Self-construals and gender. *Psychological Bulletin, 122*(1), 5–37.

Cross, W. E. (1991). *Shades of black: Diversity in African American identity.* Philadelphia: Temple University Press.

Cross, W. E. (2004). Advances in the study of black identity: Theory and research. Paper presented at the Society for Research on Adolescence, Baltimore.

Cross, W. E., & Fhagen-Smith, P. (1996). Nigrescence and ego identity development: Accounting for differential black identity patterns. In Paul B. Pedersen, Juris G. Draguns, et al. (Eds.), *Counseling across cultures* (4th ed.) (pp. 108–123). Thousand Oaks, Calif.: Sage.

Cross, W. E., & Strauss, L. (1998). The everyday functions of African American identity. In J. K. Swim & C. Stangor (Eds.), *Prejudice: The target's perspective* (pp. 267–279). San Diego: Academic Press.

Cunningham, M. (1999). African American adolescent males' perceptions of their community resources and constraints. *Journal of Community Psychology, 27*(5), 569–588.

Cunningham, M., & Meunier, L. N. (2004). The influence of peer experiences on bravado attitudes among African American males. In N. Way & J. Y. Chu (Eds.), *Adolescent boys: Exploring diverse cultures of boyhood* (pp. 219–232). New York: New York University Press.

Damon, W. (1998). Political development for a democratic future: A commentary. *Journal of Social Issues, 54*(3), 621–628.

Damon, W., Menon, J., & Bronk, K. C. (2003). The development of purpose during adolescence. *Applied Developmental Science, 7*(3), 119–128.

Dawkins, P. A. (1999). Apologizing for being a black male. *Essence, October,* 64.

Debats, D. L. (1999). Sources of meaning: An investigation of significant commitments in life. *Journal for Humanistic Psychology, 39*(4), 30–57.

De Beauvoir, S. (1952). *The second sex.* New York: Knopf.

DeFrancisco, V. L., & Chatham-Carpenter, A. (2000). Self in community: African American women's views of self-esteem. *Howard Journal of Communications, 11,* 73–92.

Denton, N. A. (1997). Racial identity and census categories: Can incorrect categories yield correct information? *Law and Inequality, 15*(1), 83.

Denzin, N. K. (2001). Symbolic interactionism, poststructuralism, and the racial subject. *Symbolic Interaction, 24*(2), 243–249.

Deutsch, N. L. (2004). Positionality and the pen: The process of becoming a feminist researcher and writer. *Qualitative Inquiry, 10*(6), 885–902.

Deutsch, N. L. (2005). "I want to treat others as others treat me": The development of prosocial selves in an urban youth organization. In D. B. Fink (Ed.), *Doing the right thing: Ethical development across diverse environments* (pp. 89–105). San Francisco: Jossey-Bass.

Deutsch, N. L. (2007). From island to archipelago: Narratives of relatedness in an urban youth organization. In R. Josselson, A. Lieblich, and D. P. McAdams (Eds.), *The meaning of others: Narrative studies of relationships* (pp. 75–91). Washington, D.C.: American Psychological Association.

Deutsch, N. L., & Hirsch, B. (2002). A place to call home: Youth organizations in the lives of inner city adolescents. In T. Brinthaupt & R. Lipka (Eds.), *Understanding early adolescent self and identity* (pp. 293–320). Albany: SUNY Press.

Deutsch, N. L., & Hirsch, B. (2005). Gender wars in the gym. In B. J. Hirsch (Ed.), *A place to call home: Community based after school programs for urban youth.* Washington, D.C./New York: American Psychological Association/Teachers College Press.

DeVault, M. (1995). Ethnicity and expertise: Racial-ethnic knowledge in sociological research. *Gender and Society, 9*(5), 612–631.

De Vries, R. E. (2003). Self, in-group, and out-group evaluation: Bond or breach? *European Journal of Social Psychology, 33*(5), 609–621.

Diamond, I., & Hartsock, N. (1998). Beyond interests in politics: A comment on Virginia Sapiro's "When are interests interesting? The problem of political representation of women." In A. Phillips (Ed.), *Feminism and politics* (pp. 193–202). New York: Oxford University Press.

di Leonardo, M. (1999). "Why can't they be like our grandparents?" and other racial fairy tales. In J. A. Reed (Ed.), *Without justice for all: The new liberalism and our retreat from racial equality* (pp. 29–64). Boulder, Colo.: Westview.

Dill, B. T. (1987). The dialectics of black womanhood. In S. Harding (Ed.), *Feminism and methodology* (pp. 97–108). Bloomington: Indiana University Press.

Dimitriadis, G. (2001). Border identities, transformed lives, and danger zones: The mediation of validated selves, friendship networks, and successful paths in community-based organizations. *Discourse: Studies in the Cultural Politics of Education, 22*(3), 361–374.

Donne, J. (1624). *Devotions upon emergent occasions and several steps in my sickness.* London: A Mathews for T. Iones.

Doss, R. C., & Gross, A. M. (1994). The effects of black English and code-switching on intraracial perceptions. *Journal of Black Psychology, 20*(3), 282–293.

Dressel, P. (1988). Gender, race and class: Beyond the feminization of poverty in later life. *Gerontologist, 28*(2), 177–180.

DuBois, D., Burk-Braxton, C., Swenson, L. P., Tevendale, H. D., & Hardesty, J. L. (2002). Race and gender influences on adjustment in early adolescence: Investigation of an integrative model. *Child Development, 73*(5), 1573–1592.

DuBois, D., & Hirsch, B. (1990). School and neighborhood friendship patterns of blacks and whites in early adolescence. *Child Development, 61,* 524–536.

DuBois, W. E. B. (1903). *The souls of black folk.* Cambridge, Mass.: University Press, John Wilson and Son.

DuBois, W. E. B. (1940). *Dusk of dawn: An essay toward an autobiography of a race concept.* New York: Harcourt, Brace.

Durlak, J., A., & Weissberg, R. P. (2007). *The impact of after-school programs that promote personal and social skills.* Chicago: Collaborative for Academic, Social, and Emotional Learning.

Dynarski, M., Pistorino, C., Moore, M., Silva, T., Mullens, J., Deke, J., et al. (2003). *When schools stay open late: The national evaluation of the 21st century community learning centers program.* Washington, D.C.: U.S. Department of Education.

Ebron, P. (1989). Rapping between men: Performing gender. *Radical America, 23*(4), 23–27.

Eccles, J. (2001). Gender and ethnicity as developmental contexts. Paper presented at the Society for Research in Child Development, Minneapolis.

Eccles, J., Midgley, C., Wigfield, A., Buchanan, C., Reuman, D., Flanagan, C., et al. (1993). Development during adolescence: The impact of stage-environment fit on young adolescents' experiences in schools and in families. *American Psychologist, 48,* 90–101.

Eccles, J. S., & Gootman, J. A. (Eds.). (2002). *Community programs to promote youth development.* Washington, D.C.: National Academy Press.

Echabe, A. E., & Castro, J. L. G. (1999). The impact of context on gender social identities. *European Journal of Social Psychology, 29,* 287–304.

Eidelman, S., & Biernat, M. (2003). Derogating black sheep: Individual or group protection? *Journal of Experimental Social Psychology, 39*(6), 602–609.

Engel, A. (1994). Sex roles and gender stereotyping in young women's participation in sport. *Feminism and Psychology, 4*(3), 439–448.

Erickson, F. (1986). Qualitative methods in research on teaching. In M. Wittrock (Ed.), *Handbook of research on teaching* (3rd ed.) (pp. 119–161). New York: Macmillan.

Erikson, E. (1959). *Identity and the life cycle.* New York: Norton.

Erikson, E. (1968). *Identity, youth and crisis.* New York: Norton.

Fagot, B. I., & Hagan, R. I. (1991). Observations of parent reactions to sex-stereotyped behaviors: Age and sex effects. *Child Development, 62,* 617–628.

Fanon, F. (1967). *Black skin, white masks.* New York: Grove Press.

Fashola, O. S. (2003). Developing the talents of African American male students during the nonschool hours. *Urban Education, 38*(4), 398–430.

Fay, B. (1975). *Social theory and political practice.* London: Allen and Unwin.

Ferguson, A. A. (2000). *Bad boys: Public schools in the making of black masculinity.* Ann Arbor: University of Michigan Press.

Filmer, P., Jenks, C., Seale, C., & Walsh, D. (1998). Developments in social theory. In C. Seale (Ed.), *Researching society and culture* (pp. 23–36). London: Sage.

Fine, M. (1992). *Disruptive voices: The possibilities of feminist research.* Ann Arbor: University of Michigan Press.

Fine, M. (1993). Sexuality, schooling, and adolescent females: The missing discourse of desire. In L. Weis & M. Fine (Eds.), *Beyond silenced voices: Class, race, and gender in United States schools* (pp. 75–99). Albany: SUNY Press.

Fine, M. (1994). Working the hyphens: Reinventing self and other in qualitative research. In N. K. Denzin & Y. S. Lincoln (Eds.), *The handbook of qualitative research* (pp. 70–82). Thousand Oaks, Calif.: Sage.

Fine, M., & Weis, L. (1998). *The unknown city: Lives of poor and working class young adults.* Boston: Beacon Press.

Fine, M., Weis, L., Centrie, C., & Roberts, R. (2000). Educating beyond the borders of schooling. *Anthropology and Education Quarterly, 31*(2), 131–151.

Flannery, D. J., Huff, C. R., & Manos, M. (1998). Youth gangs: A developmental prospective. In T. P. Gullotta, G. R. Adams, & R. Montemayor (Eds.), *Delinquent violent youth: Theory and interventions* (pp. 175–204). Thousand Oaks, Calif.: Sage.

Flum, H., & Lavi-Yudelevitch, M. (2002). Adolescents' relatedness and identity formation: A narrative study. *Journal of Social and Personal Relationships, 19*(4), 527–548.

Folbre, N. (2001). *The invisible heart: Economics and family values.* New York: New Press.

Fordham, S. (1996). *Blacked out.* Chicago: University of Chicago Press.

Fordham, S., & Ogbu, J. (1986). Black students' school success: Coping with the burden of "acting white." *Urban Review, 18*(3), 176–206.

Frable, D. E. S. (1997). Gender, racial, ethnic, sexual, and class identities. *Annual Review of Psychology, 48,* 139–162.

Fraser, N., & Gordon, L. (1994). "Dependency" demystified: Inscriptions of power in a key word of the welfare state. *Social Politics, 1,* 4–31.

French, S. E., Seidman, E., Allen, L., & Aber, J. L. (2000). Ethnic identity, congruence with the social context, and the transition to high school. *Journal of Adolescent Research, 15*(5), 587–602.

French, S. E., Seidman, E., Allen, L., & Aber, J. L. (2006). The development of ethnic identity during adolescence. *Developmental Psychology, 42*(1), 1–10.

Frosh, S., Phoenix, A., & Pattman, R. (2000). "But it's racism I really hate": Young masculinities, racism, and psychoanalysis. *Psychoanalytic Psychology, 17*(2), 225–242.

Gabriel, S., & Gardner, W. L. (1999). Are there "his" and "her" types of interdependence? The implications of gender differences in collective versus relational interdependence for affect, behavior, and cognition. *Journal of Personality and Social Psychology, 77*(3), 642–655.

Galletta, A., & Cross W. E., Jr. (2007). Past as present, present as past: Historicizing black education and interrogating "integration." In A. J. Fuligni (Ed.), *Contesting stereotypes and creating identities: Social categories, social identities, and educational participation* (pp. 15–41). New York: Russell Sage Foundation.

Gardner, W., Gabriel, S., & Lee, A. (1999). "I" value freedom, but "we" value relationships: Self-construal priming mirrors cultural differences in judgment. *Psychological Science, 10*(4), 321–326.

Gee, J. P. (1996). *Social linguistics and literacies: Ideology in discourses.* London: Taylor and Francis.

Gee, J. P., & Crawford, V. M. (1998). Two kinds of teenagers: Language, identity and social class. In D. E. Alvermann, K. A. Hinchman, D. W. Moore, S. F. Phelps, & D. R. Waff (Eds.), *Reconceptualizing the literacies in adolescents' lives* (pp. 225–245). Mahwah, N.J.: Lawrence Erlbaum Associates.

Gergen, K. (1991). *The saturated self.* New York: Basic Books.

Ghosh, R., Mickelson, R. A., & Anyon, J. (2007). Introduction to the special issue on new perspectives on youth development and social identity in the 21st century. *Teachers College Record, 109*(2), 275–284.

Gilligan, C. (1982). *In a different voice.* Cambridge: Harvard University Press.

Gilligan, C. (1993). Joining the resistance: Psychology, politics, girls, and women. In L. Weis & M. Fine (Eds.), *Beyond silenced voices: Class, race, and gender in United States schools* (pp. 143–168). Albany: SUNY Press.

Glaser, B. G., & Strauss, A. L. (1967). *The discovery of grounded theory: Strategies for qualitative research.* Chicago: Aldine.

Goldsmith, J., Arbreton, A. J. A., & Bradshaw, M. (2004). *Promoting emotional and behavioral health in preteens: Benchmarks of success and challenges among programs in Santa Clara and San Mateo Counties.* Palo Alto, Calif.: Lucile Packard Foundation for Children's Health and Public/Private Ventures.

Goodey, J. (1998). Understanding racism and masculinity: Drawing on research with boys aged eight to sixteen. *International Journal of the Sociology of Law, 26*(4), 393–418.

Gosa, T. L., & Alexander, K. L. (2007). Family (dis)advantage and the educational prospects of better off African American youth: How race still matters. *Teachers College Record, 109*(2), 285–321.

Grahame, P. R. (1998). Ethnography, institutions, and the problematic of the everyday world. *Human Studies, 21,* 347–360.

Greenberg, M. T., Weissberg, R. P., O'Brien, M. U., Zins, J. E., Fredericks, L., Resnik, H., et al. (2003). Enhancing school-based prevention and youth development through coordinated social, emotional, and academic learning. *American Psychologist, 58*(6–7), 466–474.

Greene, M. L., Way, N., & Pahl, K. (2006). Trajectories of perceived adult and peer discrimination among black, Latino, and Asian American adolescents: Patterns and psychological correlates. *Developmental Psychology, 42*(2), 218–238.

Gregory, A., Nygreen, K., & Moran, D. (2006). The discipline gap and the normalization of failure. In P. Noguera & J. Wing (Eds.), *Unfinished business: Closing the racial achievement gap in our schools* (pp. 121–150). New York: Wiley.

Grotevant, H. D., & Cooper, C. R. (1998). Individuality and connectedness in adolescent development: Review and prospects for research on identity, relationships, and context. In E. E. A. Skoe & A. L. von der Lippe (Eds.), *Personality development in adolescence: A cross national and life span perspective adolescence and society* (pp. 3–37). Florence, Ky.: Taylor and Frances/Routledge.

Gruenewald, D. A. (2003). The best of both worlds: A critical pedagogy of place. *Educational Researcher, 32*(4), 3–12.

Hall, G. S. (1905). *Adolescence.* New York: Arno Press.

Hall, J. (2001). *Canal town youth: Community organization and the development of adolescent identity.* Albany: SUNY Press.

Hall, R. E. (2001). Identity development across the lifespan: A biracial model. *Social Science Journal, 38*(1), 119–123.

Hall, R. E. (2003). Skin color as post-colonial hierarchy: A global strategy for conflict resolution. *Journal of Psychology, 137*(1), 41–53.

Hall, S. (1989). Ethnicity: Identity and difference. *Radical America, 23*(4), 9–20.

Halpern, R., Barker, G., & Mollard, W. (2000). Youth programs as alternative spaces to be: A study of neighborhood youth programs in Chicago's west town. *Youth and Society, 31*(4), 469–506.

Hamilton, S. F., Hamilton, M. A., & Pittman, K. (2004). Principles for youth development. In S. F. Hamilton & M. A. Hamilton (Eds.), *The youth development handbook: Coming of age in American communities* (pp. 3–22). Thousand Oaks, Calif.: Sage.

Hansen, D. M., Larson, R. W., & Dworkin, J. B. (2003). What adolescents learn in organized youth activities: A survey of self-reported developmental experiences. *Journal of Research on Adolescence, 13*(1), 25–55.

Harden, J. D. (1997). The enterprise of empire: Race, class, gender, and Japanese national identity. In M. diLeonardo & R. Lancaster (Eds.), *The gender/sexuality reader* (pp. 487–501). New York: Routledge.

Harding, S. (1987). Introduction: Is there a feminist method? In S. Harding (Ed.), *Feminism and methodology* (pp. 1–14). Bloomington: Indiana University Press.

Harper, D. (1986). Meaning and work: A study in photo elicitation. *Current Sociology, 34*, 24–46.

Hart, D., Atkins, R., & Ford, D. (1998). Urban America as a context for the development of moral identity in adolescence. *Journal of Social Issues, 54*(3), 513–530.

Harter, S. (1990). Self and identity development. In S. Feldman & G. Elliott (Eds.), *At the threshold: The developing adolescent* (pp. 352–387). Cambridge: Harvard University Press.

Harter, S. (1999). *The construction of the self: A developmental perspective.* New York: Guilford Press.

Harter, S., Bresnick, S., Bouchey, H. A., & Whitesell, N. R. (1997). The development of multiple role-related selves during adolescence. *Development and Psychopathology, 9*, 835–853.

Haymes, S. N. (1995). *Race, culture, and the city: A pedagogy for black urban struggle.* Albany: SUNY Press.

Heath, S. B., & McLaughlin, M. W. (1993a). Ethnicity and gender in theory and practice: The youth perspective. In S. B. Heath & M. W. McLaughlin (Eds.), *Identity and inner-city youth: Beyond ethnicity and gender* (pp. 13–35). New York: Teachers College Press.

Heath, S. B., & McLaughlin, M. W. (1993b). Identity and inner-city youth. In S. B. Heath & M. W. McLaughlin (Eds.), *Identity and inner-city youth: Beyond ethnicity and gender* (pp. 1–12). New York: Teachers College Press.

Heilman, E. (1998). The struggle for self. *Youth and Society, 30*(2), 182–208.

Helfenbein, R., Jr. (2006). Economies of identity: Cultural studies and a curriculum of making place. *Journal of Curriculum Theorizing, 22*(2), 87–100.

Hemmings, A. (2000). Lona's links: Postoppositional identity work of urban youths. *Anthropology and Education Quarterly, 31*(2), 152–172.

Hemmings, A. (2002). Youth culture of hostility: Discourses of money, respect, and difference. *Qualitative Studies in Education, 15*(3), 291–307.

Henny, L. (1986). Trend report: Theory and practice of visual sociology. *Current Sociology, 34*, 1–23.

Herman, M. (2004). Forced to choose: Some determinants of racial identification in multiracial adolescents. *Child Development, 75*(3), 730–748.

Hill, M. E. (2002). Skin color and the perception of attractiveness among African Americans: Does gender make a difference? *Social Psychology Quarterly, 65*(1), 77–91.

Hirsch, B. (2005). *A place to call home: Community based after-school programs for urban youth.* Washington, D.C./New York: American Psychological Association/Teachers College Press.

Hirsch, B., Mickus, M., & Boerger, R. (2002). Ties to influential adults among black and white adolescents: Culture, social class, and family networks. *American Journal of Community Psychology, 30*(2), 289–303.

Lerner, R. M. (2002). *Concepts and theories of human development*, 3rd ed. Mahwah, N.J.: Lawrence Erlbaum Associates.

Lerner, R. M., Almerigi, J. B., Theokas, C., & Lerner, J. V. (2005). Positive youth development: A view of the issues. *Journal of Early Adolescence, 25*(1), 10–16.

Lerner, R. M., Brentano, C., Dowling, E. M., & Anderson, P. M. (2002). Positive youth development: Thriving as the basis of personhood and civil society. *New Directions for Youth Development, 95,* 11–33.

Lerner, R. M., Lerner, J. V., Almerigi, J. B., Theokas, C., Phelps, E., Gestsdottir, S., et al. (2005). Positive youth development: Participation in community youth development programs, and community contributions of fifth-grade adolescents. *Journal of Early Adolescence, 25*(1), 17–71.

Lerner, R. M., Phelps, E., Alberts, A., Forman, Y., & Christiansen, E. D. (2007). The many faces of urban girls: Features of positive development in early adolescence. In B. J. R. Leadbeater & N. Way (Eds.), *Urban girls revisited: Building strengths* (pp. 19–52). New York: New York University Press.

Lesko, N. (2001). *Act your age: A cultural construction of adolescence.* New York: Routledge Falmer.

Li, X., Stanton, B., Pack, R., Harris, C., Cottrell, L., & Burns, J. (2002). Risk and protective factors associated with gang involvement among urban African American adolescents. *Youth and Society, 34*(2), 172–194.

Limon, J. (1994). *Dancing with the devil: Society and cultural politics in Mexican-American southern Texas.* Madison: University of Wisconsin Press.

Loder, T., & Hirsch, B. (2003). Inner-city youth development organizations: The salience of peer ties among early adolescent girls. *Applied Developmental Science, 7*(1), 2–12.

London, J. K., Zimmerman, K., & Erbstein, N. (2003). Youth-led research and evaluation: Tools for youth, organizational, and community development. *New Directions for Evaluation, 98,* 33–45.

Lopez, N., & Lechuga, C. E. (2007). "They are like a friend": Other mothers creating empowering school-based community living rooms in Latina and Latino middle schools. In B. J. R. Leadbeater & N. Way (Eds.), *Urban girls revisited: Building strengths* (pp. 97–120). New York: New York University Press.

Lorber, J. (1994). *Paradoxes of gender.* New Haven, Conn.: Yale University Press.

Luttrell, W. (2003). *Pregnant bodies, fertile minds: Gender, race, and the schooling of pregnant teens.* New York: Routledge.

Luttrell, W. (2005). Crossing anxious borders: Teaching across the quantitative-qualitative "divide." *International Journal of Research and Method in Education, 28*(2), 183–195.

Lykes, M. B. (1985). Gender and individualistic vs collective bases for notions about the self. *Journal of Personality, 53,* 356–383.

Maccoby, E. E. (1998). *The two sexes: Growing up apart, coming together.* Cambridge, Mass.: Belknap Press.

Madson, L., & Trafimow, D. (2001). Gender comparisons in the private, collective, and allocentric selves. *Journal of Social Psychology, 141*(4), 551–559.

Mahoney, J. L., Eccles, J. S., & Larson, R. W. (2004). Processes of adjustment in organized out-of-school activities: Oppportunities and risks. *New Directions for Youth Development, 101,* 115–143.

Marcia, J. E. (1980). Identity in adolescence. In J. Adelson (Ed.), *Handbook of adolescent psychology* (pp. 159–187). New York: Wiley.

Marcus, G. E. (1986). Contemporary problems of ethnography in the modern world system. In J. Clifford & G. E. Marcus (Eds.), *Writing culture: The poetics and politics of ethnography* (pp. 165–193). Berkeley: University of California Press.

Markus, H. R., & Kitayama, S. (1994). Culture and the self: Implications for cognition, emotion, and motivation. *Psychological Review, 98,* 224–253.

Markus, H. R., & Nurius, P. (1986). Possible selves. *American Psychologist, 41,* 954–969.

Marshall, C., & Rossman, G. B. (1999). *Designing qualitative research.* Thousand Oaks, Calif.: Sage.

Marshall, N. (2003). Introduction: Social construction of gender in childhood and adolescence. *American Behavioral Scientist, 46*(10), 1289–1295.

Maton, K. I., & Salem, D. A. (1995). Organizational characteristics of empowering community settings: A multiple case study approach. *American Journal of Community Psychology, 23*(5), 631–657.

May, D. (2001). *Adolescent fear of crime, perceptions of risk, and defensive behaviors: An alternative explanation of violent delinquency.* Lewiston, N.Y.: Edwin Mellon Press.

McAdams, D. P. (1993). *The stories we live by: Personal myths and the making of the self.* New York: William Morrow.

McAdams, D. P. (2001). The psychology of life stories. *Review of General Psychology, 5,* 100–122.

McAdams, D. P., & Bowman, P. J. (2001). Narrating life's turning points: Redemption and contamination. In D. P. McAdams, R. Josselson, & A. Lieblich (Eds.), *Turns in the road: Studies of lives in transition* (pp. 3–34). Washington, D.C.: American Psychological Association.

McAdams, D. P., Diamond, A., de St. Aubin, E., & Mansfield, E. (1997). Stories of commitment: The psychosocial construction of generative lives. *Journal of Personality and Social Psychology, 72*(3), 678–694.

McCoy, S. K., & Major, B. (2003). Group identification moderates emotional responses to perceived prejudice. *Personality and Social Psychology Bulletin, 29*(8), 1005–1017.

McLaughlin, M. (1993). Embedded identities: Enabling balance in urban contexts. In S. B. Heath & M. W. McLaughlin (Eds.), *Identity and inner-city youth: Beyond ethnicity and gender* (pp. 36–67). New York: Teachers College Press.

McLaughlin, M. (2000). *Community counts: How youth organizations matter for youth development.* Washington, D.C.: Public Education Network.

McLaughlin, M., Irby, M., & Langman, J. (1994). *Urban sanctuaries: Neighborhood organizations in the lives and futures of inner city youth.* San Francisco: Jossey-Bass.

Mead, G. H. (1934). *Mind, self, and society from the standpoint of a social behaviorist.* Chicago: University of Chicago Press.

Mead, M., & Baldwin, J. (1971). *A rap on race.* New York: Lippincott.

Mies, M. (1983). Towards a methodology for feminist research. In G. Bowles & R. D. Klein (Eds.), *Theories of women's studies* (pp. 117–139). Boston: Routledge and Kegan Paul.

Miles, M. B., & Huberman, A. M. (1994). *Qualitative data analysis: An expanded sourcebook,* 2nd ed. Thousand Oaks, Calif.: Sage.

Miller, B. M. (2005). *Pathways to success for youth: What counts in after-school.* Massachusetts After-School Research Study Report. Arlington/Wellesley, Mass.: Intercultural Center for Research in Education and Natuional Institute on Out-of-School Time.

Miller, J. B. (1976). *Toward a new psychology of women.* Boston: Beacon Press.

Miller, J. B. (1990). The development of women's sense of self. In C. Sanardi (Ed.), *Essential papers on the psychology of women* (pp. 437–454). New York: New York University Press.

Moje, E. (2004). Doing identity: On the complexities of researching social identities with urban youth. Paper presented at the Society for Research on Adolescence, Baltimore.

Moynihan, P. (1965). *The Negro family: The case for national action.* Washington, D.C.: U.S. Government Printing Office.

Musick, J. (1993). *Young, poor, and pregnant: The psychology of teenage motherhood.* New Haven, Conn.: Yale University Press.

Myers, L. W. (1998). The effects of urban education on the self-esteem of African American men. *Challenge: A Journal of Research on African American Men, 9*(2), 57–66.

Nasir, N. S., & Kirshner, B. (2003). The cultural construction of moral and civic identities. *Applied Developmental Science, 7*(3), 138–147.

Nasir, N. S., & Saxe, G. (2003). Ethnic and academic identities: A cultural practice perspective on emerging tensions and their management in the lives of minority students. *Educational Researcher, 32*(5), 14–18.

National Research Council, & Institute of Medicine. (2002). *Community programs to promote youth development.* Washington, D.C.: National Academy Press.

Negy, C., Shreve, T. L., Jensen, B. J., & Uddin, N. (2003). Ethnic identity, self-esteem, and ethnocentrism: A study of social identity versus multicultural theory of development. *Cultural Diversity and Ethnic Minority Psychology, 9*(4), 333–344.

Newman, B. M., & Newman, P. R. (2001). Group identity and alienation: Giving the we its due. *Journal of Youth and Adolescence, 30*(5), 515–538.

Noblit, G. W., & Hare, R. D. (1988). *Meta-ethnography: Synthesizing qualitative studies*. Newbury Park, Calif.: Sage.

Noguera, P. A. (2003). The trouble with black boys: The role and influence of environmental and cultural factors on the academic performance of African American males. *Urban Education, 38*(4), 431–459.

Noguera, P. A. (2004). Social capital and the education of immigrant students: Categories and generalizations. *Sociology of Education, 77*(2), 180–183.

Nonn, T. (1998). Hitting bottom: Homelessness, poverty, and masculinity. In M. Kimmel & M. Messner (Eds.), *Men's lives* (pp. 318–327). Boston: Allyn and Bacon.

Oboler, S. (2002). The politics of labeling: Latino/a cultural identities of self and others. In C. G. Velez-Ibanez & A. Sampaio (Eds.), *Transnational Latina/o communities: Politics, processes, and cultures* (pp. 73–89). New York: Rowman and Littlefield.

O'Connor, C. (1999). Race, class, and gender in America: Narratives of opportunity among low-income African American youths. *Sociology of Education, 72*(3), 137–157.

O'Connor, C. (2003). The [dynamic and processual] significance of race: Re-articulating the promise of Wilson's macro-historical framework. *Ethnic and Racial Studies, 26*(6), 1006–1028.

Ogbu, J. (1988). Understanding cultural diversity and learning. *Educational Researcher, 21*(8), 5–14.

Okin, S. M. (1998). Gender, the public and the private. In A. Phillips (Ed.), *Feminism and politics* (pp. 116–141). New York: Oxford University Press.

Olesen, V. (1994). Feminisms and models of qualitative research. In N. K. Denzin & Y. S. Lincoln (Eds.), *The handbook of qualitative research* (pp. 158–174). Thousand Oaks, Calif.: Sage.

Olesen, V. (2005). Early millennial feminist qualitative research: Challenges and contours. In N. K. Denzin & Y. S. Lincoln (Eds.), *The Sage handbook of qualitative research*, 3rd ed. (pp. 235–278). Thousand Oaks, Calif.: Sage.

Olsen, C. S. (1996). African-American adolescent women: Perceptions of gender, race, and class. *Marriage and Family Review, 24*(1/2), 105–121.

Orellana, M. (1999). Space and place in an urban landscape: Learning from children's views of their social worlds. *Visual Sociology, 14*, 73–89.

Oyserman, D. (1999). African American identity in adolescence. *African American Research Perspectives, 5*(1), 57–67.

Oyserman, D., Gant, L., & Ager, J. (1995). A socially contextualized model of African American identity: Possible selves and school persistance. *Journal of Personality and Social Psychology, 69*(6), 1216–1232.

Oyserman, D., & Harrison, K. (1998). Implications of cultural context: African

American identity and possible selves. In J. K. Swim & C. Strangor (Eds.), *Prejudice: The target's perspective* (pp. 281–300). San Diego: Academic Press.

Oyserman, D., Kemmelmeier, M., Fryberg, S., Brosh, H., & Hart-Johnson, T. (2003). Racial-ethnic self-schemas. *Social Psychology Quarterly, 66*(4), 333–347.

Oyserman, D., & Markus, H. R. (1990a). Possible selves and delinquency. *Journal of Personality and Social Psychology, 59*(1), 112–125.

Oyserman, D., & Markus, H. R. (1990b). Possible selves in balance: Implications for delinquency. *Journal of Social Issues, 46*(2), 141–157.

Oyserman, D., & Markus, H. (1998). Self as social representation. In U. Flick (Ed.), *The psychology of the social* (pp. 107–125). New York: Cambridge University Press.

Pagano, M. E. (2001). Non-parental social support and the well-being of low-income, minority youth. Dissertation Abstracts International: Section B: The Sciences and Engineering. Vol 61(11-B), Jun 2001, 6166. US: University Microfilms International.

Pastor, J., McCormick, J., & Fine, M. (1996). Makin' homes: An urban girl thing. In B. Leadbeater & N. Way (Eds.), *Urban girls: Resisting stereotypes, creating identities* (pp. 15–34). New York: New York University Press.

Patterson, O. (2006, March 26). A poverty of the mind. *New York Times,* p. 13.

Pedersen, S., Seidman, E., Yoshikawa, H., Rivera, A. C., Allen, L., & Aber, J. L. (2005). Contextual competence: Multiple manifestations among urban adolescents. *American Journal of Community Psychology, 35*(1/2), 65–82.

Pew Research Center (2007). *Optimism about Black progress declines: Blacks see growing values gap between poor and middle class.* Washington, DC: Pew Research Center.

Phillips, T. M., & Pittman, J. F. (2003). Identity processes in poor adolescents: Exploring the linkages between economic disadvantage and the primary task of adolescence. *Identity, 3*(2), 115–129.

Phinney, J. S. (1989). Stages of ethnic identity development in minority group adolescents. *Journal of Early Adolescence, 9,* 34–49.

Phinney, J. S., Cantu, C. L., & Kurtz, D. A. (1997). Ethnic and American identity as predictors of self-esteem among African American, Latino, and white adolescents. *Journal of Youth and Adolescence, 26*(2), 165–185.

Phinney, J. S., & Chavira, V. (1992). Ethnic identity and self-esteem: An exploratory longitudinal study. *Journal of Adolescence, 15*(3), 271–281.

Phinney, J. S., & Rosenthal, D. A. (1992). Ethnic identity in adolescence: Process, context, and outcome. In G. R. Adams, T. P. Gullotta, & R. Montemayer (Eds.), *Adolescent identity formation: Advances in adolescent development* (pp. 145–172). Thousand Oaks, Calif.: Sage.

Phinney, J. S., & Tarver, S. (1988). Ethnic identity search and commitment in black and white eighth graders. *Journal of Early Adolescence, 8,* 265–277.

Poston, W. (1990). The biracial identity development model: A needed addition. *Journal of Counseling and Development, 69*(2), 152–155.

Pringle, R., & Watson, S. (1998). "Women's interests" and the poststructuralist state. In A. Phillips (Ed.), *Feminism and politics* (pp. 203–223). New York: Oxford University Press.

Proweller, A. (1998). *Constructing female identities: Meaning making in an upper middle class youth culture.* Albany: SUNY Press.

Quadagno, J., & Fobes, C. (1995). Welfare state and the cultural reproduction of gender: Making good girls and boys in the Job Corps. *Social Problems, 42*(2), 171–190.

Quintana, S. (2004). Race, ethnicity, and culture in child development. *Child Development, 75*(4), v–vi.

Quintana, S. M., & Segura-Herrera, T. A. (2003). Developmental transformations of self and identity in the context of oppression. *Self and Identity, 2*(4), 269–285.

Rappaport, J. (1995). Empowerment meets narrative: Listening to stories and creating settings. *American Journal of Community Psychology, 23*(5), 795–808.

Rappaport, J. (2000). Community narratives: Tales of terror and joy. *American Journal of Community Psychology, 28*(1), 1–24.

Rattansi, A., & Phoenix, A. (2005). Rethinking youth identities: Modernist and postmodernist frameworks. *Identity, 5*(2), 97–123.

Reichert, M. C., Stoudt, B., & Kuriloff, P. (2006). Don't love no fight: Healing and identity among urban youth. *Urban Review, 38*(3), 187–209.

Reimer, K. (2003). Committed to caring: Transformation in adolescent moral identity. *Applied Developmental Science, 7*(3), 129–137.

Reynolds, L. T. (2003a). Early representatives. In L. T. Reynolds & N. J. Herman-Kinney (Eds.), *Handbook of symbolic interactionism* (pp. 59–81). New York: Altamira.

Reynolds, L. T. (2003b). Intellectual precursors. In L. T. Reynolds & N. J. Herman-Kinney (Eds.), *Handbook of symbolic interactionism* (pp. 39–58). New York: Altamira.

Rhodes, J. E., Davis, A. A., Prescott, L. R., & Spencer, R. (2007). Caring connections: Mentoring relationships in the lives of urban girls. In B. J. R. Leadbeater & N. Way (Eds.), *Urban girls revisited: Building strengths* (pp. 142–156). New York: New York University Press.

Rich, A. (1980). Compulsory heterosexuality and lesbian existence. *Signs, 5,* 631–660.

Rich, A. (1984). *The fact of a doorframe: Poems selected and new 1950–1984.* New York: Norton.

Ridgeway, C. L., & Smith-Lovin, L. (1999). The gender system and interaction. *Annual Review of Sociology, 25,* 191–216.

Riggs, N. R., & Greenberg, M. T. (2004). After-school youth development programs: A developmental-ecological model of current research. *Clinical Child and Family Psychology Review, 7*(3), 177–190.

Riley, P. J., & Kiger, G. (1999). Moral discourse on domestic labor: Gender, power and identity in families. *Social Science Journal, 36*(3), 541–548.

Robinson, T. L., & Ward, J. V. (1995). African American adolescents and skin color. *Journal of Black Psychology, 21*(3), 256–274.

Roderick, M. (2003). What's happening to the boys? Early high school experiences and school outcomes among African American male adolescents in Chicago. *Urban Education, 38*(5), 538–607.

Roffman, J. G. (2001). Non-parent support figures in the lives of inner-city youth. *Dissertation Abstracts International: Section B: The Sciences and Engineering.* Vol 61(11-B), Jun 2001, 6167. US: University Microfilms International.

Roffman, J. G., Pagano, M. E., & Hirsch, B. (2001). Youth functioning and the experiences of inner-city after-school programs among age, gender, and race groups. *Journal of Child and Family Studies, 10*(1), 85–100.

Rogoff, B. (2003). *The cultural nature of human development.* New York: Oxford University Press.

Rosenbaum, J. E. (2001a). *Beyond college for all: Career paths for the forgotten half.* New York: Russell Sage Foundation.

Rosenbaum, J. E. (2001b). *High schools' role in college and workforce preparation: Do college-for-all policies make high school irrelevant?* Philadelphia: Mid-Atlantic Laboratory for Student Success.

Rosenbloom, S. R., & Way, N. (2004). Experiences of discrimination among African American, Asian American, and Latino adolescents in an urban high school. *Youth and Society, 35*(4), 420–451.

Rosenthal, H. (2001). Discussion paper—working towards inclusion: "I am another other." *Educational Psychology in Practice, 17*(4), 385–392.

Roth, J., Brooks-Gunn, J., Murray, L., & Foster, W. (1998). Promoting healthy adolescents: Synthesis of youth development program evaluations. *Journal of Research on Adolescence, 8*, 423–459.

Rotheram-Borus, M., & Wyche, K. (1994). Ethnic differences in identity development in the United States. In S. Archer (Ed.), *Interventions for adolescent identity development* (pp. 62–83). Thousand Oaks, Calif.: Sage.

Rubinstein-Avila, E. (2006). Publishing "equinox": Broadening notions of urban youth development after school. *Anthropology and Education Quarterly, 37*(3), 255–272.

Ruble, D. N., & Martin, C. L. (1998). Gender development. In N. Eisenberg (Ed.), *Handbook of child psychology,* Vol. 3: *Social, emotional, and personality development,* 5th ed. (pp. 933–1016). New York: Wiley.

Ryan, R. M., & Deci, E. L. (2000). The darker and brighter sides of human existence: Basic psychological needs as a unifying concept. *Psychological Inquiry, 11*(4), 319–338.

Ryan, R. M., Deci, E. L., & Grolnick, W. S. (1995). Autonomy, relatedness, and the self: Their relation to development and psychopathology. In D. Cicchetti & D. J. Cohen (Eds.), *Developmental psychopathology,* Vol. 1: *Theory and methods* (pp. 618–655). New York: Wiley.

Sabo, D. F., Miller, K. E., Farrell, M. P., Barnes, G. M., & Melnick, M. (1998). *The women's sports foundation report: Sport and teen pregnancy.* East Meadow, N.Y.: Women's Sports Foundation.

Said, E. (1978). *Orientalism.* New York: Vintage Books.

Sapiro, V. (1998). When are interests interesting? The problem of political representation of women. In A. Phillips (Ed.), *Feminism and politics* (pp. 161–192). New York: Oxford University Press.

Schein, L. (1997). The consumption of color and the politics of white skin in post-Mao China. In M. diLeonardo & R. Lancaster (Eds.), *The gender/sexuality reader* (pp. 473–486). New York: Routledge.

Schwalbe, M., Godwin, S., Holden, D., Schrock, D., Thompson, S., & Wolkomir, M. (2000). Generic processes in the reproduction of inequality: An interactionist analysis. *Social Forces, 79*(2), 419–452.

Schwartz, S. J. (2005). A new identity for identity research: Recommendations for expanding and refocusing the identity literature. *Journal of Adolescent Research, 20*(3), 293–308.

Scott, L. D., Jr. (2003). The relation of racial identity and racial socialization to coping with discrimination among African American adolescents. *Journal of Black Studies, 33*(4), 520–538.

Seale, C. (1998). Qualitative interviewing. In C. Seale (Ed.), *Researching society and culture* (pp. 202–216). London: Sage.

Seaton, G. (2004). Coping across context: The functionality of black hypermasculinity. Paper presented at the Society for Research on Adolescence, Baltimore.

Secondulfo, D. (1997). The social meaning of things: A working field for visual sociology. *Visual Sociology, 12,* 33–45.

Sedikides, C., & Brewer, M. (2001). Individual self, relational self, and collective self: Partners, opponents or stranger? In C. Sedikides & M. Brewer (Eds.), *Individual self, relational self, collective self* (pp. 1–4). Philadelphia: Psychology Press.

Sherrod, L. R., Flanagan, C., & Youniss, J. (2002). Dimensions of citizenship and opportunities for youth development: The what, why, when, where, and who of citizenship development. *Applied Developmental Science, 6*(4), 264–272.

Shorter-Gooden, K., & Washington, N. C. (1996). Young, black and female: The challenge of weaving an identity. *Journal of Adolescence, 19,* 465–475.

Singelis, T. M. (1994). The measurement of independent and interdependent self-construals. *Personality and Social Psychology Bulletin, 20*(5), 580–591.

Smedley, A. (1998). "Race" and the construction of human identity. *American Anthropologist, 100*(3), 690–702.

Smith, D. (1987). *The everyday world as problematic: A feminist sociology.* Boston: Northeastern University Press.

Smith, D. (1999). From women's standpoint to a sociology for people. In J. L. Abu-Lughod (Ed.), *Sociology for the twenty-first century: Continuities and cutting edges* (pp. 65–82). Chicago: University of Chicago Press.

Smith, E. P., Walker, K., Fields, L., Brookins, C. C., & Seay, R. C. (1999). Ethnic identity and its relationship to self-esteem, perceived efficacy and prosocial attitudes in early adolescence. *Journal of Adolescence, 22*(6), 867–880.

Snow, D. A. (2001). Extending and broadening Blumer's conceptualization of symbolic interactionism. *Symbolic Interaction, 24*(3), 367–377.

Spencer, M. B. (2001). Resiliency and fragility factors associated with the contextual experience of low resource urban African American male youth and families. In A. C. Crouter (Ed.), *Does it take a village?* (pp. 51–77). Mahwah, N.J.: Lawrence Erlbaum Associates.

Spencer, M. B. (2003). A theoretical and empirical examination of identity as coping: Linking coping resources to the self processes of African American youth. *Applied Developmental Science, 7*(3), 181–188.

Spencer, M. B., Dupree, D., & Hartmann, T. (1997). A phenomenological variant of ecological systems theory (PVEST): A self-organization perspective in context. *Development and Psychopathology, 9,* 817–833.

Spencer, M. B., Fegley, S., Harpalani, V., & Seaton, G. (2004). Understanding hypermasculinity in context: A theory-driven analysis of urban adolescent males' coping responses. *Research in Human Development, 1*(4), 229–257.

Spencer, M. B., & Markstrom-Adams, C. (1990). Identity processes among racial and ethnic minority children in America. *Child Development, 61*(2), 290–310.

Spergel, I. A. (1992). Youth gangs: An essay review. *Social Service Review, 66*(1), 121–140.

Stack, C. (1996). Writing ethnography: Feminist critical practice. In D. Wolf (Ed.), *Feminist dilemmas in fieldwork* (pp. 96–106). Boulder, Colo.: Westview.

Steele, C. (1997). A threat in the air: How stereotypes shape intellectual identity and performance. *American Psychologist, 52*(6), 613–629.

Steele, C., & Aronson, J. (1995). Stereotype threat and the intellectual test performance of African Americans. *Journal of Personality and Social Psychology, 69*(6), 797–811.

Steinberg, L. (1990). Autonomy, conflict, and harmony in the family relationship. In S. S. Feldman & G. R. Elliott (Eds.), *At the threshold: The developing adolescent* (pp. 255–276). Cambridge: Harvard University Press.

Stevens, J. W. (1995). Adulthood status negotiation among poor urban African-American pregnant and non-pregnant late age adolescent females. *Journal of Applied Social Sciences, 20*(1), 39–50.

Stevens, J. W. (1997). African American female adolescent identity development: A three-dimensional perspective. *Child Welfare, 76*(1), 145–173.

Stevenson, H. C. (2004). Boys in men's clothing: Racial socialization and neighborhood safety as buffers to hypervulnerability in African American adolescent males. In N. Way & J. Y. Chu (Eds.), *Adolescent boys: Exploring diverse cultures of boyhood* (pp. 59–77). New York: New York University Press.

Stewart, A. J. (1994). Toward a feminist strategy for studying women's lives. In C. E. Franz & A. J. Stewart (Eds.), *Women creating lives: Identities, resilience and resistance* (pp. 11–35). San Francisco: Westview.

Stoler, A. (1997). Carnal knowledge and imperial power: Gender, race and morality in colonial Asia. In M. D. Leonardo & R. Lancaster (Eds.), *The gender/sexuality reader* (pp. 13–36). New York: Routledge.

Stoltenberg, J. (1994). Toward gender justice. In P. F. Murphy (Ed.), *Feminism and masculinities* (pp. 41–49). New York: Oxford University Press.

Story, L. (2005, September 20). Many women at elite colleges set career path to motherhood. *New York Times,* p. A1.

Strauch, B. (2003). *The primal teen: What the new discoveries about the teenage brain tell us about our kids.* New York: Anchor Books.

Strausberg, C. (2003, April 30). Atty Meyers to churches: Form armies of black males to teach youths "code of honor." *Chicago Defender,* p. A3.

Strauss, A., & Corbin, J. (1994). Grounded theory methodology: An overview. In N. K. Denzin & Y. S. Lincoln (Eds.), *Handbook of qualitative research* (pp. 273–285). Thousand Oaks, Calif.: Sage.

Strauss, A. L. (1998). *Basics of qualitative research: Techniques and procedures for developing grounded theory.* Thousand Oaks, Calif.: Sage.

Stryker, S. (1980). *Symbolic interactionism: A social structural version.* Menlo Park, Calif.: Benjamin/Cummings.

Stryker, S. (1987). The vitalization of symbolic interactionism. *Social Psychology Quarterly, 50*(1), 83–94.

Tajfel, H. (2001). Experiments in intergroup discrimination. In M. A. Hogg & D. Abrams (Eds.), *Intergroup relations: Essential readings* (pp. 178–187). Philadelphia: Psychology Press.

Tajfel, H., & Turner, J. C. (1986). The social identity theory of intergroup behavior. In S. Worchel & W. G. Austin (Eds.), *Psychology of intergroup relations* (pp. 7–24). Chicago: Nelson-Hall.

Tarrant, M., North, A. C., Edridge, M. D., Kirk, L. E., Smith, E. A., & Turner, R. E. (2001). Social identity in adolescence. *Journal of Adolescence, 24,* 597–609.

Tatum, B. D. (1997). *"Why are all the black kids sitting together in the cafeteria?" and other conversations about race.* New York: Basic Books.

Taylor, C. S., Smith, P. R., & Taylor, V. A. (2007). Businesswomen in urban life. In B. J. R. Leadbeater & N. Way (Eds.), *Urban girls revisited: Building strengths* (pp. 338–359). New York: New York University Press.

Thorne, B. (1990). Children and gender: Constructions of difference. In D. Rhodes (Ed.), *Theoretical perspectives on sexual difference* (pp. 100–113). New Haven, Conn.: Yale University Press.

Thorne, B. (1993). *Gender play: Girls and boys in school.* New Brunswick, N.J.: Rutgers University Press.

Tice, D. M., & Baumeister, R. F. (2001). Primacy of the interpersonal self. In C. Sedikides & M. Brewer (Eds.), *Individual self, relational self, collective self* (pp. 71–88). Philadelphia: Psychology Press.

Tolman, D. L. (1994). Doing desire: Adolescent girls' struggles for/with sexuality. *Gender and Society, 8*(3), 324–342.

Tolman, D. L. (1996). Adolescent girls' sexuality: Debunking the myth of the urban girl. In B. Leadbeater & N. Way (Eds.), *Urban girls: Resisting stereotypes, creating identities* (pp. 255–271). New York: New York University Press.

Tolman, D. L., Spencer, R., Harmon, T., Rosen-Reynoso, M., & Striepe, M. (2004). Getting close, staying close: Early adolescent boys' experiences with romantic relationships. In N. Way & J. Y. Chu (Eds.), *Adolescent boys: Exploring diverse cultures of boyhood* (pp. 235–255). New York: New York University Press.

Triandis, H. C. (1989). The self and social behavior in differing cultural contexts. *Psychological Review, 96,* 506–520.

Umana-Taylor, A. J., Diversi, M., & Fine, M. A. (2002). Ethnic identity and self-esteem among Latino adolescents: Distinctions between the Latino populations. *Journal of Adolescent Research, 17*(3), 303–327.

Verkuyten, M. (2005). Ethnic group identification and group evaluation among minority and majority groups: Testing the multiculturalism hypothesis. *Journal of Personality and Social Psychology, 88*(1), 121–138.

Vigil, J. D. (1988). Group processes and street identity: Adolescent Chicano gang members. *Ethos, 16*(4), 421–445.

Vigil, J. D. (2003). Urban violence and street gangs. *Annual Review of Anthropology, 32,* 225–242.

Villenas, S. (2001). Latina mothers and small-town racisms: Creating narratives of dignity and moral education in North Carolina. *Anthropology and Education Quarterly, 32*(1), 3–28.

Walker, B. M. (2004). Frames of self: Capturing working-class British boys' identities through photographs. In N. Way & J. Y. Chu (Eds.), *Adolescent boys: Exploring diverse cultures of boyhood.* New York: New York University Press.

Walsh, D. (1998). Doing ethnography. In C. Seale (Ed.), *Researching society and culture* (pp. 217–232). London: Sage.

Ward, J. V. (1996). Raising resisters: The role of truth telling in the psychological development of African American girls. In B. Leadbetter & N. Way (Eds.), *Urban girls: Resisting stereotypes, creating identities* (pp. 85–99). New York: New York University Press.

Ward, J. V. (2007). Uncovering truths, recovering lies: Lessons of resistance in the socialization of black girls. In B. J. R. Leadbeater & N. Way (Eds.), *Urban girls revisited: Building strengths* (pp. 243–260). New York: New York University Press.

Waterman, A. S. (1990). Personal expressiveness: Philosophical and psychological foundations. *Journal of Mind and Behavior, 11,* 47–73.

Waterman, A. S. (1993). Finding something to do or someone to be: A eudaimonist perspective on identity formation. In J. Kroger (Ed.), *Discussion on ego identity* (pp. 147–167). Hillsdale, N.J.: Lawrence Erlbaum Associates.

Waters, M. (1996). The intersection of gender, race, and ethnicity in identity development of Caribbean American teens. In B. Leadbetter & N. Way (Eds.), *Urban* girls: Resisting stereotypes, creating identities (pp. 65–81). New York: New York University Press.

Way, N. (1996). Between experiences of betrayal and desire: Close friendships among urban adolescents. In B. Leadbeater & N. Way (Eds.), *Urban girls: Resisting stereotypes, creating identities* (pp. 173–192). New York: New York University Press.

Way, N. (1998). *Everyday courage: The lives and stories of urban teenagers.* New York: New York University Press.

Way, N. (2004). Intimacy, desire, and distrust in the friendships of adolescent boys. In N. Way & J. Y. Chu (Eds.), *Adolescent boys: Exploring diverse cultures of boyhood* (pp. 167–196). New York: New York University Press.

Way, N. (2007). Preface to B. J. R. Leadbeater & N. Way (Eds.), *Urban girls revisited: Building strengths* (pp. xiii–xvi). New York: New York University Press.

Way, N., & Chen, L. (2000). Close and general friendships among African American, Latino, and Asian American adolescents from low-income families. *Journal of Adolescent Research, 15*(2), 274–301.

Way, N., & Chu, J. Y. (2004a). Introduction to N. Way & J. Y. Chu (Eds.), *Adolescent boys: Exploring diverse cultures of boyhood* (pp. 1–10). New York: New York University Press.

Way, N., & Chu, J. Y. (Eds.). (2004b). *Adolescent boys: Exploring diverse cultures of boyhood.* New York: New York University Press.

Weigert, A. J., & Gecas, V. (2005). Symbolic interactionist reflections on Erikson, identity, and postmodernism. *Identity, 5*(2), 161–174.

Weis, L. (1990). *Working class without work: High school students in a de-industrializing economy.* New York: Routledge.

Weis, L. (1993). White male working class youth: An exploration of relative privilege and loss. In L. Weis & M. Fine (Eds.), *Beyond silenced voices: Class, race, and gender in United States schools* (pp. 237–258). Albany: SUNY Press.

Weis, L., & Fine, M. (Eds.). (2000). *Construction sites.* New York: Teachers College Press.

Weisz, J. R., Sandler, I. N., Durlak, J. A., & Anton, B. S. (2005). Promoting and protecting youth mental health through evidence-based prevention and treatment. *American Psychologist, 60*(6), 628–648.

West, C. (1993). *Race matters.* Boston: Beacon Press.

West, C., & Zimmerman, D. (1981). Doing gender. *Gender and Society, 1*(2), 125–151.

Western, B. (2006). *Punishment and inequality in America.* New York: Russell Sage Foundation.

Williams, B. F. (1996). Skinfolk, not kinfolk: Comparative reflections on the identity of participant-observation in two field situations. In D. Wolf (Ed.), *Feminist dilemmas in fieldwork* (pp. 72–95). Boulder, Colo.: Westview.

Wilson, B., White, P., & Fisher, K. (2001). Multiple identities in a marginalized culture: Female youth in an "inner-city" recreation/drop-in center. *Journal of Sport and Social Issues, 25*(3), 301–323.

Wilson, W. J. (1987). *The truly disadvantaged: The inner city, the underclass, and public policy.* Chicago: University of Chicago Press.

Wingrove, E. (1999). Interpellating sex. *Signs, 24,* 869–893.

Winston, C. (2004). Identity and success of African American students: What does race have to do with it? Paper presented at the Society for Research on Adolescence, Baltimore.

Wolf, D. (1996). Situating feminist dilemmas in fieldwork. In D. L. Wolf (Ed.), *Feminist dilemmas in fieldwork* (pp. 1–55). Boulder, Colo.: Westview.

Wolf, D. L. (1996). *Feminist dilemmas in fieldwork.* Boulder, Colo.: Westview.

Wollstonecraft, M. (1792). *Vindication of the rights of women.* London: J. Johnson.

Wong, C. A., Eccles, J. S., & Sameroff, A. (2003). The influence of ethnic discrimination and ethnic identification on African American adolescents' school and socioemotional adjustment. *Journal of Personality, 71*(6), 1197–1232.

Wong, J. (2002). What's in a name? An examination of social identities. *Journal for the Theory of Social Behaviour, 32*(4), 451–463.

Wood, M., Furlong, M. J., Rosenblatt, J. A., Robertson, L. M., Scozzari, F., & Sosna, T. (1997). Understanding the psychosocial characteristics of gang-involved youths in a system of care: Individual, family, and system correlates. *Education and Treatment of Children, 20*(3), 281–295.

Worrill, C. W. (2001). Taking a deeper look at ourselves. *Michigan Citizen, 23*(46), A7.

Yoder, A. E. (2000). Barriers to ego identity status formation: A contextual qualification of Marcia's identity status paradigm. *Journal of Adolescence, 23*(1), 95–106.

Youniss, J., McLellan, J. A., & Yates, M. (1997). What we know about engendering civic identity. *American Behavioral Scientist, 40*(5), 620–631.

Youniss, J., & Yates, M. (1999). Youth service and moral-civic identity: A case for everyday morality. *Educational Psychology Review, 11*(4), 361–376.

Index

■ ■ ■ ■ ■ ■ ■ ■ ■

About the Author

Nancy L. Deutsch is Assistant Professor in the Curry School of Education at the University of Virginia.